THE RISE of the CANTERBURY TALES

Baba Brinkman

Illustrated by Erik Brinkman

Talonbooks
Vancouver

Talonbooks
P.O. Box 2076, Vancouver, British Columbia, Canada V6B 3S3
www.talonbooks.com

Typeset in Adobe Garamond and Priori and printed and bound in Canada.

First Printing: 2006

The publisher gratefully acknowledges the financial support of the Canada Council for the Arts; the Government of Canada through the Book Publishing Industry Development Program; and the Province of British Columbia through the British Columbia Arts Council for our publishing activities.

Audio recordings of *The Rap Canterbury Tales* and other projects by Baba Brinkman can be found online at www.babasword.com. All rights reserved by the author.

Library and Archives Canada Cataloguing in Publication

Brinkman, Baba, 1978–

  The rap Canterbury Tales / Baba Brinkman ; illustrated by Erik Brinkman.

Includes bibliographical references.

ISBN 0-88922-548-6

  1. Chaucer, Geoffrey, d. 1400. Canterbury tales--Adaptations. I. Brinkman, Erik, 1980– II. Chaucer, Geoffrey, d. 1400. Canterbury tales. III. Title.

PS8603.R56R36 2006   C811'.6   C2006-901750-6

ISBN-10: 0-88922-548-6
ISBN-13: 978-0-88922-548-0

CONTENTS

For Sheila, the muse and queen of her court, where I was once among the pages.

Whoso shal telle a tale after a man,
He moot reherce as ny as evere he kan
Everich a word, if it be in his charge,
Al speke he never so rudeliche and large,
Or ellis he moot telle his tale untrewe,
Or feyne thyng, or fynde wordes newe.

Like its namesake, this is a book about storytelling, and about the way stories are carried on through different forms, languages, cultures, and centuries. The simplest version goes like this: a few years ago I took some stories from a fourteenth-century manuscript and rewrote them into a contemporary rhyme style and they are printed here. We could leave it at that and simply allow these stories to have their impact (skip to page 66 for this option), but stories tend to produce stories of their own, and the ones I chose to translate seem to have accumulated some density. In the general prologue you will also learn how my source created his stories, and why he chose to use iambic pentameter couplets to tell them, and why I chose a more recent rhyme format for my translation, and where those two different forms come from and how they are related. In fact, over the past few years I have found it impossible to tell the stories in *The Rap Canterbury Tales* without also telling the story of how their creation came about, which now deserves an explanation.

This book began as the solution to a problem. Geoffrey Chaucer wrote *The Canterbury Tales* over the last two decades of the fourteenth century, and it has brought him over six hundred years of imitation and reverence. However, today Chaucer's poetry is only generally accessible to scholars and students of Middle English. The rhyming verse in *The Canterbury Tales* is explicitly designed for oral recitation, as was most poetry in the Middle Ages, but the language is too different from our own to retain its original impact. The problem, as I saw it, was that Chaucer's literary importance has always been a function of his popularity, and his popularity was waning. I wanted to bring these stories back to life, but translating them into prose would only stifle the lyricism in Chaucer's narrative voice. On the other hand, translating them into a contemporary iambic pentameter would still feel archaic to the modern ear. What I needed was a new medium that would capture the same ethos as Chaucer did for his age: a live performance mode rich in wordplay and lyrical nuance, with a technique that could grab a live audience's attention and hold it long enough to tell a complex story.

At the same time, I saw this translation project as the solution to another problem. I have been involved with hip-hop culture and rap music (hip-hop's oral expression), either as an avid listener or as an artist, since the age of eleven, and I see it as the embodiment and essence of what poetry should be, and once was. Hip-hop is the site where literature is produced before it is recognized as literature: the pen, the pad, the stage, the performer, and the crowd. Whether or not any individual creation is recognized as literature is the business of forensic scholars; what is more important today is hip-hop's emerging status as the source of more creative juice than any other musical or literary genre. This is partially a function of its simplicity and accessibility, since rhyme, rhythm, and storytelling are such universal human instincts. However, at this point hip-hop must be recognized as the primary creative source because it is now the preferred medium of expression for the first-ever globally connected generation. This unifying potential should be a cause for celebration, but previous generations still tend to resent and fear hip-hop culture and denounce it as a corrupting influence, mostly because of widespread misrepresentation of the culture's core values in the media.

The humble ambition that inspired me to write *The Rap Canterbury Tales* was a desire to resurrect Chaucer's brilliant stories from their vellum mausoleum by giving them a new form that would once again delight and edify live listening audiences, while at the same time redeeming hip-hop in the eyes of my parents' generation. Since Chaucer is an unassailable icon of literary culture and the old guard, I saw his poetry as a valuable tool to dismantle the widespread prejudice against hip-hop culture, which gave birth to the art form I love. Also, since hip-hop is an unassailable icon of contemporary cool, I saw it as the perfect medium to deliver Chaucer's message to a younger generation growing indifferent to the delights of archaic literature.

I chose to translate only the specific *Canterbury Tales* that would work best in a live performance context—stories with a coherent narrative thread, a solid and conclusive ending, and intrigues involving those old stalwarts of pop culture: sex and violence. For the past six years I have performed various incarnations of these stories in front of thousands of people around the world, as well as setting them to a hip-hop soundtrack and recording them in the form of a rap album. Until now, they have existed only in the form of sound waves and digital files and never on paper, except in my notebook. They are presented here, along with Chaucer's original Middle English and my explanatory introductions, as the best possible way of telling the story of how these stories came about, and what they were meant to do. There is more here than I could ever get a live audience to sit through, and it is only at this point in the story's evolution that I am willing to leave the listener behind, briefly. It is my hope, however, that reading this book will do more for your appreciation of poetry *off* the page than anything I could say to you in person, or in rhyme. Experience precedes formulation, and the spoken word precedes the written, but once you have read, I invite you to listen.

Recordings of these *Tales* are available at www.babasword.com.

GENERAL PROLOGUE

Ther is no newe gyse, that it nas old.

This story begins in April, when spring rains engender flowers, birds sing, and people start to think about going on pilgrimages. In the first April of the new millennium I was busy finishing my English honours thesis, "Competitive Poetics: A Comparison of Speaker/Audience Relationships in Hip-hop Lyrics and *The Canterbury Tales*." When my last assignments were handed in I would leave the city to work in the mountains for the summer, planting trees. I was also busy making travel plans for autumn, the beginning of my hard-earned post-graduation year off. My plan was to go to England to perform my newly minted hip-hop adaptation of Geoffrey Chaucer's *Knight's Tale* at the Canterbury Festival 2000, a celebration marking the six-hundredth anniversary of the poet's death. This was amazing synchronicity, I thought.

> But he that departed is in everi place
> Is nowher hol, as written clerkes wyse.
> What wonder is, though swich oon have no grace?
> Ek wostow how it fareth of som servise,
> As plaunte a tree or herbe, in sondrey wyse,
> And on the morwe pulle it up as blyve!
> No wonder is, though it may nevere thryve.

You may ask yourself, how did I get here? The idea came to me about nine months earlier. I was at my summer job, planting trees on a muddy clear-cut, thinking about rap music and about traditional English poetry, and for the first time I recognized them as part of the same continuum. My reasoning was simple: if Shakespeare is poetry, then rap is poetry. This is not to say that any living rapper is necessarily on par with Shakespeare as a poet, but rather that rap fills virtually the same social niche: live performances of oral storytelling and lyrical entertainment. The general perception of rap as a popular form unsuited to literary subject matter only reinforces the correlation, since Shakespeare's plays were also a form of populist entertainment, and were only later adopted by academics and hailed as great literature in hindsight.

Storytelling and language arts once existed only as live performances, and our appetite for literature today has its roots in that experience. Perhaps rap has succeeded by speaking directly to that instinct in a way that contemporary poetry rarely does. If the enduring relevance of literature is a function of popular appeal rather than intellectual pretensions, then rap music may be the Elizabethan theatre of our time. The specific connection to Chaucer didn't occur to me at first, simply because I was less familiar with him, but I was sure this correlation would extend far beyond Shakespeare.

Associating rap with literature made immediate sense to me logically, but the connection also became a source of creative inspiration. I had recently started writing lyrics and performing as a hip-hop artist, and my intention was to make it professionally. However, I was also three years into an English degree and clearly the demands on a scholar's time were not compatible with launching a music career. At least by making hip-hop lyrics my subject I could advance my understanding of the art form in tandem with my skills. Hip-hop appealed to me as a creative outlet partially because it makes such brilliant use of rhyme and rhythm, devices that traditionally marked the difference between poetry and prose. Hip-hop artists and literary poets of the past are united by their use of structured language, while contemporary poets tend to reject formal devices in favour of free verse. In Shakespeare's *Much Ado About Nothing*, Benedick complains, "I was not born under a rhyming planet," as if skill with rhymes were an innate quality that some people are simply endowed with, either by providence or by genetic disposition. However, if rhyming planets do exert an influence on poetic form, then most of the twentieth century has been a bit of a dark age, and scientists have yet to discover a lyrical gene to correct the problem. Yet rappers now routinely claim to be possessed by rhyme in the same fatalistic way, as in the words of Bubba Sparxxx, "I ain't choose to rhyme; rhymin' chose me." I realized that there had to be a connection between the formal parallels (rhyme and rhythm) and the parallels in function (live entertainment), all of which seemed to put both hip-hop and traditional English poetry at odds with today's published free verse. The inspiration I felt that day in the summer of 1999 was not so much an epiphany as an overwhelming sense of curiosity, compelling me to explore.

> Diverse scoles maken parfyt clerkes,
> And diverse practyk in many sundry werkes

As with many theories, I began with an intuitive certainty and then faced the daunting challenge of proving the correlation with evidence. When I returned to university in September for my final year I immediately announced to my supervisors that rap lyrics would be the subject of my honours thesis, and that I wanted to connect rap with literary history. They actually took this better than you might expect. The main caveat I got was that I wouldn't get away with doing less research simply because I had picked a "fun" subject. So I hit the library, and was surprised to find quite a few books on hip-hop culture waiting for me, shattering my assumption that the study of rap would be relatively virgin academic territory. However, most of these books and articles discussed hip-hop in terms of political science and cultural studies rather than literature, tracing the music's roots in the oral traditions of the African Diaspora. The only explicit connections I could find between rap artists and literary poets were references within the lyrics themselves. While cultural scholars were pronouncing rappers the inheritors of the Nigerian griot storyteller, Black Thought from The Roots was rapping, "My style's got the rhythm that of an Anglo Saxon"; Q-Tip from A Tribe Called Quest proclaimed, "It's the Abstract Poet, prominent like Shakespeare"; and my favourite thinking-man's rapper at the time, Canibus, growled, "I'm breakin' the laws of physics with metaphors and lyrics / Speakin' to dead poets by conjuring up their spirits / From Shakespeare to Edgar Allen / Yo, the whole Dead Poet's Society couldn't mess around with the talent."

What I also discovered when I began to research rap in earnest was that its cultural context was far larger and more complex than I had imagined. By 1999 rap had spread from its origins in New York City in the seventies into every urban centre on the planet. I read about rappers in Asia, Africa, the Middle East, Europe, South America, and dozens of other places I had never imagined hip-hop to exist. I also found that each of these sub-cultures had managed to claim hip-hop for its own, adapting the art form to local needs and circumstances. Even its roots were being debated. Most of the books and articles treated hip-hop specifically as a black cultural phenomenon, but one article that stood out for me was about the Latino roots of hip-hop. The argument was that the origins of hip-hop were equal parts black and Latino but blacks had unfairly taken full credit for it, and these early Latino rappers could trace their cultural roots back to the ancient Aztec warrior poets of Mexico. This immediately gave me pause to think about my own intentions, since I was reading articles by black writers about rap's African roots, articles by Latinos about rap's Aztec roots, and I was planning to make an argument connecting rappers to white Europeans.

Apparently each person who engages with hip-hop culture, either as an artist or a critic (if there's a difference), tends to imagine hip-hop in the context of their own heritage, but these perspectives can't all have equal historical merit. If the people who invented hip-hop were all black and Latino then theirs are the roots of the culture, yet few would argue that hip-hop is of pure stock in the same way as, say, pre-contact indigenous peoples' traditions. Hip-hop's original roots didn't grow in a vacuum; they were quickly grafted from all sides and nurtured in the American urban melting pot under the influence of post-industrial European institutions. However, I wasn't out to claim hip-hop's roots as European, only to show that hip-hop has grown into the cultural space once filled by European poets, who themselves were the inheritors of bards and oral storytellers. The challenge with oral traditions is that they leave no physical record, so they can't be studied in the same way as the written word. It is usually only possible to discuss them through the work of ethnographers and anthropologists, or sometimes in terms of written texts that employ oral storytelling techniques. Rappers, on the other hand, write their lyrics down and mass-produce them for resale, activities more familiar to post-literate European poets than pre-literate African griots. However, when it comes to oral traditions it could be said that all roads lead to Africa, since modern humans are all descended from African ancestors. African Americans are more directly connected to this heritage, but if you trace any culture's oral tradition back far enough it will lead to the same place. Some rappers even see hip-hop as Africa's gift to the world, a form of global creative redemption by way of slavery and the Diaspora. This view is explained by Common, a rap artist from Chicago: "[Black people] are obviously shining our light to the world, and went through these trials and tribulations for a certain reason."

Besides navigating this cultural labyrinth, my real challenge was narrowing the subject down to more concrete terms without losing sight of the greater trend. I began to hunt through the canon for stylistic analogies and discovered some interesting parallels. For instance, the rhymed short-line verse structure of John Skelton's sixteenth-century poem "Phillip Sparrow" is almost identical to DMX's rhyme style in "Rough Rider's Anthem," which was a hit song at the time. I also found dozens of parallels in the content of traditional poetry and rap lyrics, such as Thomas Wyatt, "Then seek no more out of thyself to find / The thing that thou hast sought so long before / For thou shalt feel it sitting in thy mind," and Blackalicious, "The final destination used to be my main question / But then I looked and all that I was searching for was present." This was a scavenger hunt though, yielding interesting tidbits but no smoking gun. That same semester I was also enrolled in my first full course on Chaucer's poetry, and I began to get into his world through close readings in tutorial. Historically Chaucer seemed like an excellent candidate for comparison with hip-hop because of his closeness to the oral traditions of England and the extent of his influence on future generations of poets, including Shakespeare, and also because Chaucer's particular dialect of English was later accepted as the written standard. For these and many other reasons he has been recognized for centuries as the "father of English poetry," and thus Chaucer and hip-hop could be seen as bookends representing the earliest and latest expressions of rhymed narrative verse in the English language.

> And though I nat the same wordes seye
> As ye han herd, yet to yow alle I preye
> Blameth me nat; for, as in my sentence,
> Shul ye nowher fynden difference

The most remarkable analogies I found between Chaucer and hip-hop were not only historical, however; they were also reflected explicitly in the organizational structure of *The Canterbury Tales*. The text consists of a collection of stories that Chaucer wrote over the course of about fifteen years towards the end of his life. Some of the *Tales* were apparently composed before he began the compilation, while others were obviously tailor-made for the project. To bring all of these different stories together into one, Chaucer creates a fictional company of pilgrims riding on horseback from London to Canterbury, who all decide to play a game to help pass the time along the way: a storytelling contest. Each tale represents an entry in the contest by one of the pilgrims, and Chaucer ascribes certain personality traits to each of them, which are then reflected in their tales. What begins on the surface as a religious pilgrimage soon takes a profane turn when the stories become a vehicle for challenges and insults aimed at the other pilgrims. Chaucer employs the competition as a unifying principle, but also as a device to expose social tensions among the pilgrims, while showcasing their different storytelling techniques and levels of ability.

The clearest analogy for this storytelling contest model in hip-hop culture is the phenomenon of the freestyle battle, a live performance event that underlies the majority of recorded rap lyrics either in style or content. By definition, a freestyle is a rap that is unwritten and unrehearsed, composed by the rapper in the moment of performance, with rhymes that are improvised on beat and, when required, on topic. A freestyle battle is when two or more rappers compete in this way head to head, using punch lines, boasts, and insults to out-rhyme and outwit their opponents. The two terms aren't interchangeable though, since written rhymes are sometimes used in battles, and freestyles are often simple demonstrations of ability rather than direct competitions. Freestyle and battling perform the same function in hip-hop culture as Chaucer's storytelling competition does in *The Canterbury Tales*, dramatizing social tensions among rappers and showcasing different techniques and levels of ability. These systems were developed in response to the particular conditions of hip-hop's genesis.

Hip-hop first appeared in the mid-1970s in the Bronx borough of New York as a dance party phenomenon, the result of extreme creativity fostered under conditions of extreme poverty. Innovative DJs like Kool Herc, Grandmaster Flash, and Afrika Bambaataa entertained crowds at block parties by playing a new style of music, blending together only the "break beat" or percussion breakdown sections of records selected from various musical genres. The point was to keep people dancing by never letting the beat stop or falter in intensity. Before rap lyrics were ever recorded, DJs would hook up microphones to their mixers and have someone (or themselves) hype up the crowd with simple rhymed phrases like "Throw your hands in the air, and wave 'em like you just don't care." These hype-men came to be known as MCs, for "Master of Ceremonies" or "Mic Controller" or Rakim's interpretation: "No mistakes allowed / 'Cause to me, MC means 'Move the Crowd.'" It was during this period in the mid- to late seventies that the core elements of hip-hop culture all appeared in the Bronx: turntablism, rapping, break-dancing, beat-boxing, and graffiti art, all characterized by the need to find outlets for creative energy (musical, lyrical, kinetic, percussive, artistic) using only the limited resources of the urban ghetto.

Hip-hop was intensely competitive from the beginning, with decibel battles between sound systems, b-boy battles among break-dancers, territorial battles among graffiti writers, battles over DJ skills, and lyrical battles for prestige among MCs. This was partly because the Bronx was a centre of gang activity in the seventies, and the performance battles of hip-hop culture were invented to take the place of physical encounters. Rappers began channelling other oral traditions such as signifying (insult contests) into their live performances, and the competitive atmosphere increased the pressure on rappers to distinguish their styles and be clever and innovative with their wordplay. There wasn't a culture of celebrity around the rappers yet, however; they were part of larger sound crews and their primary function was to support the DJs, who were the culture's real pioneers. There also wasn't much money in hip-hop in its embryonic phase, but there was respect to be gained, and those crews with the most recognition were soon doing paid gigs at clubs.

> And therefore every man this tale I telle,
> Wynne whoso may, for al is for to selle;

In 1979 the first commercially successful hip-hop record, "Rapper's Delight," was released as a single on the label Sugar Hill Gang. Up until "Rapper's Delight," the only way to make money from hip-hop was by performing live, but with that one song's immense success there was an immediate shift in the aspirations of artists towards recording projects. There is still a lot of nostalgia in hip-hop culture today about this pre-commercial period when rappers were defined strictly by their live performance skills and not by their corporate promotional backing, but rap music's pop-culture status remains a paradox that even the strictest purists can't escape. Without "Rapper's Delight" and the parade of commercial hits that followed, the phenomenon we call hip-hop wouldn't necessarily still exist, or most people wouldn't have heard of it. When rap was adopted by the popular music industry in full force throughout the eighties and beyond, it permanently changed the face of the culture, but surprisingly little of the essential elements of hip-hop's foundation were altered. Instead, the sites of hip-hop cultural production were split loosely into two camps with different functions, underground and mainstream. The mainstream manifests itself whenever hip-hop crosses over successfully into mass media, while the underground maintains the same live performance aesthetic that defined the culture's origins.

When I first started rapping I didn't realize how crucial both freestyle and battling are to hip-hop culture. I started off simply writing rhymes and memorizing them, ready to recite to anyone who would listen. On a few occasions I would spout off in front of an MC about how I was an MC too, and I often got the same response: "You're an MC? Okay, let's hear you freestyle." I would answer that I couldn't do it, and would repeatedly be told, "If you can't freestyle, you're not an MC." At the same time I started noticing this distinction in hip-hop lyrics as well; for instance, a New York MC called Wordsworth declares, "I'm from an environment where freestyle's the requirement / I bought every album; then my parents had to hide the rent." It was also repeated often in books on hip-hop: a rapper is someone who writes rhymes and memorizes and records them, while an MC has the ability to write and memorize but can also freestyle and battle other MCs in a live setting. In other words, every MC is a rapper, but not every rapper is an MC. Live performances are inherently less profitable than selling records because of the physical limitations of the audience, so freestyle and battling skills alone are not usually enough to sustain a career in hip-hop. Instead, live performances function as a training ground for artists, who are expected to pay their dues before graduating to the recorded medium. MCs aren't required to continue battling and freestyling regularly once their music careers take off, but they must be *able* to demonstrate their skills if challenged. Constant battling is counter-productive when you're making records, so in this case the readiness is all. Some rappers naturally try to subvert this process, recording radio singles without building any live skills first, but MCs tend to denounce this as an unfair cop-out or shortcut, since they consider their skills harder won. On the other hand, some battle MCs never make the transition to becoming recording artists, and the greatest success comes from balancing live performance skills with record sales. This is where the tension arises between the underground and mainstream, and hip-hop culture is produced in the ebb and flow of this tension.

Hip-hop's underground and mainstream veins interact much like organisms in symbiosis, or like parts of the psyche. The underground functions as hip-hop's conscience, while the mainstream functions as its ego. The underground accuses the mainstream of selling out, and the mainstream accuses the underground of player hating. The underground provides the mainstream with talented new artists reluctantly eager to cross over, while the mainstream ensures hip-hop's dominance in the public media, keeping underground artists motivated by the distant promise of fame and fortune. Neither side can exist without the other. Anyone who complains about the negativity of rap—the violence, misogyny, and jewelry-obsessed materialism that have come to define the majority of mainstream artists' content—is in essence mistaking the mainstream for the culture as a whole. However, this is an illusion of visibility, like watching a summer blockbuster and instantly dismissing cinema as an inherently superficial art form. The reason MTV and Top 40 hip-hop are rife with criminality and the objectification of women is because gratuitous sex and violence are universally marketable subjects. This also explains the commercial success of pulp fiction novels, prime-time television, and Hollywood movies. Mainstream hip-hop is marketed and distributed entirely by a handful of profit-driven corporations, and they predictably guide mainstream artists' content in a profitable direction. This is a constant source of frustration for underground MCs at the top of their game, as expressed in Immortal

Technique's rant, "And now they say they wanna get me signed to the majors / If I switch up my politics and change my behaviour." However, many hip-hop fans would consider "signing to the majors" a betrayal in itself, regardless of content. Likewise, this is a constant source of frustration for commercially successful artists who don't feel like their content has suffered as much as their credibility simply for being popular, which prompts Wyclef to mock, "Hip-hop fans, you're like the woman in my house / No matter how loyal I am, you still have your doubts / Talkin' about, 'is he real in this relationship? / Or did he "go pop" and on the side get a mistress?'"

> For what man that is entred in a pley,
> He nedes moot unto the pley assente.

Around the time I started learning about the role of freestyle battling in hip-hop culture, I also started watching live battles and freestyle performances in my hometown of Vancouver. I was aware that most rappers typically cut their teeth freestyling in the schoolyard or on the corner, but I was insulated from this community during my first year as an MC (or proto-MC) since I didn't know many rappers. It also took me a while to accept the fact that I was going to have to learn to freestyle on demand if I wanted to get even a nod from other artists. Freestyle is a skill that seems nearly impossible when you first try it, and gets easier and easier as you practise, as with any instrument combining sound and rhythm, but it also requires a cognitive attention to meaning. Paradoxically, thinking too much about your words is totally paralyzing, so freestyle requires a balance between intense mental focus and absolute faith, allowing the words to come from somewhere unknown (either the subconscious or the spiritual realm, depending on your beliefs). This is also the source of traditional English dream poetry such as the Venerable Bede's "Account of Caedmon" or Samuel Taylor Coleridge's "Kubla Khan," which is not rationally "composed" in a cognitive sense. Freestyle is not free from structure, however, only from pre-composition: its quality is determined by the ingenuity and harmony of the rhymes, and the way they react to the beat. There is an element of freestyle in all writing, in so far as every word is produced in a given moment, but solitary composition affords the option to edit and rearrange. Hip-hop freestyle, on the other hand, is a continuous linguistic flow that exists only in the moment and cannot be captured or revised; it is a live event that offers a cross-section of the performer's mental landscape, history, personality, and skill level, revealing as much in the rhyme patterns and syntax as in the content of the words. Of course, it takes a trained ear to sort through it, but from the number of things I've surprised myself by saying in freestyles I imagine it could be of great use to psychologists, if anything is.

I remember feeling extremely discouraged at first by how awful I sounded. I can also remember a dream I had near the beginning of my experiments with freestyle (speaking of psychology). There was a bespectacled black Rastafarian hip-hopper with dreadlocks sitting on the hood of a car, and when I approached him he confronted me with the now-familiar, "Oh, you're an MC? Okay, let's hear you freestyle." My freestyle skills in the dream were equal to my skills in reality, virtually non-existent, and after a few awkward lines I stopped. Then he proceeded to demonstrate the possibilities of the art form, conjuring rhymes that rendered our surroundings in striking terms, using metaphors that defied anticipation, and twisting words and phrases into indescribable new forms. I remember thinking, in the dream, that I couldn't learn to freestyle that well if I spent the rest my life practising. I awoke with that same feeling of hopelessness, but later it occurred to me that on some level I had actually created *all* of the lyrics in my dream, both his and mine. Although I couldn't remember what was said, I was certain the words were real and intelligible, and I realized that this elusive ability was actually latent within me, perhaps within everyone. Soon my freestyle sessions took on the quality of uncovering something half-buried internally, rather than striving after something outside of myself. After all, I was already confident that I could write, and freestyle was just a matter of writing out loud, under pressure, much faster, continuously, while using rhyme and rhythm. It came slowly, but I built my confidence and my abilities in tandem, with Talib Kweli egging me on: "If you can talk you can sing, / If you can walk you can dance."

I was freestyling my head off (in private) by the time I launched into my thesis research in the autumn of 1999, but was still too green to enter real battles. I also resisted the idea of battling for a long time because I wanted to take a rhetorical stand against it as an MC. The first rhymes I wrote followed the standard "I/You" hip-hop formula where a phantom opponent (you) is insulted in contrast to one's own prowess (I), as in Lauren Hill's opening salvo in *The Score*: "Claimin' that you got a new style, / Your attempts are futile, / Oooh child, you're puerile, / Brain waves are sterile / You can't create; / You just wait to take my tape." This battle formula can be found in the majority of mainstream rap lyrics largely because most rappers develop their techniques through underground competitions before getting a record deal. However, it felt awkward and contrived to me, since most raps are actually delivered to an audience rather than an opponent (and Lauren is probably not calling her fans puerile, although some rappers do). So I decided to break from tradition and began addressing my "you" to the audience if I used the word at all, in both my written rhymes and freestyles. This gave me a broader frame of reference in my content than the standard battle metaphors, but it also made it harder for me to get my head into battle mode when I finally tried to make the switch.

> I can not se that arguments avayle:
> Thanne semeth it there moste be batayle

My initial ambivalence towards battling was transformed into pure reverence when I witnessed my first live event. It is impossible to capture the tension and excitement of a live battle in a mere description, but I can highlight some of the qualities that make it so fraught. Proper freestyle battles are rigidly structured, with time limits for the raps and clear standards of judgment. Competing MCs are usually organized into head-to-head battles in heats, eliminating half of the competitors in each round. In my first battle there were over fifty MCs signed up, so the organizers held a mass qualifying round right at the beginning to determine who would make the final three rounds (I did not). This sudden surge of interest was spurred by the release of Eminem's semi-fictional biopic, *8 Mile*, which rekindled widespread interest in battling as an art form. Of course, battles still happened regularly before *8 Mile* came out, but I had never heard of fifty MCs signing up for one. It was proof that there were closet rappers everywhere.

Since the purpose of a battle is to test MCs and also to entertain hip-hop fans, the audience is always an integral part of the performance. At the beginning of a battle the host will usually announce something like this to the crowd: "If you feel what these guys are sayin' you better make some noise for them, and if you think it's weak, well, you better let 'em know it." The invitation to participate effectively puts the audience in the judge's seat, since battles are usually decided by crowd response. Rappers sometimes pack the crowd with their friends to bias the outcome, so a few individual judges are often designated to make a final call. However, judging also introduces the possibility of corruption into the battle arena, since it's generally easier to bribe or influence an individual than a mob, which is why most MCs would rather lose to a biased crowd than a biased judge. Despite this slight grey area, in 99 percent of battles the judges go with the crowd, and the winner is usually obvious to everyone. It is also the audience's belief in their own supremacy that spurs them to participate, and it is the MCs' subjection to the crowd's will that keeps them humble and at the same time gives them their confidence. This confidence comes from the knowledge that there is no elusive essentialist standard by which your raps will be judged in a battle; there is only you, your opponent, and the crowd. Win the crowd and you win the contest. Winning the crowd is harder than it sounds, however, since hip-hop crowds are notoriously hostile to performers. There is no appreciation given for effort or good intentions, only a frank and raucous appraisal of each MC's entertainment value from moment to moment. To win a battle you have to draw on a combination of quick thinking, rhythmic delivery, cleverness, and confidence, all live on stage while being analyzed and insulted by your opponent. If you falter, stutter, or fail to be generally entertaining, the crowd will take the opportunity to loudly heckle you off stage, interrupting you even before your minute is up.

The thing that makes freestyle battling such an effective test of an MC's ability is that it is virtually impossible to fake. Once MCs get on stage it quickly becomes obvious whether or not they are able to compete, because of the intense pressure applied by the audience. Occasionally rappers will attempt to pass their written rhymes off as freestyles in a battle, but this is an old trick and the crowd is always looking for it. Battle freestyles have to use the immediate setting as a source of material, by rhyming on the opponent's name and appearance, and especially by responding to things that were said in the last rap. This serves as a test of MCs' ability to focus and think on their feet, which increases the entertainment value of the performance; it also signifies to the crowd that the rhymes aren't regurgitated. If an MC is battling with lines that sound too abstract, or the rhyme schemes are too obviously structured, the crowd will often harangue and make a gesture in the air like a pen writing, calling, "Booooo! Written! Written!" I have seen MCs get disqualified from battles because their rhymes, while effective in every other way, were exposed by the crowd's response as pre-written.

> For soothly, he that precheth to hem that listen nat
> heeren his wordes, his sermon hem anoieth.

The result of this heavy scrutiny and the structured simplicity of the battle format is that most rappers, like myself, eventually have to concede that the only way to win battles is to practise obsessively and build your skills until you have the confidence and command of language necessary to perform under those conditions. There is no way to circumvent the paying of dues in this context, which ensures that only those who are serious about being hip-hop artists can succeed, although even with commitment there is no guarantee. In a battle you can't expect the crowd's indulgence just because you are exposing them to your personal art, nor can you attribute a hostile response from the crowd to their lack of taste, or insightfulness, or discernment. These are excuses that have exposed countless audiences to stupefying drivel at the hands of inept performers, whatever the genre. In a battle the only valid definition of taste, skill, authenticity, originality, craftsmanship, quality, genius, or any other criteria that we use to distinguish great art from mediocre, all flows directly from the crowd in the moment of the performance, and anyone with enough talent and dedication can capture this current. It is also irrelevant what you have achieved in the past, how rich you are, what colour you are, or what your reputation is; all that matters is how you perform. Evidence, one of the MCs from Dilated Peoples, says it best: "Fuck what you've done; if you've got skills, reveal it."

There is something appealing about the inherent fairness of this system. No one planned or designed it; it simply evolved along with hip-hop culture as a way to test the skills and dedication of artists, preventing posers and amateurs from dominating the stage. The reason this mechanism evolved is obvious: there were simply more people who wanted to be rappers than there were people willing to support them. This is described by Pras of the Fugees in terms of a competition for resources: "Too many MCs, not enough mics." The existence of freestyle battling and live performance as a necessary trial for underground MCs acts as a form of natural selection or quality control for hip-hop culture as a whole, demanding a level of commitment from artists that isn't imposed by the recording industry. Record companies don't care whether their artists can battle, only whether they sell records. Reciprocally, underground hip-hop heads care more about an artist's skills and authenticity than about Sony's profit margin. Freestyle and battling evolved in response to local challenges, namely the disproportionate number of aspiring rappers; however, the unintended result has been an impressive talent pool that contributes to hip-hop's continued dominance of the music industry and global popular culture. This relationship also steeps hip-hop culture in the ideal of meritocracy, where creativity is rewarded and fraud is punished. Of course, this ideal is constantly frustrated and perforated in reality by record companies and the market-driven mainstream media responsible for broadcasting the message, but this only feeds into the underground's commitment to self-determination.

As I gradually came to understand the function of freestyle battling and live performance in hip-hop culture, I also began reading Chaucer's poetry through the lens of my experience. The result was that it became impossible for me to conceive of Chaucer outside of the context of what I was learning about hip-hop. I viewed live hip-hop shows as field research, and my close readings of Chaucer as lab work. Whether you attribute it to the power of positive thinking or to the pattern-recognition neurosis that plagued John Nash, I found exactly what I was looking for in *The Canterbury Tales*. Chaucer seems to have designed his pilgrim storytelling contest around the exact same principles and guidelines that govern hip-hop's underground, and I believe he uses these devices for the exact same function they perform in hip-hop culture. I would even argue that Chaucer *anticipates* hip-hop in a number of important ways, by dramatizing live performance and competition explicitly in his content, by drawing attention to different stylistic choices, and by raising questions about the poet's place in society at large, all within the playful context of a fictional game.

In the *General Prologue* to *The Canterbury Tales*, Chaucer establishes the setting, introduces his characters, and sets up the framework for everything that follows. He tells us that he was resting at a Southwark inn, near London, preparing to leave the next day on a pilgrimage to Canterbury, when a group of twenty-nine other pilgrims arrived at the inn with the same purpose. By the end of that day, Chaucer tells us, he has already spoken to each of these pilgrims and learned virtually everything about them, and he goes on to describe their history, appearance, and personality, one by one. There is an element of magic realism in this narrative already (or simply tall-tale telling), since the details Chaucer gives are more complex than anyone could possibly have learned from an afternoon of conversations, no matter how sharp their networking skills. This will not be the last time he makes use of his fictional licence for the purpose of the story. Once the pilgrims have been introduced, we meet the innkeeper, described as a large man, bold and impressive, whom Chaucer refers to as "our Host" throughout. The Host proposes a game for the "sport" and "comfort" of the journey, a storytelling contest in which each pilgrim will tell a tale as they ride along (actually the proposed scope of the work has each pilgrim telling two tales on the way to Canterbury and two on the way back for a total of 120 tales, but Chaucer died before completing them all and never revised the introduction). According to the Host, the stories must be "aventures that whilom han bifalle," (things that happened in the past), and whoever "bereth hym best of alle" (performs the best) will win the prize, which is a "soper at our aller cost" (a free meal). The criteria for judging the tales will be based on two factors, "best sentence" and "moost solaas" (most solace), which is generally taken to mean the tales with the most meaningful content and the most entertainment value. This balancing act between a story's ability to edify and entertain is based on the old Latin maxim *delectare et docere* (to delight and to teach), a classical literary ideal that is returned to throughout the *Tales*. The Host also declares that he will join the pilgrimage and act as a judge for the contest, like the mediator of a freestyle battle. Chaucer even begins by calling the Host a "marchel in an halle," or Master of Ceremonies (MC).

> Though I right now sholde make my testament,
> I ne owe hem nat a word that it nys quit.

The Knight opens the contest with an epic tale of chivalric romance, the longest and most complicated of *The Canterbury Tales*. When *The Knight's Tale* finally ends, the Miller declares that he is going to "quite" the Knight, a word that in Chaucer's time meant "respond to" or "pay back," the root of our word "unrequited." The Miller goes on to tell a tale in which the Knight's themes are all reversed, chivalry is lampooned, and the rich old carpenter John is humiliated. This aggravates another pilgrim, the Reeve, who is a carpenter by trade, and he responds with a tale in which a miller is humiliated in a similar way. The Reeve claims self-defence: "[L]eveful is with force force of-showve" (it is right to respond to force with force). This theme of "quiting" is carried on throughout the tales, with rivalries cropping up among the pilgrims over their social standing, their personalities, and their conflicting views. Sometimes these rivalries are mediated and defused by the Host, and other times he seems to fuel them and stir up his own conflicts. As the journey unfolds, Chaucer usually remains in the background as an observer, telling us what the other pilgrims are saying and doing without getting himself involved.

"Quiting" is also one of the most important factors in a freestyle battle, since the crowd demands an interactive event, looking for constant evidence of improvisation. Although Chaucer never explicitly tells us whether the stories in *The Canterbury Tales* are being improvised or recited verbatim from memory, the presence of "quiting" in the text implies that at least the *choice* of tale is flexible, since each narrative may be required to respond to the previous one. If they are meant to be improvised stories, it is obviously only within the fictional world Chaucer creates in the text, since text is relatively static by definition. This would make them like the scripted battles in *8 Mile*, which are not literally improvised but are meant to signify real freestyles within the fiction of the movie. Of course, the improvisation required of rappers in a freestyle battle is not expected to be absolute either. Many of the rhymes will have been used before in other freestyles or written songs, and common themes and refrains allow the mind to move from topic to topic without stumbling. What is required, however, is novelty in the word order within lines, and if material is being transplanted from other performances it must fit the specific context of the battle, proving that the rapper can interact with his environment. This is precisely the way storytellers have traditionally functioned in oral cultures throughout history, constantly retelling old stories with new words, improvising only in the details. One of the only published links I found between hip-hop and European oral traditions in my research was an essay comparing hip-hop freestyle to Homer's versification techniques in *The Iliad*, both of which require the poet to master a range of rhythmic and descriptive patterns within which to fit their improvised lines. This is also how I read Chaucer's *Canterbury Tales*; the pilgrims are telling familiar stories of the past, but the individual lines and rhymes are being improvised, at least fictionally. This is much more believable from the perspective of verisimilitude as well, since it is much easier to learn the general plots of stories than it is to memorize them word for word.

> Whiche layes with hir instrumentz they songe
> Or elles redden hem for hir plesaunce

To get a better sense of Chaucer's treatment of oral traditions in *The Canterbury Tales*, it is important to consider his historical context. Chaucer was writing in the latter part of the fourteenth century, which was a transitional period for poetry in medieval English society. Court records show that up until the twelfth and thirteenth centuries, minstrels were regularly receiving aristocratic support for their services as both musicians and storytellers, so that poetry and music were inextricably linked during this time. By the fourteenth and fifteenth centuries, however, there is a well-documented change in the social function of minstrels, who were specializing into a more narrowly defined role as musicians and singers, rather than poets and storytellers. Of course, many minstrels may have continued to compose and perform poetry, but there is virtually no further record of them being paid for this service, only for their music. One explanation that has been offered for this shift is the rise of what Richard Firth Green calls the "household poet." As medieval culture generally grew more literate, aristocratic households were increasingly filled with amateur poets whose performances placed them in competition with the minstrels who had traditionally monopolized the role of oral storyteller. Gradually this trend caused the mystique to disappear from the poet's role, since poetry was now practised so commonly it was no longer worth paying for. Minstrels survived this transformation by increasingly specializing as musicians, for which they were still in high demand, but poetry became something far more communal and democratic, open to anyone who cared to join in, as opposed to an exclusive class of trained professionals.

One of the most dramatic effects of this trend was a collapse of the sense of separation that had once defined the relationship between poet and audience. Minstrels had previously enjoyed a certain aura of mystery around their status as performers and guardians of social and spiritual tradition, similar to oral storytellers in pre-literate cultures. In contrast, the amateur household poets who succeeded them were far less privileged, since any member of the audience might also be a performer waiting to participate. As a result poetry became a more accessible activity, but at the same time there was less assurance of quality, leaving it up to the audience to decide what was acceptable. Also, with the barriers broken down, the audience now had far more freedom to provide instant feedback, which increased the pressure on poets to meet a certain performance standard or suffer the consequences. One important outcome of these combined factors was an increase in competition among amateur poets, which found its expression in various literary games, such as riddles and verse improvisation contests.

Another important effect of this shift was that poetry became more closely associated with writing as opposed to the spoken word. While minstrels were expected to improvise and recite without any text on hand, the amateur household poet was a versifier who wrote his lines down. Of course, writing was still understood as a blueprint for recitation and poetry was generally read out loud, but the increased use of text certainly had an effect on the poet's imagined reception (a.k.a. ego), which could now include absent readers as well as present listeners. Chaucer's was a manuscript culture, which combined elements of the oral with elements of the textual; however, the printing press was still over a century away and manuscripts were far more expensive than most people could afford. Thus, there was an inherent conflict in the fact that this move towards text happened at a time when poetry was no longer a paid vocation. The only way for a poet to produce a manuscript was to gain the recognition necessary to have it paid for by a wealthy patron, and this was rare. The relationship between written and spoken poetry in Chaucer's time was therefore analogous to the relationship between hip-hop's mainstream and underground components today. Record labels now function as the patrons who support artists with sufficient recognition among their peers, and hip-hop albums, like manuscripts, are meant to capture the essence of the oral performances that preceded them, and stand as a blueprint for the performances to come. Poets with a patron in the fourteenth century also had less freedom to choose their content, like artists signed to a major label, since the patron would commission poems on certain prescribed subjects (such as their own magnificence). So was Chaucer underground or mainstream? Of all the records of his life that survive, there is not one that refers to Chaucer as a professional poet, and there is no direct evidence that he was ever paid for his writing. However, there is ample evidence from the writing of his contemporaries, and from his own ironic self-references, that Chaucer was the most respected and prolific poet of his time writing in the English language; in other words, he was an underground legend.

> Also I prey yow to foryeve it me,
> Al have I nat set folk in hir degree
> Heere in this tale, as that they sholde stonde.
> My wit is short, ye may wel understonde.

The changing relationship between poets and their audiences that followed the displacement of minstrels by household poets is dramatized more clearly in *The Canterbury Tales* than in any other medieval text. None of the pilgrims enjoys a position of privilege over the others when it comes to telling their story. Of course, some pilgrims are treated more respectfully than others on the surface because of their social standing, but the tale-telling contest serves as a great leveller and subverter of the social hierarchy within the text. The Knight is from the highest social class, and he is "quited" by the Miller, who is among the lowest. As in a freestyle battle, the quality of the tales is rated only through the response of the audience, and a few of the performances are actually interrupted in mid-line because they are deemed unworthy to finish. Throughout the contest the Host functions alternately as the mediator and spokesman for the group, although he doesn't monopolize debate. This raises the same questions of bias as appointed judges in a freestyle battle, but in this case Chaucer was probably just using the Host as his fictional audience's mouthpiece for the sake of simplicity, saving him the trouble of thirty speeches after each performance. This is implied when he says "oure Hoost hadde the wordes for us alle" and also by the fact that none of the pilgrims ever contradicts anything the Host says about a tale. The function of audience feedback takes its most extreme form in the episode surrounding Chaucer's own submission to the storytelling contest, *The Tale of Sir Thopas.*

Throughout the frame story of *The Canterbury Tales* Chaucer remains mostly invisible as a witness, but at one point the Host notices him and calls him forward, demanding a tale. Although Chaucer certainly had a reputation in England as a great poet by the time of its composition, within the fiction of the text he is anonymous until the Host summons him: "What man artow?" All of the other pilgrims are named after their profession, so Chaucer would perhaps bear the title of "the Poet," but the beauty of his irony lies in its self-deprecation, and this scene is his masterpiece. The Host introduces Chaucer to the other pilgrims with a series of insults: "Thou lookest as thou wouldest find an hare, / For evere upon the ground I se thee stare" (Chaucer is staring meekly at the ground as if he is looking for a rabbit, a sure sign of stage fright). He goes on to mock Chaucer's appearance: "He in the waast is shape as wel as I; / This were a popet in an arm t'enbrace / For any womman" (He has a fat belly, like a puppet on a woman's arm), and also his shyness and mysteriousness: "He semeth elvyssh by his countenance, / For unto no wight dooth he daliaunce" (He is so antisocial that he seems like an elf or a fairy). The Host then commands Chaucer to "tell us a tale of mirth," and Chaucer's humble response is, "[O]other tale certes kan I noon, / But of a rym I lerned longe agoon" (I don't know any stories except for this one rhyme I learned long ago). Chaucer's claim that he only knows one story could be seen as a deliberate deception of the Host, but this is unlikely since the episode that follows would make it an uncharacteristically prolonged deception. Instead, Chaucer the master storyteller is presenting his fictional character within the text as a total amateur, and the tale he goes on to tell is deliberately crafted to stand out as the most pathetic entry in the competition.

On the surface *The Tale of Sir Thopas* is obviously meant to be a parody of bad romantic verse. It is overwrought and pretentious with an excess of pointless details, shallow caricatures instead of dynamic characters, and a plot that meanders about without really progressing. It is divided into short stanzas with irregular metre and trite rhymes that scholars have demonstrated by comparison to be below Chaucer's usual versifying standards. One typical passage reads:

> Sire Thopas wax a doughty swayn;
> Whit was his face as payndemayn,
> His lippes rede as rose;
> His rode is lyk scarlet in grayn,
> And I yow telle in good certain
> He hadde a semely nose.
>
> (Sir Thopas was a tough customer;
> His face was white as French bread,
> His lips red as rose;
> His complexion was like fine red cloth,
> And I can tell you truly
> He had an elegant nose.)

The content of the poem is manifestly shallow, its point deriving from its pointlessness, but Chaucer is still saying a great deal stylistically. *Sir Thopas* stands out in that it is the only one of the *Canterbury Tales* to be told in tetrameter tail-rhyme stanzas (lines with four alternating stresses combined with shorter lines), which was the favoured format of the metric romances popular in England for most of the fourteenth century, a style closely associated with minstrelsy. Chaucer is using this sing-song style to parody other poets and minstrels, but there may be an implied self-criticism as well, since he himself used tetrameter in most of his early verse. The significance of this contrast also lies in the continental European influences behind these techniques. Like most of Chaucer's earlier poems, the tetrameter of the English metric romance tradition was derived from French sources, but later in his career Chaucer encountered the poetry of the Italians, Dante, Petrarch, and Boccaccio, who were all writing in iambic pentameter (lines with five alternating stresses). Chaucer imported this form from Italy and adapted it to the cadences of Middle English, a great innovation for which he had no previous English models. Iambic pentameter couplets are less restrictive and thus better suited to narrative verse than the old tetrameter form, and once Chaucer made the switch he never returned, with the prominent exception of *The Tale of Sir Thopas*.

This sudden change in technique leaves the reader wondering what kind of joke Chaucer is trying to pull, since he seems to have affected a kind of prescient quixotic madness over a century before Cervantes. The story stumbles along as Sir Thopas dreams of an elf queen and goes prancing (Chaucer repeatedly uses the verb "pricking") through the fields to find her. He meets a three-headed giant called "Sir Oliphaunt," who challenges him to a duel, but he retreats back to town to drink and listen to minstrels with his friends. The climax comes as Sir Thopas is preparing to return for the duel, when the poem is interrupted in mid-line, "Til on a day –" and the Host cuts in rudely with the verdict:

> "Namoore of this, for Goddes dignitee,"
> Quod oure Hooste, "for thou makest me
> So wery of thy verray lewednesse
> That, also wisly God my soule blesse,
> Myne eres aken of thy drasty speche.
> Now swich a rym the devel I biteche!
> This may wel be rym dogerel," quod he.

> ("No more of this, for God's sake,"
> Said the Host, "you make me
> So weary of your utter vulgarity
> That, God forgive me,
> My ears hurt from your crappy speech.
> I condemn this rhyme to the devil!
> This may well be rhyme doggerel.")

Mercifully, Chaucer has returned to his trademark iambic pentameter couplets for the Host's response, a form that feels comparatively refreshing after the cluttered rhymes of *Sir Thopas*. Carrying on the dramatic irony, Chaucer acts wounded and defensive:

> "Why so?" quod I, "why wiltow lette me
> Moore of my tale than another man,
> Syn that it is the beste rym I kan?"

> ("Why won't you let me
> Tell my tale like the others,
> Since it's the best rhyme I know?")

This provokes a further attack from the Host:

> "By God," quod he, "for pleynly, at a word,
> Thy drasty rymyng is nat worth a toord!
> Thou doost noght elles but despendest tyme.
> Sire, at o word, thou shalt no lenger ryme."

> ("By God, because, in a word,
> Your crappy rhyming isn't worth a turd!
> You're doing nothing but wasting time.
> You shall no longer rhyme.")

This scene is so reminiscent of a hip-hop battle that I find it hard to believe it's over six hundred years old. Virtually everything the Host says to Chaucer can also be found in combative hip-hop lyrics. For example, Talib Kweli parallels the criticism of Chaucer's time-wasting and poor rhyming skills: "I don't get on stage and waste your time, / MCs got a lot to say, but they just can't rhyme." Eminem echoes the sentiment about empty speech: "Nowadays everybody wanna talk like they got somethin' to say / But nothin' comes out when they move their lips / Just a bunch of gibberish," as does Pharoah Monch: "A million MCs and they ain't sayin' nothin'!" The claim that Chaucer's rhymes aren't worth a turd has been reiterated in practically every battle I've ever witnessed.

> And whan this wise man saugh that hym wanted audience, al shamefast he sette hym doun agayn. For Salomon seith: "Ther as thou ne mayst have noon audience, enforce thee nat to speke."

When the Host says to Chaucer, "Thou shalt no longer rhyme," it seems like his turn must be over, but then the Host's speech takes on a conciliatory tone:

> "Lat se wher thou kanst tellen aught in geeste,
> Or telle in prose somwhat, at the leeste,
> In which ther be som murthe or som doctrine."

> ("Let's see if you can use alliteration,
> Or tell us something in prose at least,
> In which there is some mirth or meaning.")

As punishment for his ineptitude in *The Tale of Sir Thopas*, Chaucer is barred not from speaking, but from rhyming, and he is given the option to continue using either prose or alliteration (repetition of the first letter or sound in each word). Chaucer then goes on to tell *The Tale of Melibee*, a prose tract on compassion and good governance. The Host seems to be identifying a formal hierarchy within the storytelling competition, with rhymes representing the most difficult and thus the highest form, followed by alliteration, and finally prose, which is rated "at the leeste." This hierarchy is based on the complexity of each form's constituent parts, since rhymes use whole words for their effect, alliteration uses only one or two letters, and prose represents a complete forfeiture of verse structure. The idea of free verse would have been completely absurd to Chaucer, or he would have simply recognized it as a form of obscure prose broken up into shorter lines.

The scene that follows *The Tale of Sir Thopas* dramatizes many of the formal debates Chaucer would have encountered as a poet during the later part of the fourteenth century. "Geeste" or alliterative verse was the native form used in Old English texts like *Beowulf*, and was associated with the oral tradition transmitted by minstrels and the storytellers that Chaucer refers to as "geestours for to tellen tales." Rhyme had already started to usurp the place of alliteration in English poetry, but there was an alliterative revival in the fourteenth century, represented by *Sir Gawaine and the Green Knight* and *Piers Ploughman*, so it was certainly a form still available for Chaucer to use. However, the only sustained use of alliteration in all of Chaucer's writing occurs in *The Knight's Tale*, where he draws on the clamour of clashing consonants to represent the sounds of battle: "He thurgh the thikkeste of the throng gan threste; / Ther stomblen steedes stronge, and doun gooth al." Here Chaucer is paying tribute to the most resilient feature of alliteration: its aptitude for describing violence. But the absence of alliteration in virtually all of his writing suggests a deliberate position against it on Chaucer's part, perhaps because he considered it an archaic form or perhaps because he simply took more pleasure in rhyme.

The intersection of forms in this scene also allows Chaucer to draw attention to different rhyming techniques, to great ironic effect. The tetrameter romance rhymes criticized by the Host are meant to parody the older minstrel style that Chaucer had used himself in his earlier work, a style that was still being used by practically every other rhyming poet in England at the time. The iambic pentameter couplets employed in the scene itself and in the bulk of *The Canterbury Tales* were Chaucer's own innovation, and stand out as an obviously superior narrative form in comparison to *Sir Thopas*. The reason for this is obvious; the addition of two extra syllables in each line allows for more variation in stress and therefore more metrical freedom in telling a story, without losing the coherence between rhymes. Thus, by insulting and mocking his fictional pilgrim character within the text, Chaucer is ironically pointing to the success of his own work in comparison to everyone else's. He is subtly challenging both alliterative poets and metrical romance poets, intensifying the battle ethos.

Sir Thopas is also key to understanding *The Canterbury Tales* because of what it tells us about the fictional competition among the pilgrims. The story is used to set an example for the others, showing everyone in no uncertain terms what happens to a poet who fails to please his audience. When the Host tells Chaucer that his replacement tale must have some "mirth or some doctrine," this goes back to the original criteria of "sentence" and "solaas" established in the *General Prologue*. Evidently *The Tale of Sir Thopas* is terminated because it fails to be either enjoyable or enlightening. The Host's aggravated outburst is essentially a dramatization of every performing poet's worst fear: the fear of an audience rebellion. It is also an acknowledgement of the new relationship between poets and audiences that followed the popularization of poetry in the Middle Ages. Chaucer may cut a pathetic figure in the *Sir Thopas* episode, but I think he is actually paying tribute to the necessary functions of competition and audience feedback, which combine to increase the pressure on poets to build their skills, exactly like battling in hip-hop culture. The purpose of *Sir Thopas* is to enrich the overall quality of the material by offering itself in contrast to the other *Tales* and also through the implicit pressure to perform it puts on the other pilgrims. Chaucer's decision to deliver the worst tale himself within this fictional competition is thus an ironic act of altruistic self-sacrifice, like the rabbit that stops and beats the ground with its foot to warn the others of a predator's approach, only to be devoured.

> Thou liknest it also to wilde fyr;
> The moore it brenneth, the moore it hath desir
> To consume every thing that brent wole be.

Sir Thopas serves to remind the pilgrims that the game they are playing has rules and stakes, but Chaucer is also pointing to the principles that govern the natural and social sciences. Chaucer's poetry is filled with references to history, philosophy, medicine, alchemy, and astronomy, and there is no doubt that he had an inquiring mind; however, what I find most interesting is not what he knew, but what he anticipated. For instance, Chaucer's treatment of audience feedback in *The Canterbury Tales* could be seen as a foreshadowing of the recent findings around the action of feedback loops. A feedback loop is any cycle or system in which some part of the output is returned to the beginning, affecting further output. Feedback loops have been identified by researchers in virtually every field, from population ecology and behavioural psychology to economics and political science. These feedback loops come in two distinct forms, positive and negative. Positive feedback loops amplify themselves indefinitely, since their output increases their input, which in turn further increases their output. The classic positive feedback loop is the whine of microphone feedback through a power amplifier. An excellent literary example of a positive feedback loop occurs in Shakespeare's *Hamlet*, when Hamlet describes his parents' relationship before his father's murder: "Why, she would hang on him / As if increase of appetite had grown / By what it fed on." I have witnessed positive feedback loops at work in battles many times: when a rapper falters or misses a word the crowd's jeering will cause him to lose concentration and commit further errors, which will provoke more hostility from the crowd and so on. These conditions often cause otherwise talented rappers to fail completely in the battle arena. Reciprocally, positive feedback loops can lead just as quickly to success, as the cheers of the crowd increase the rapper's confidence, which leads to a more impressive performance and thus to more cheering. This gives a double meaning to the term "positive feedback," but positive feedback loops are generally associated with negative effects, since they quickly lead to the extremes of either complete implosion or gross over-inflation.

The second model is the negative feedback loop, which has a stabilizing rather than an amplifying effect. A negative feedback loop is defined in *The Academic Press Dictionary of Science and Technology* as "Any control system in which feedback is used to compare actual performance with a standard representing the desired performance." This is an exact description of the Host's feedback within *The Canterbury Tales*. The actual performance of each pilgrim is measured against the performance desired by the highly demanding audience, a form of quality control. When feedback exists, poets are forced to anticipate it by submitting themselves to the audience's will, which increases their effectiveness as performers. When feedback is absent, poets are free to imagine themselves as being effective regardless of what anyone else thinks, which results in a general deterioration of the audience's experience. Given the obvious advantages to the audience (and to the overall quality of the poetry), it is not surprising that Chaucer put such an emphasis on audience feedback in *The Canterbury Tales*.

Another idea that Chaucer seems to have anticipated with his system of competition and feedback in *The Canterbury Tales* is Charles Darwin's theory of evolution by means of natural selection. Chaucer's ideas about poetry resulted from observing the interactions between poets and their audiences in England in the fourteenth century. He realized that the poetic techniques available showed considerable variation in their effectiveness in pleasing an audience, which resulted in different levels of success in terms of the survival of each performance under the potential hostility of audience feedback. Chaucer was also aware that literary trends are inherited through the influence of poets on future generations of poets, as stories are passed on through translation and adaptation. Each generation's challenge lies in adapting the universal stories and themes of the past into a context that is acceptable to the audience of the present. Both Darwin and Chaucer recognized competition as the key to growth and development, and sought a framework within which positive results could be distinguished from negative, and competitive energy could be harnessed for individual success *and* overall progress. Chaucer's area of interest was different from Darwin's, but the insight that produced *The Origin of Species* is also present in *The Canterbury Tales*, the definitive manual for the function of poets in society.

> And for ther is so gret diversite
> In Englissh and in writyng of oure tonge,
> So prey I God that non myswrite the,
> Ne the mysmetre for defaute of tonge;
> And red wherso thow be, or elles songe,
> That thow be understonde, God I beseche!
> But yet to purpos of my rather speche:

The storytelling competition that Chaucer employs as his framing device tells us a great deal about the different types of poetry that influenced him, but it also raises the question of his own influence on others. By the end of his life Chaucer was well aware of his growing reputation, and he must have considered the impact of his ideas and techniques on his imitators and inheritors. By assigning audience feedback and competition central roles in *The Canterbury Tales*, Chaucer is addressing one of the main problems threatening the future of his craft. The storytelling torch had recently passed from the hands of specialized minstrels into the hands of anyone who cared to participate. This democratization process carried the danger of diluting poetry into irrelevance, but also the potential of diversifying and revitalizing it. The key difference between these two outcomes lay in maintaining a direct connection between poetry and its listening audience. In *The Canterbury Tales*, Chaucer has created a fictional world in which all members of society, from the lowliest Cook to the primmest Prioress, are potentially capable of producing excellent narrative poetry upon demand. The *Tales* succeed to various degrees in delighting the audience and teaching them something, while still celebrating each pilgrim's distinct perspective. Also, the presence of a potential reward for outstanding performance, "a soper at our aller cost," provides a necessary incentive to excel: the most deserving poets will be generously supported by society. However, the pilgrims who fail to deliver are equally important to this fictional world, since they reveal the mechanism through which the utopian effect has been achieved. The tyranny of the audience is introduced as a populist solution to the tyranny of inept performers. This mechanism works as a form of fictional quality control within the text, but it can also be seen as a prescription for the future of English literature as a whole, a way of encouraging poets to innovate and excel. *The Canterbury Tales* was Chaucer's blueprint for building towards a continually evolving ideal of literature.

So what happened? How did poetry go from the model Chaucer put forward—competitive, descriptive, rhyming narrative verse—to the printed free verse that we call poetry today? Even more importantly, how did poetry evolve from its roots in popular entertainment and communal play into something elitist and inaccessible, virtually irrelevant to most people's lives? The changes in poetry's form and social function over the past six centuries were introduced piecemeal by generations of poets experimenting with different styles, each movement influencing the next. Complex as they were, these changes were all stimulated by one momentous paradigm shift in technology: the invention of the printing press. In Chaucer's time poetry could not be separated from its sense of a listening audience, since its primary purpose was to be recited; even verse written in a manuscript was understood as a representation of an oral event to be used for communal recitation. Communality was necessary because hand-written manuscripts were laborious and expensive to produce. However, after Guttenberg's printing press arrived in England about eighty years after Chaucer's death, reading and writing were further democratized by the reduced cost of mass production. Along with writers in every other genre, poets gained access to a much broader potential readership, which completely changed the way they imagined their place in society. The elements of live performance, competition, and audience feedback that Chaucer considered crucial to the development of poetic technique were eventually replaced by the editorial whims of publishers catering to niche markets, a form of artificial selection. This exchanged one set of environmental factors for another, but it was a Faustian bargain that cost poets their sense of connection to a live listening audience. The changes took hold so slowly and the immediate benefits of print were so numerous that this expense passed virtually unnoticed—most poets had no problem giving up ten listeners in exchange for the potential of a thousand readers.

Stylistic choices necessarily anticipate the reception of any work of art, and when poets exchanged their listening audience for a silent readership this also affected the relationship between verse form and its function. In the sixteenth century, Philip Sidney raised this question in his *Defense of Poesy*, in which he rejects verse form as a defining quality of poetry: "[B]eing but an ornament and no case to poetry, since there have been many most excellent poets that never versified, and now swarm many versifiers that need never answer to the name of poets." The "excellent poets who never versified" were all foreign and classical figures writing in other languages, however, while poetry in English had previously been structured by definition. Completely unrhymed poetry in English first appeared in sixteenth-century drama in the form of blank verse (unrhymed iambic pentameter), which was used by Christopher Marlowe and Shakespeare. Going one step further, John Milton attached a preface to his blank verse masterpiece, *Paradise Lost*, denouncing rhyme as "the Invention of a barbarous Age" and an unnatural impediment to great poetry. William Wordsworth's *Preface to the Lyrical Ballads* also sought to "naturalize" poetry and carve away the "elevations of style" that had characterized eighteenth-century verse. Although the *Ballads* themselves made extensive use of rhyme, in 1802 Wordsworth had no problem writing, "[T]he language of every good poem can in no respect differ from that of good prose." The crossbreeding potential of prose and poetry was fully explored a few decades later in Walt Whitman's *Leaves of Grass*, which rejected both rhyme and metre and ushered in an era that extends to the present day, defined by the dominance of free verse. Whitman's influence can be found in W. B. Yeats, Ezra Pound, T. S. Eliot, and virtually every significant modernist poet of the twentieth century. Of course, there were no laments being sung for the death of rhyme; instead, free verse was heralded as the final liberation of poetry from the unnatural burden imposed by the repressive structure of rhyme and rhythm.

> I kan nat geeste 'rum, ram, ruf,' by lettre,
> Ne, God woot, rym holde I but litel bettre

The idea that devices like rhyme and rhythm are unnatural to poetry would have been ridiculous in Chaucer's time, since they were precisely what distinguished poetry from prose; you might as well have said alcohol was unnatural to beer, ruining an otherwise perfectly good beverage. Over the centuries, poets who defended and employed rhyme were preserving the English literary tradition going back to well before Chaucer, and poets who rejected rhyme were trying to break from that tradition and adapt to the times, and to the conditions of print culture. Of course, poetry never stopped being recited out loud; this simply ceased to be its primary function, which transformed the sound qualities of poetry from defining characteristics into mere superficial ornaments to be gradually dispensed with. Some poets struggled hard against this trend, but the greater financial incentives offered by publishing constantly acted as a selective force, favouring increased freedom of expression and the eventual rejection of all structure in verse. The process was perpetuated by both writers and readers; after all, if rhyming feels quaint and old-fashioned to poets then it will certainly feel that way to their readers, and vice versa. One result was a gradual merging of prose and poetry, once formal distinctions, which became more and more subjectively defined as they grew together. The other result was that poetry went from being a source of entertainment and communal play to being an academic discipline, practised by educated people for the gratification of other educated people in the name of abstract literary principles with measurements of quality separate from the experience of the rapidly diminishing audience. This separation has led to an unhealthy reverence at staged readings of published poems, which are often assumed to be so elusive and precious in value that the audience must be stupid for not getting anything from the listening experience. In most cases, however, the emperor is naked.

The changes in literary style that gradually followed the rise of print culture were also perpetuated by historical and political factors. The false reverence currently afforded published free verse is a consequence of the audience's alienation from the creative process, but it also has roots in the social upheavals of the nineteenth century. In the wake of the French

Revolution, and with the rise of skepticism from the likes of Hume and Voltaire, poets were hailed as the only possible redeemers of bankrupt social and religious institutions. Percy Shelley declared poets "the unacknowledged legislators of the World," and one of the most influential thinkers of the time, Thomas Carlyle, prophesied a future where poetry would replace religion: "Literature is but a branch of Religion, and always participates in its character: however, in our time, it is the only branch that still shows any greenness; and, as some think, must one day become the main stem." This re-privileging of poets as the keepers of society's political and spiritual identity hailed back to the minstrels of the twelfth and thirteenth centuries, who had enjoyed the validation of wealthy patrons—secular and religious— as well as the general populace. However, modern poets failed to fulfill this promise; they had lost their public voice and no longer had an audience to legitimize them, so they continued their retreat into academia.

While historical and cultural factors do exert an influence on literary trends, often these trends can ultimately be traced to changes in technology. Video killed the radio star; photography killed realism in the visual arts; and the printing press killed rhyme. Thanks to human ingenuity and creativity, each of these deaths has also led to the birth of new art forms and new styles, but sometimes an invention can have an unexpected revitalizing effect on a lost tradition as well. The resurrection of rhyme that hip-hop culture has achieved in three short decades was enabled by the invention of recorded sound by Thomas Edison in 1877. The importance of sound is diminished in a printed poem, so poets naturally responded by shifting their emphasis away from sound and onto nuances of meaning, discarding rhyme and rhythm and other remnants of the oral tradition in the process. This was partially in consideration of the fact that readers appreciate different qualities of a poem than listeners, as implied by Margaret Atwood's comment, "I don't think what poetry does is express emotion. What poetry does is to evoke emotion from the reader, and that is a very different thing." As effective as Atwood and many other free verse poets can be in achieving this end, it is also a very different thing to evoke emotion from the *listener* (as opposed to the reader). However, the phonograph solved the problem created by the printing press, since it enabled both sound and text to reach the same potentially mass audience. This had wide-reaching implications for the direction poetry could take in terms of rhyme and rhythm. Before the invention of sound recording technology, the effect of rhyme had only ever been enjoyed in the form of an ethereal live performance, but now this effect could be captured and mass-produced. Hip-hop owes its success to many factors, but the ultimate factor is the medium of transmission. Recorded sound allows rappers to reach millions of people with their oral performances, imagining themselves in the context of posterity in a way that only published poets have done historically, as in Eminem's plea: "Just let our spirits live on / Through our lyrics that you hear in our songs." Edison may not have intended his invention to lead to the revitalization of rhyme as an art form, but it is somehow fitting that the first thing he recorded was the sound of himself reciting "Mary Had a Little Lamb," a rhyming poem.

> Ye knowe ek that in forme of speche is chaunge
> Withinne a thousand yeer, and wordes tho
> That hadden pris, now wonder nyce and straunge
> Us thinketh hem, and yet thei spake hem so

To understand what is happening in hip-hop right now with regard to rhyme, it is necessary to consider both the device's history and its general effect, a field referred to loosely as "rhyme theory." Rhyme in poetry has four recognized functions: mnemonic (memory), schematic (organization), melodic (sound), and semantic (meaning). All four of these functions of rhyme go back to the prehistoric roots of human oral traditions. Rhyme in this case would be more properly generalized as repetition, since all poetic devices, including rhyme, alliteration, consonance (repeated consonant sounds), assonance (repeated vowel sounds), metre, and even rhythm more generally, are all defined by the repetition of a particular sound or stress. Rhyme is simply the most complex form of this phenomenon of linguistic repetition, since it is based on entire words or syllables rather than on smaller parts of speech. Repetition provides a structure in which to set stories and myths, acting as a series of signposts or markers for the mind to follow. In other words, repetition uses sound to make connections between words and ideas that aren't necessarily connected in meaning, linking them through melody and rhythm. This was crucial to the function of storytellers in traditional oral cultures because it aided memorization and also allowed their words to harmonize with music. Before the written word was invented only about five thousand years ago, human culture was passed on from generation to generation almost entirely in the form of oral stories, so every culture on earth has its roots in these archetypal linguistic elements of memory and melody. The sound qualities of poetry embodied in rhyme and repetition resonate with us on an instinctual level partially because they are the qualities that formed our distant ancestors' first awareness of their place in the world.

Every culture and language on earth will have its own story about how the archaic roots of rhyme in the oral tradition have been transformed through the impact of writing and technology. The only one of these stories that I can contribute to at the moment is the story of the English language. The Germanic ancestor of English, which we call Old English, is first recognized as a distinct language about thirteen hundred years ago. Old English poetry, exemplified by *Beowulf*, is generally composed of lines with four stressed syllables using alliteration rather than rhyme, with each line divided into two halves by a pause or "caesura." However, rhyme was certainly known in England at this time, since it was used in Latin hymns in the church, so its absence from virtually all Old English poetry implies that it was deliberately avoided in favour of alliteration. Rhyme only appears in common use in English poetry after 1066, when the Norman conquest established French as the language of government and the aristocracy. Although the French poetry of the time was rhymed rather than alliterative, the Normans can't be said to have "introduced" rhyme into England, since it was already there in other forms but was previously being ignored. One likely explanation lies in the differences in stress and inflection among Indo-European languages, which can limit the effectiveness of rhyme. Philip Sidney pointed this out in 1595 in his *Defense of Poesy*, and modern linguistics has recently expanded the picture. Old English was a Germanic language that expressed variations in the meaning of words by using unstressed suffixes. Since the effect of rhyme is based on stress, and on creating a sound connection between two words that aren't otherwise connected in meaning, languages that express themselves with unstressed suffixes historically tend to avoid rhyme in favour of other forms of repetition. It is not hard to see why this is the case, since words like "seduced" and "created" don't really rhyme even though they share the same endings. By contrast, the words "syntax" and "relax," which also share only their last two letters, make for excellent rhymes because the endings are stressed and their common sound is coincidental to their meaning. Now try to imagine sustained rhyming in a language where unstressed suffixes were the norm instead of the exception. When Norman French mixed with Old English after 1066, it caused many of the Germanic unstressed suffixes to be abandoned, which led to much greater variation in syllable stress at the ends of words, making rhyme a more effective device. The resulting Middle

English hybrid provided excellent raw materials for the crafting of rhyming verse, a potential that Chaucer was the first to fully explore.

The introduction of rhyme into English in the Middle Ages was made possible by changes in the language as it mixed with French, but there is some evidence to suggest that the use of rhyme also contributed to those changes. In surveys of the linguistic roots of words used in a variety of Middle English poetry, rhymes at the end of lines are more frequently found to be foreign imports than other words in the poem. This is because rhyme forces the poet to find a matching sound for each word, while still adhering to a certain story or subject. Given the unsuitability of many Old English words to the requirements of rhyme, multilingual poets in the Middle Ages who were stuck for a word would often simply take one from French, Norse, Latin, or Italian. English at the time was a vernacular language with no standardized dictionary or index, so once the word was used in a poem written in English it would often be accepted later as an English word. This is yet another way in which rhyme is capable of producing meaning through the creative pressure it puts on poets; there are literally hundreds of words in common use that were adopted into the English language in this way. For example, the word "experience" appears for the first time in English as a rhyme in Chaucer's poetry: "In wommen vinolent is no defence – / This knowen lecchours by experience." There was no Old English word with a meaning exactly equivalent to "experience" in this context, nor was there a word with a similar sound, so Chaucer simply adopted the French *experience* as an English word to suit both his verse and his narrative requirements. Since the significance of words is often altered by different usages when they jump from one language into another, the meaning we associate with the word "experience" today owes something to the way Chaucer decided to use it in his rhyming practice (which happens to be the same as the French meaning). Using foreign words also allowed Chaucer to avoid the effect of obvious or trivial rhyme.

> I kan right now no thrifty tale seyn
> That Chaucer, thogh he kan but lewedly
> On metres and on rymyng craftily,
> Hath seyd hem in swich Englissh as he kan

Of the four functions of rhyme—mnemonic, schematic, melodic, and semantic—only the semantic function is capable of losing its potency. Over-familiarity does not alter the value of a rhyme as a memory aid, as a marker of scheme (for instance, to distinguish sonnets from limericks), or as a sound effect. However, rhymes that are overused tend to lose their semantic value, unless poets can find creative ways of refreshing them. The reason for this terminal shelf life lies in the potential for meaning creation inherent in rhyme, which is a neurological function. In common speech we naturally connect words to one another through associations of meaning, which are based on perceived connections between the ideas or objects represented by the words. When a rhyme connects two words using an effect of sound, it forces us to think about those two words in a new way, creating a new synaptic connection between neurons in the brain, accompanied by a pleasure response. This is the reason for the so-called "punch line" effect of rhyme, and the reason rhyme is often associated with humour. Like rhyme, humour often presents us with circumstances that seem to be separate and then finds an unexpected way of connecting them. Rhyme theorists generally agree that the more creative the semantic link between the two words used, the more effective the rhyme will be. This is also one reason why English is better suited to rhyme than most languages. Since English is cobbled together from more diverse foreign sources than any other contemporary language, its rhyming pairs are more likely to be based on semantic differences rather than common linguistic roots (such as suffixes), which increases the potential for meaning creation. When rhymes that have been used too often become predictable, such as "moon/june" and "true/blue," the process of meaning-creation is subverted, replacing the delight of invention with the tediousness of routine.

Chaucer was the first poet to draw attention to this quality of rhyme. When the Host says to Chaucer, "This may well be rhyme dogerel," this is the first written record we have of the final word, which means bad or trivial rhyming verse. Chaucer may have been using a common term or he may have invented it specifically for this scene, but either way *The Tale of Sir Thopas* remains the first definitive example we have of self-consciously awkward rhyming. So what is the difference between doggerel rhyme and effective rhyme? Some verse theorists have proposed that it is a quality of surprise that makes rhyme effective, which would seem to fit with the criteria of meaning creation, but if surprise were really primary then good rhymes would cease to impress after the second or third pass. This is manifestly not the case, however; a superbly crafted rhyme continues to produce the same effect indefinitely, sometimes even gaining potency with increased exposure. The quality of a rhyme must therefore be a creative essence captured by the poet in the moment of its composition, such that its effect can be conjured each time the words are brought to mind. In this case doggerel is not actually caused by over-familiarity with rhyme; instead, it is simply a product of ineptitude or laziness on the poet's part in choosing semantic links that are too obvious. Granted, the more rhymes become familiar the greater the mind's creative reach must be to keep their usage fresh, but the challenge lies in the inventiveness of poets, not in any innate quality of the device.

There are various techniques that poets have traditionally used to refine their rhyming practice, many of which can be traced back to Chaucer, the first great rhyme technician in English. One is simply a sense of mindfulness about which rhymes are becoming too obvious to be effective without some kind of twist. For instance, a survey comparing Chaucer's rhymes for "knight" with two other metric romances of his time revealed five rhymes Chaucer shared with both poems, six shared with one or the other exclusively, and six rhymes not found in either romance. The one conspicuous pairing that was commonly used by both of the other poets but found nowhere in any of Chaucer's writing is with "fight." Considering the obvious semantic link between knights and fights there is no chance this omission on Chaucer's part was a coincidence. Rather, it was the obviousness of the pairing that had caused it to be overused by other poets and thus avoided by Chaucer. Another of Chaucer's innovations was to end his sentences and clauses in the middle of lines rather than at the end, which allows the story to flow past the rhymes without pausing repetitively after each one. This can be seen in the *Prologue* to *Sir Thopas*: "'Ye, that is good,' quod he; 'now shul we heere / som deyntee thing, me thynketh by his cheere.'" Chaucer's subtle arrangement prevents the rhyme "heere/cheere" from dominating the line's natural cadence, so that you hardly hear it unless it is deliberately emphasized. Comparisons have shown that other medieval poets are more prone to end each line with a punctuation mark, as if their thoughts were stumbling over the rhymes rather than gliding past them. Chaucer's technique shows a degree of sophistication beyond anything that came before him, and much of what came after, prompting Sidney to say of him in *The Defense of Poesy*: "I know not whether to marvel more, either that he in that misty time could see so clearly, or that we in this clear age go so stumblingly after him."

Who koude ryme in Englyssh proprely?

Hip-hop artists employ all of Chaucer's techniques and more to maintain the vitality of their rhymes. They first expanded the range of possibility by using rhymes based on sound rather than spelling. Rhymes like the classic "love/prove" pairing are useless in hip-hop, which relies on common stressed vowel sounds rather than consonants, as in Lauren Hill's "create/wait/take/tape" combination. Sometimes words that ought not to rhyme at all are made to sound the same through deliberate mispronunciation, as in Eminem's "I shouldn't have to pay these shrinks / These eighty G's a week to say the same things tweece / Twice, whatever, I hate these things." However, the innovation that has had the widest-reaching impact on hip-hop lyrics is polysyllabic rhyme (also called "multi-syllable rhyme" and "rhyming patterns" in the U.K.). Originally hip-hop employed strictly one- and two-syllable rhymes in masculine (e.g. air/care) and feminine (e.g. lazy/crazy) constructions, as in 1982's "The Message" featuring Melle Mel: "Don't push me 'cause I'm close to the edge / I'm tryin' not to lose my head / It's like a jungle sometimes; it makes me wonder / How I keep from goin' under." These two varieties had been the staple of rhyming verse in English for centuries, but hip-hop's intensely competitive conditions produced a much faster rate of stylistic innovation. Polysyllabic rhyme was introduced to resolve rhyme's tendency towards obsolescence. Since rhyme patterns can constantly be refreshed in the form of new arrangements, they are not exhaustible in the same way that monosyllabic rhymes are. The difference between monosyllabic and polysyllabic rhymes for versifiers is like the difference between addition and algebra for mathematicians, or between primary colours and blended pigments for painters.

The dominance of polysyllabic rhyme in hip-hop today is a cumulative result of decades of competitive one-upmanship, but there are three artists whose impact stands out. The first rapper to fully explore the potential of polysyllabic rhyme was Rakim in 1986, whose first song, "I Ain't No Joke," on his first album, *Paid In Full,* contained the lyrics:

> Write a rhyme in graffiti and every show you see me in,
> Deep concentration, 'cause I'm no comedian.
> Jokers are wild; if you wanna be tame,
> I treat you like a child, and you're gonna be named

Another enemy, not even a friend of me
'Cause you'll get fried in the end when you pretend to be
Competin', 'cause I just put your mind on pause
And I complete when you compare my rhyme with yours.

Other rappers had occasionally experimented with polysyllabic rhyme before, but Rakim managed to develop it into a powerful and sustained flow, combining end rhyme combinations like "mind on pause / rhyme with yours" with constant internal rhymes like "competin' / complete when." It was as if he had broken rhyme down into its smallest constituent parts and built something greater out of them, and it had the effect of raising the bar for the next generation of rappers, who felt they had to try to match Rakim's rhymes or admit defeat. This continued to reverberate until Nas upped the ante for rhyme complexity again in 1994 with *Illmatic*, taking Rakim's concept to the next level by stretching repeated rhyme patterns in longer sequences: "Packin' like a Rasta in the weed spot / Vocals will squeeze glocks / MCs eavesdrop / Though they need not," and also by filling lines with more complicated combinations of rhyme references: "When I attack there ain't a army that could strike back / 'Cause I react never calmly on a hype track." The bar was raised again in 1999 with Eminem's *Slim Shady LP*, which got so much attention in the media for the controversial content that the innovations in form were generally overlooked, at least outside of hip-hop circles. Eminem, claiming Rakim as one of his main lyrical influences, combined polysyllabic rhymes in tighter and more prolonged series than anyone before him: "I feel like I'm walkin' a tightrope without a circus net / Poppin' Percaset / I'm a nervous wreck / I deserve respect / But I work a sweat / For this worthless cheque / I'm 'bout to burst this tech / In somebody to reverse this debt." These three albums and many others transformed polysyllabic rhyme from an optional standing challenge for rappers into a virtual requirement that now permeates the lyrics of almost every song, mainstream and underground, at least in English. However, polysyllabic rhyme functions much like freestyling and battling in hip-hop culture: it doesn't necessarily bring success, but it must be mastered and eventually integrated into an artist's overall technique. It can be counter-productive to focus too obsessively on rhyme patterns while sacrificing clarity of content, but rappers must be *able* to draw on them effortlessly when needed, even in pursuit of lyrical simplicity. There is a difference between Picasso's stick figures and the scribbling of an infant.

> Diverse folk diversely they seyde,
> But for the moore part they loughe and playde.

Polysyllabic rhyme, like freestyle battling, is a spontaneous invention of hip-hop artists that also has antecedents in the English literary tradition. Chaucer often uses them in the form of rich rhyme combinations like "cleped us/precius" and "wyvys/alyve is," and also occasionally in more complex arrangements, such as in *The Knight's Tale*: "Swownynge, and baar hire fro the corps away. / What helpeth it to tarien forth the day," and in *The Franklin's Tale*: "And with my deth I may be quyt, ywis. / Hath ther nat many a noble wyf er this." Internal rhyme and chiasmus (inverted rhyme patterns) can also be found in *The Canterbury Tales*, such as in *The Miller's Tale*: "For curteisie, he sayde, he wolde noon. / The moone, whan it was nyght, ful brighte shoon." These and other examples show a certain linguistic playfulness on Chaucer's part, but he never experimented further than the odd line. The first poet to use polysyllabic rhyme consistently as a device was Samuel Butler in the seventeenth century, in his anti-Puritan satire *Hudibras*, which contains the lines: "Beside, he was a shrewd philosopher / And had read every text and gloss-over," and "Profound in all the nominal / And real ways beyond them all." The tone of the poem is sardonic and humorous, and Butler intersperses these complex rhymes with simpler constructions like "gabble/Babel" and imperfect rhymes like "disparage/porridge" to achieve a deliberately absurd effect befitting the story's mock hero. This technique came to be known as "Hudibrastic rhyme" after Butler's creation, and was also used to great effect in the nineteenth century by Lord Byron in his more playful mock epic *Don Juan*. Byron plays his unusual rhymes for comedy, using them to make clever connections that are surprising because they seem obvious: "What men call gallantry, and gods adultery, / Is much more common where the climate's sultry." The best and most often cited example of *Don Juan's* polysyllabic rhyme is the couplet: "But – Oh! ye lords of ladies intellectual, / Inform us truly, have they not hen-peck'd you all?" Byron explains his verse structure in the poem as a matter of temperament rather than any kind of statement: "Prose poets like blank-verse, I'm fond of rhyme," but he still can't resist taking an oblique shot at prose poets when he adds: "Good workmen never quarrel with their tools." Other poets of the nineteenth century also experimented with internal rhyme and polysyllabic rhyme, most notably Gerard Manley Hopkins, who appropriately described his poetry as "oratorical – less to be read than heard." However, these constructions never took hold as common practice, probably because most poets did not think of their poetry in Hopkins's terms.

Polysyllabic rhyme became common practice in hip-hop because of the conditions the culture imposes on rappers. Rhyme inherently limits a poet's options in terms of word choice, creating tension in the flow of ideas or narrative, and polysyllabic rhyme amplifies this tension exponentially when the patterns involved become more complex. The mental and lexical dexterity required to navigate this tension acts as a source of distinction among rappers, a game that is used to measure differences in skill level with greater objectivity. Polysyllabic rhyme also creates greater variation in stress and emphasis, especially when used internally, and the nuance and texture produced by overlapping rhymes prevent lines from ending in repetitive pauses, which is a quality of doggerel. In the best rap flows there is hardly any sense of where lines end or begin, only a constant lyrical stream with rhyme patterns interspersed. However, pauses at the end of lines can still be used for emphasis, and especially for the comedy effect of punch lines. One reason polysyllabic rhyme only finds limited expression in literary poetry is that it couldn't be fully separated from the humorous context of its original use in Butler's *Hudibras*, which also exploits the punch line effect. The twist of meaning that results from juxtaposing unusual combinations of words in each rhyme often simply surprises us into laughter. However, Rakim and the rest of hip-hop's polysyllabic pioneers didn't carry this traditional baggage of association; they were simply using rhyme patterns to produce a more textured soundscape in their lyrics, and also to flaunt a greater command of language, adapting to hip-hop's hyper-competitive environment. As a result, rappers could establish mood using tone and context without trivializing their subject, and employ polysyllabic rhymes as a device for expressing everything from euphoria to anguish and rage to political insight.

The only example I have found of consistent polysyllabic rhyme in a serious literary context occurs in J. R. R. Tolkien's *Lord of the Rings* trilogy. Tolkien intersperses his prose in the text with frequent songs and poems chronicling the histories and legends of the Elves, Dwarves, Ents, Hobbits, and Men, most of which follow traditional metre and rhyme schemes. The only exception is one of Bilbo's final poems, "The Song of Eärendil," composed during his retirement in Rivendell, which contains the most exquisite polysyllabic rhyming patterns in the English language prior to the appearance of hip-hop. The entire poem is set to a rolling rhythm evocative of the Old English oral storytelling tradition, but Tolkien also follows a strict plan that requires every other line to rhyme internally with the end rhyme pattern from the last. One exemplary passage reads:

> Through Evernight he back was borne
> On black and roaring waves that ran
> O'er leagues unlit and foundered shores
> That drowned before the Days began,
> Until he heard on strands of pearl
> Where ends the world the music long,
> Where ever-foaming billows roll
> The yellow gold and jewels wan.

Although the language is solemn and literary, rhymes like "waves that ran / Days began" and "foundered shores / drowned before" would be perfectly at home in the lyrics of any serious hip-hop song. The pattern has been noted and discussed occasionally in fanzine newsletters and online forums, but scholars of verse form have failed to acknowledge it as a significant innovation on Tolkien's part, which is indicative of his general exclusion from the canon of English literature. Tolkien was a great medievalist and Chaucerian, and a great writer, who strictly disavowed any of the allegorical undertones to his fiction, which has typically caused academics to ignore him, although this may have been precisely his intent. Nevertheless, while I was working on the rap/Chaucer thesis, a friend of mine was crusading actively for the inclusion of Tolkien in the English literature syllabus, while one of my professors taught Quentin Tarantino film scripts in our twentieth-century drama class. This is how the academic canon maintains its integrity, and also how it evolves: nothing is accepted into English coursework until someone persuasively argues for its worth.

> But nathelees, this meditacioun
> I putte it ay under correccioun
> Of clerkes, for I am nat textueel;
> I take but the sentence, trusteth weel.

The idea for *The Rap Canterbury Tales* came from a class project, in which a group of us was assigned to adapt one of Chaucer's tales into a dramatic presentation. The tale we chose was *The Knight's Tale* and I was given the task of reworking it into a script. This was in October of 1999, when I was still in the research phase of my thesis, and it occurred to me that adapting Chaucer's poetry to rap would be a great way to creatively reveal the affinity between them. I wrote a rough version over the course of a single weekend, resulting in a twenty-minute performance in front of the class with live music and students in costume playing the parts of the various characters; I played Palamon. At the time I was listening to a number of storytelling rappers, including Mos Def, Talib Kweli, Common, Nas, Big Punisher, Pharoahe Monch, and The Roots. Slick Rick and Outkast had recently dropped a track called "The Art of Storytelling," which pretty much summed up my entire interest in the study of literature. I was especially impressed by the rich polysyllabic rhymes in their various narrative techniques, since narrative poetry presents a much greater challenge to rhyme in that it must stick to a script. It is easier to be lyrically complex if you change topic every other line. Mos Def tells a story of race discrimination on an airplane when a flight attendant was suspicious of him being in a first-class seat: "Showed her my boarding pass / And then she sorta gasped / All embarrassed, puttin' extra lime in my water glass / An hour later here she come by walkin' past: / 'I hate to be a pest but my son would love your autograph.'" The rhymes carry the story rather than impede its clarity, even though they are assembled from combinations of up to three words ("sorta" being two). However, Big Punisher still takes the tongue-twisting prize for the way he sets the scene in a story about a mafia double-cross: "Then in the middle of Little Italy little did we / Know that we riddled to middlemen who didn't do diddly." Of course, if every line were this intricate then the content would suffer, but it works perfectly in grabbing the listener's attention for the tale that follows.

I set myself the task of adapting Chaucer's *Knight's Tale* into the most intricate polysyllabic rhymes I could devise, while still speaking as plainly and remaining as true to the original story as possible. Most of Chaucer's detailed descriptions had to be abridged, as well as the long speeches and many other elements, but the thrust of the story, names of characters, and historical context remain the same. I used Chaucer's own adaptation process as my model. Chaucer borrows his *Canterbury Tales* from a wide range of sources, some popular and some highly literary. This is a great balancing act, in which he fills raunchy tavern stories like *The Miller's Tale* with sophisticated rhetoric and classical allusion, while adapting great poets like Petrarch and Ovid to common Middle English, a popular vernacular language that was thought to be better suited to minstrel romances than to real poetry. The goal of this harmonizing process seems to have been universality, since Chaucer makes every line plain and accessible on its surface, while also infusing his poetry with multiple layers of irony and social criticism. The result is a text that can be read for enjoyment, or to learn something about human nature, or as a historical document, or for its near-infinite depth of ironic complexity, depending on how closely you want to look. Since Chaucer was partially writing to popularize elitist literature, I found his current status as an inhabitant of dusty libraries a little ironic in itself, and felt no qualms about adapting him into the popular vernacular language of hip-hop, which is generally thought to be better suited to radio singles than to real poetry. Performing my hip-hop version of *The Knight's Tale* as a live oral storytelling experience seemed to restore the poem to its original purpose, since Middle English simply can't speak to an audience today as it did in Chaucer's time.

> For whoso wol of every word take hede,
> Or reulen hym by every wightes wit,
> Ne shall he nevere thryven, out of drede;

Around that time someone gave me a pamphlet advertising the Canterbury Festival 2000, and I decided I had to attend. My rationale was that I needed to go on a pilgrimage to Canterbury myself to complete the story, but my pilgrimage would be in search of an audience rather than a monument. I contacted the festival organizers and pitched my show, receiving some lukewarm encouragement. In April of 2000 I completed my thesis and graduated, and went on to spend the entire summer revising the rough draft of *The Knight's Tale* that I had churned out in four days for the class presentation back in October. A lot of this revision took place in the same setting as my original inspiration of the summer before, planting trees on clear-cuts in the interior of British Columbia. I taught myself to rap to the rhythm of those repetitive motions—stab the shovel, open the hole, plant the tree, close the dirt, take three steps, stab the shovel. I would freestyle all day to that beat, and also compose lines in my head and write them down when I got home each night. The final version of *The Knight's Tale* printed here was completed in August of that summer. I remember putting the last words in place and then counting the number of lines I had ended up with: 410. Then I went back to Chaucer's version as printed in the *Riverside Chaucer*; his *Knight's Tale* is composed of 2249 lines, a free adaptation of Boccaccio's Italian poem *Il Teseida*, which has 9904 lines. This was not planned, nor is it perfect, but apparently there are algorithms at work in the adaptation process as well, since the story was reduced in length by roughly 80 percent each time. It is difficult to imagine a version of only 80 lines, but I am not one to underestimate the vernaculars of the future.

My pilgrimage to find an audience in Canterbury had mixed results, and I ended up going to graduate school the following year to explore these ideas further. Between 2001 and 2004 I went on to adapt *The Miller's Tale*, *The Pardoner's Tale*, and *The Wife of Bath's Tale*, in the order in which they are printed here. Some might say there is an element of hypocrisy in the fact that they are printed at all, given my purported feelings about poetry on the page. However, this publication follows hundreds of performances in front of live audiences around the world, in which the words were first refined and given life. Like a manuscript, the verses in this book are intended as a representation of a live oral event, and as a blueprint for recitation out loud, allowing the rhymes to achieve their sound effect. Although I have been described as "an enemy of free verse," I actually count free verse poems among my all-time favourites, and draw some of my greatest inspiration from poetry on the page. However, using Chaucer and Shakespeare as my models, I believe that poetry must be entertaining first, or have some quality that appeals to a live audience, before any of its other qualities become relevant; where there is no solace, there will be no sentence. The best poetry strikes a balance between the two, but they are not equal in importance or function. This awareness is something that rappers live and breathe, knowing that they dismiss their audience's needs at their own peril. Talib Kweli proves himself an inheritor of Chaucer's aesthetic when he raps, "I speak in schools a lot 'cause they say I'm intelligent. / No, it's 'cause I'm dope; if I was wack I'd be irrelevant." Spoken Word poets are also masters of cadence and live performance, and watching them always challenges my devotion to rhyme, since they manage to hold audiences spellbound using it only sparingly, or not at all. Free verse poetry has an important role to play in literature, but its dominance has come at the cost of my generation's interest in participating, threatening poetry's relevance as an art form. Ultimately I can't blame anyone's indifference towards poetry on the influence of television or the sensationalist media; I can only blame it on poets.

When I first set out to find analogies for hip-hop in English literature my goal was to find a poet with enough stylistic similarity to rap that a fruitful comparison could be made. The parallels I found in Chaucer were so extraordinary that even though many of them were revealed to me years ago I am still amazed by them. Chaucer laid out a blueprint in *The Canterbury Tales* for an evolving ideal of poetry's role in society, based on live competitive events controlled by audience feedback, with rhymed narrative verse as its highest expression, empowering the voices of people from all levels of society, a populist poetic meritocracy. Hip-hop could hardly be a more perfect fulfillment of Chaucer's vision. The imbalance in favour of text-based poetry introduced by the printing press and resolved by the phonograph (call it the "Guttenberg-Edison Gap") is one of the reasons it took six hundred years for this vision to come about. The competition that Chaucer designed for his pilgrims has naturally evolved in hip-hop in the form of freestyle battling, which exists as a training ground for artists rather than as an end in itself. Without this interactive mechanism the diversity of perspective and level of talent found in hip-hop music today wouldn't be nearly as pronounced, and the culture as a whole wouldn't be nearly as influential. By promoting this merit-based competitive realm as fundamental to the identity of the culture, hip-hop has managed to spread around the world without falling victim to excessive corruption or distortion of its principles. I'm sure this statement will be disputed, but only by those whose primary understanding of hip-hop comes from MTV. Underground hip-hop is defined by constant innovation and lyrical virtuosity, and by maintaining a direct connection to live audiences, who know they are expected to set the bar high for rappers. The result is an entire generation of aspiring MCs worldwide, who are all using the raw materials of their own language and culture to adapt hip-hop into new forms, challenging themselves to put words together in striking ways, and stimulating a revitalization of the oral tradition: a rhyme renaissance.

THE RHYME RENAISSANCE

This time we live in is a Rhyme Renaissance,
And this history lesson is five minutes long;
If hip-hop is bringin' it, fine, let's get it on,
And consider it official when I finish this song.

My goal is to redefine the whole history of rhyme,
'Cause the only way to free the soul is to free the mind,
And no wisdom as old as this should be confined
To total mystery, so we'll just read the signs
And Da Vinci codes, and try to see the science
In this linguistically composed pristine design.
It goes deep—suppose we could just rewind
To when we first rose to our feet and left the trees behind;
We'd see tribes of bipedal australopithecines
Trying to survive, as species divide and interbreed,
Attending to basic needs, like safe places to sleep,
Raising seeds and making sure they had things to eat,
So they started solving problems by evolving language genes.
It probably started from the need to follow wildebeest herds,
Or the need to distinguish between weeds and herbs,
Or from mimicking the mimicking screams of red and green birds.
It's a chicken/egg riddle: Which came first,
Plain speech or verse? 'Cause as long as there's been words,
There's been awareness of relationships between words,
And when rhymes connect them, new meanings emerge.
The history of languages has been researched

By linguists and traced back to a singular birth,
So the ability to speak rhythmically and sing works
To intrinsically link every human being on this earth.

But I wonder what percent of what happens is meant to happen,
'Cause in the genesis of rap, what has to be factored in
Is that this chapter was invented by black men,
And all human beings are descended from Africans
Who spread across the map in every different direction,
And adapted to every place under the sun,
So their faces started changing as the race was run,
Just as every language came from the same mother tongue,
Since each one directly relates to another one.
From the open plainsmen to the rainforest dwellers,
Every people needed designated storytellers
To pass on their culture orally from the elders,
And rhythm and repetition and rhymes and refrains
Allow performers to organize storylines in their brains,
And memorize more kinds of important signs and names,
And make changes based on the needs of each performance.
Feats of endurance are needed to describe deeds of enormous
Historical importance, like the Trojan-Greek war,
And the horse used to breach the fortress; in the aforementioned
Tradition of reciting, writing was a natural invention
For kings to catalogue things, with practical intentions,

And the offspring, of course, was the birth of the author,
From Homer to Virgil to the immortal words of Chaucer,
The father of modern verse and first formal border-crosser.

But the birth of the author was also the birth of the ego;
Celebrity seems to bring the worst out of people,
Especially with the invention of the printing press,
Which instantly made poetry so much less intimate,
'Cause suddenly poems were mostly written to be read
Alone, instead of written to be said aloud to crowds of listening heads,
And in just a few centuries, rhyme and rhythm were dead,
And forty thousand years of lyricism were watered down,
And exposed to careless prose, on mostly Modernist grounds,
And poets found that the old supportive crowds were not around,
But they hardly even noticed, 'cause they were published
    and important now.
But then recorded sound started with Thomas Edison,
One of the most intelligent inventions there's ever been,
And ever since, a person's words can be heard across the globe,
And the emergence of the Rhyme Renaissance was possible.
But it really started off in the Bronx in the seventies,
When kids with limited means produced monster melodies.
High Fidelity beats made their speech more compelling,
When ghetto teens resurrected rhymes and storytelling,
And used ancient wisdom as a system for rebelling.

The rhythm was thrilling, swelling the competition,
And millions of brilliant minds fought for the top positions,
And people finally seem to be starting to sit up and listen,
I'm just tryin' to give 'em a bit of a nudge with this composition.

And the epilogue? It's been about twenty-nine years
Since hip-hop first appeared and confirmed the worst fears
Of the powers that be, 'cause now it's in every urban sphere,
Assaulting virgin ears; it's like a massive attack,
'Cause every language on this planet can be adapted to rap.
It's like a gigantic amoeba that's having a snack,
A generation thinking vocally, acting locally,
Speaking openly, and having an impact globally.

'Cause this time we live in is a Rhyme Renaissance,
And this history lesson was five minutes long.
If hip-hop is bringin' it, fine, let's get it on,
And consider it official when I finish this song,
And it's on …

A Note on the Text

> For myne wordes, heere and every part,
> I speke hem alle under correccioun
> Of yow that felyng han in loves art,
> An putte it al in youre discrecioun
> To encresse or maken dymynucioun
> Of my langage, and that I yow biseche.
> But now to purpos of my rather speche.

The Canterbury Tales has been preserved in dozens of manuscripts from the fifteenth century, but there are no surviving pages that were written during Chaucer's lifetime. Since we have no text written in his own hand, every edition of Chaucer's poetry must therefore admit the possibility of editorial corruption, either by the copying scribe, or in printed versions by the editor, who must by necessity make selections from among the many sources available. This edition is no exception, but its primary purpose is to offer an *interpretation* of the *Tales* for the general reader, with Chaucer's words accompanied by both the modern rap translations and the illustrations for the sake of accessibility and enjoyment, abandoning any pretence of perfect fidelity to the elusive original. As an interpretation, this book presents ideas and methods that will be and should be debated, but my intention has always been to follow the spirit of Chaucer's poetry, rather than the letter of any single historical text.

In accordance with this approach, the Middle English verses printed here were taken from an open-source text on the Internet (of which there are at least half a dozen available), and edited by cross-referencing a number of other editions. The most important of these were *The Riverside Chaucer*, which contains the premier scholarly edition of *The Canterbury Tales* currently available, and a facsimile of *The Ellesmere Chaucer*, which is one of the earliest and best surviving manuscripts of the work. Punctuation was edited in accordance with my sense of the metre and general context of the poem; in hip-hop parlance the lines were edited for their flow. The line references in the notes section at the end of this book follow *The Riverside Chaucer*'s citation format, and I have also referred to it often for research purposes in writing the general introduction. *The Riverside Chaucer* has been my constant companion since I first encountered the *Canterbury Tales*, and I recommend it highly to readers interested in exploring Chaucer further.

The interpretive footnotes glossing the Middle English in this book were mostly derived from internal contextual evidence, while a number of dictionaries and glossaries were consulted and cross-referenced for specific definitions. The footnotes use accessibility and congruity of context as their guiding principles, and they are meant to provide only as much information as is needed to understand the story. However, for greater detail about Chaucer's sources and traditional interpretations, a scholarly edition should be consulted. The glossary in this book is limited to words and phrases too dissimilar to their modern equivalent to be easily recognized. Since most Middle English words differ from modern words only in their spelling, every word that is not glossed should be readable with a little effort. Often the easiest way to recognize a cognate word is to sound it out; for instance, *compaignye* is "company," and *narwe* is "narrow." Chaucer's words get increasingly easier to read as they grow more familiar, so don't get discouraged if it seems difficult at first.

The pronunciation of Middle English remains as elusive today as Chaucer's exact intentions for the text. Like every dialect that preceded sound recording technology, Middle English speech can no longer be heard aurally, so medieval scholars have two main sources of evidence for its pronunciation. The first form of evidence comes from dialects currently spoken in relatively isolated rural English communities that are believed to have changed their speech very little in the past six hundred years. The second form of evidence is rhyme, since it is often assumed that Chaucer and other medieval versifiers tended to use perfectly harmonious sounds for their rhyming pairs. Obviously neither of these two forms of evidence can be relied on with any certainty, so the pronunciation of Middle English remains a source of constant debate. For this reason I encourage readers to begin by pronouncing Chaucer's words as you would modern ones, or however they sound most comfortable to you. If your enjoyment and curiosity are sufficient to want to proceed further, *The Riverside Chaucer* also provides a useful pronunciation guide, currently the best educated guess available.

The order of Chaucer's *Tales* in this book is based on the temporal order in which I adapted them to rap versions, which for the most part also parallels their order in the *Ellesmere*. *The Canterbury Tales* survives in ten fragments, which have been pieced together differently by different editors. Internal evidence makes it clear that *The Knight's Tale* was meant to appear first in *The Canterbury Tales*, followed directly by *The Miller's Tale*, and that *The Parson's Tale* was meant to appear last, but many of the other *Tales* have been rearranged by various editors to suit different interpretations of Chaucer's intended order. *The Wife of Bath's Tale* usually appears before *The Pardoner's Tale*, but I translated *The Wife of Bath's Tale* last and usually perform it last; it is also printed last here because the Wife of Bath is Chaucer's most popular and generally endearing character, and her *Tale* seems to leave the reader/listener with the best aftertaste. I have also abridged the version of Chaucer's *Knight's Tale* printed here, shortening some of the longer speeches and descriptions of ancient rituals and scenery. This was necessary because the rap version required me to focus mainly on the forward thrust of the narrative, since live audiences tend to tune out during lingering descriptions of physical detail. My focus on the dramatic rather than the visually descriptive elements left a number of pages of Chaucer's *Knight's Tale* with no corresponding rap translation, and it is these pages I have omitted here. Chaucer was always mindful of the *experience* of a story, and this has been my guiding principle in the editing, adapting, and presentation of the *Tales* in this book.

✝HE KNIGH✝'S ✝ΛLE

Chaucer opens the contest with *The Knight's Tale*, the longest and most detail-rich of *The Canterbury Tales*. It stands out partly because Chaucer apparently wrote an early version before he conceived of the pilgrimage frame story, which means he created the character of the Knight to fit the tale, rather than writing the tale to fit the character as with most of the others. The tale was revised to fit its new context, but the scope and complexity of the narrative remain at odds with the other *Tales*, which Chaucer generally kept shorter to fit the fictional setting of live recitation. Listening to the entire *Knight's Tale* in Middle English recited at one sitting would stupefy even the most devout pilgrim. The Knight is described as a "worthy man" who "loved chivalrie, / Trouthe and honour, fredom and curteisie." His portrait in the *General Prologue* consists of a list of the foreign battles he fought in, as well as a stream of praise for his impeccable conduct, high reputation, good manners, prudence, and courage, culminating in the final stroke: "He was a verray, parfit gentil knyght" (He was a very perfect noble knight).

The Knight's Tale takes place in ancient Greece, and begins with Theseus, the governor of Athens, taking his army on a campaign to conquer the Amazon women, capturing their Queen Ypolita for his wife, and her younger sister Emelye as a ward. From the first few lines of the tale Chaucer's perfect gentle knight begins to reveal a deep naivety about the human impact of war and the contradictions inherent in the chivalric code. This incongruity can be seen in the fourth couplet of the tale: "What with his wisdom and his chivalrie, / He conquered all the regne of Femenye" (With his wisdom and his chivalry he conquered the land of the Amazons). Although the Amazons were known to be fierce warriors, Chaucer uses the title "Femenye" (which translates literally as "land of women"), making Theseus's campaign an ironic parody of masculine aggression, which "wisely and honourably" sets out to conquer and subdue femininity. Theseus's hawkish arrogance is revealed again on his way home, when he encounters the former queen of the neighbouring city of Thebes, who has recently been exiled after an internal conflict in which an outsider usurped the city. Her husband, the former king of Thebes, was left unburied to be eaten by dogs, and she and her fellow widows are dressed in black, kneeling on the side of the road and wailing for help. Upon seeing this company of ladies in mourning making such an awful noise that "in this world nys creature lyvynge / That herde swich another waaymentynge" (There wasn't a creature living in this world who had heard such an awful wailing), Theseus's first reaction is:

> "What folk been ye, that at myn homcomynge
> Perturben so my feste with criynge?"
> Quod Theseus. "Have ye so greet envye
> Of myn honour, that thus compleyne and crye?"

> ("Who are you, that at my homecoming
> Disturbs my festivities with your crying?"
> Said Theseus, "Are you so envious
> Of my honour that you complain and cry?")

His first guess proves to be off the mark, but when Theseus learns of the real reason for the women's distress he immediately takes his army to Thebes and lays siege to the city, and after conquering it he "rente adoun bothe wall and sparre and rafter" (tore down wall and beam and rafter). Once the city has been levelled in this shock-and-awe campaign, and the usurper, Creon, has been subjected to a regime change, Theseus restores the bodies of the unburied to their wives, and orders his men to ransack and pillage the dead. During the looting they come across two badly wounded knights, Palamon and Arcite, who are cousins of royal Theban birth, and Theseus condemns them to be locked in the tower in Athens for life.

The action in *The Knight's Tale* centres on the various prisoners of war Theseus has taken in these two campaigns. Palamon and Arcite both see Emelye the Amazon princess walking in the garden below the tower where they are imprisoned, and they both fall in love with her and begin to bicker over who saw her first and who loves her more. They renounce their friendship and battle repeatedly over Emelye, who is not interested in either of them, since she is a captive herself and would rather be free to "walken in the wodes wilde" (walk in the wild woods). Although the story takes place in ancient Greece, the Knight steeps the characters in the language of courtly love and chivalry, creating a constant tension through cultural contrast and anachronism, a tension that is magnified in the rap version by the use of contemporary language. Emelye is a fierce Amazon, presumably with one breast cut off to improve her archery, but Palamon and Arcite discuss her in conventional medieval romance terms, "my lady, whom I love and serve," making her the object of their petty rivalry, with her virginity as the prize. The voice of the Knight is either oblivious to or complicit in this aggression as he earnestly describes their strife and the final intervention of the gods. For the rap version I have taken these undercurrents and brought them more to the forefront, although my Knight is only slightly less subtle than Chaucer's. The narrator of the tale is generally uncritical of the violent arrogance behind Theseus's governance and the carnal possessiveness behind Palamon and Arcite's feelings for Emelye, either ignoring these contradictions or winking at them. However, he is still an excellent storyteller, using striking images and sophisticated philosophy to weave the tale and bring the characters to life. The Knight's status among the pilgrims and his worldliness and battle experience would make him a figure like Rakim or KRS-One in hip-hop culture, an old-school veteran whose skills and influence are uncontested, respected even by those who don't share his views.

The Knight's Tale: Part One

1   **W**hilom, as olde stories tellen us,

2   Ther was a duc that highte Theseus;

      Of Atthenes he was lord and governour,

4   And in his tyme swich a conquerour

      That gretter was ther noon under the sonne.

      Ful many a riche contree hadde he wonne;

      What with his wysdom and his chivalrie,

8   He conquered al the regne of Femenye,

9   That whilom was ycleped Scithia,

      And weddede the queene Ypolita,

      And broghte hir hoom with hym in his contree,

12   With muchel glorie and greet solempnytee,

13   And eek hir yonge suster Emelye.

      And thus with victorie and with melodye

      Lete I this noble duc to Atthenes ryde,

16   And al his hoost in armes hym bisyde.

17   And certes, if it nere to long to heere,

      I wolde have toold yow fully the manere

      How wonnen was the regne of Femenye

      By Theseus, and by his chivalrye,

21   And of the grete bataille for the nones

      Bitwixen Atthenes and Amazones,

23   And how asseged was Ypolita

      The faire hardy queene of Scithia,

25   And of the feste that was at hir weddynge,

1/ Whilom = Once. 2/ duc = duke; highte = was called. 4/ swich = such. 8/ regne of Femenye = land of women (the Amazons). 9/ whilom was ycleped = once was called. 12/ solempnytee = ceremony. 13/ eek = also. 16/ hoost = army. 17/ certes = certainly; nere = were not. 21/ nones = occasion. 23/ asseged = besieged. 25/ feste = feast.

As history teaches us, it happened to be
That Theseus, the governor of Athens in Greece,
Attacked and besieged, with wisdom and honour,
The land of the Amazon women, and conquered,
And wedded their queen, Ypolita; along with her
Young sister Emelye, his plundered possessions,
Theseus met them with a humble reception,
And he let them come back with him, under protection
From hundreds of weapons, to Athens and kept them.

26   And of the tempest at hir hoom-comynge;
27   But al that thyng I moot as now forbere;
28   I have, God woot, a large feeld to ere,
29   And wayke been the oxen in my plough,
      The remenant of the tale is long ynough.
31   I wol nat letten eek noon of this route;
32   Lat every felawe telle his tale aboute,
      And lat se now who shal the soper wynne;
      And ther I lefte, I wol ayeyn bigynne.
         This duc of whom I make mencioun,
      Whan he was come almoost unto the toun,
37   In al his wele and in his mooste pride,
38   He was war, as he caste his eye aside,
      Where that ther kneled in the hye weye
40   A compaignye of ladyes, tweye and tweye,
      Ech after oother, clad in clothes blake;
      But swich a cry and swich a wo they make,
43   That in this world nys creature lyvynge
44   That herde swich another waymentynge;
45   And of this cry they nolde nevere stenten,
46   Til they the reynes of his brydel henten.
         "What folk been ye, that at myn hom-comynge
48   Perturben so my feste with criynge?"
      Quod Theseus. "Have ye so greet envye
      Of myn honour, that thus compleyne and crye?

26/ tempest = storm. 27/ moot as now forbere = must leave out. 28/ ere = plow.
29/ wayke = weak. 31/ letten = delay; eek = also; route = group. 32/ aboute = in turn.
37/ wele = success. 38/ war = aware. 40/ tweye and tweye = two by two. 43/ nys = is no.
44/ waymentynge = wailing. 45/ nolde = would not; stenten = stop. 46/ henten =
grabbed. 48/ feste = celebration.

Upon his return to Greece, Theseus learned of these
Awful and shameful dishonoured injustices
Brought to the name of the monarch entrusted with
Keeping the city of Thebes.

51   "Or who hath yow mysboden or offended?
        And telleth me if it may been amended,
        And why that ye been clothed thus in blak."
             The eldeste lady of hem alle spak –
55   Whan she hadde swowned with a deedly cheere,
56   That it was routhe for to seen and heere –
        And seyde, "Lord, to whom Fortune hath yiven
        Victorie, and as a conqueror to lyven,
59   Nat greveth us youre glorie and youre honour,
60   But we biseken mercy and socour.
        Have mercy on oure wo and oure distresse;
62   Som drope of pitee thurgh thy gentillesse
        Upon us wrecched wommen lat thou falle;
        For certes, lord, ther is noon of us alle
        That she ne hath been a duchesse or a queene.
66   Now be we caytyves, as it is wel seene,
        Thanked be Fortune, and hir false wheel,
68   That noon estaat assureth to be weel.
69   And certes, lord, to abyden youre presence,
        Heere in the temple of the goddesse Clemence
71   We han ben waitynge al this fourtenyght;
72   Now help us, lord, sith it is in thy myght!
             "I, wrecche, which that wepe and waille thus,
        Was whilom wyf to kyng Cappaneus,
75   That starf at Thebes – cursed be that day! –

~

51/ mysboden = abused. 55/ swowned = fainted; deedly cheere = ill complexion.
56/ routhe = pitiful. 59/ Nat greveth us = we aren't upset by. 60/ biseken = seek; socour
= comfort. 62/ gentillesse = nobility. 66/ caytyves = outcasts; wel seene = obvious.
68/ estaat = estate; weel = well. 69/ abyden = wait for. 71/ han ben = have been. 72/ sith
= since. 75/ starf = died.

In the dust with his
Power obsolete in a coward's defeat,
He now was deceased and cast out in the streets,

"And alle we that been in this array
And maken al this lamentacioun,
We losten alle oure housbondes at that toun,
Whil that the seege theraboute lay.

80 And yet now the olde Creon, weylaway!
That lord is now of Thebes the citee,
Fulfild of ire and of iniquitee,

83 He, for despit and for his tirannye,
84 To do the dede bodyes vileynye,
85 Of alle oure lordes, whiche that been yslawe,
86 Hath alle the bodyes on an heep ydrawe,
87 And wol nat suffren hem, by noon assent,
88 Neither to been yburyed nor ybrent,
89 But maketh houndes ete hem in despit."

90   And with that word, withouten moore respit,
91 They fillen gruf, and criden pitously,
    "Have on us wrecched wommen som mercy
93 And lat oure sorwe synken in thyn herte."
94 This gentil duc doun from his courser sterte
95 With herte pitous, whan he herde hem speke;
    Hym thoughte that his herte wolde breke,
97 Whan he saugh hem so pitous and so maat,
98 That whilom weren of so greet estaat.
99 And in his armes he hem alle up hente,
100 And hem conforteth in ful good entente,

~

80/ weylaway! = alas! 83/ despit = spite. 84/ vileynye = dishonour. 85/ yslawe = slain.
86/ on an heep ydrawe = piled in a heap. 87/ suffren hem = allow them. 88/ yburyed
nor ybrent = buried nor burned. 89/ in despit = out of spite. 90/ respit = delay.
91/ fillen gruf = fell face down. 93/ sorwe = sorrow. 94/ courser = horse; sterte =
stepped. 95/ pitous = piteous. 97/ pitous = pitiful; maat = dejected. 98/ whilom = once.
99/ hem alle up hente = took them up. 100/ in ful good entente = with good will.

Where the hounds with their teeth would devour his meat.

His widow, the queen, in her hour of need,

Showered pleas on Theseus from down on her knees.

And swoor his ooth, as he was trewe knyght,
102   He wolde doon so ferforthly his myght
103   Upon the tiraunt Creon hem to wreke,
That all the peple of Grece sholde speke
How Creon was of Theseus yserved
As he that hadde his deeth ful wel deserved.
107   And right anoon, withouten moore abood,
His baner he desplayeth, and forth rood
To Thebes-ward, and al his hoost biside;
110   No neer Atthenes wolde he go ne ride,
Ne take his ese fully half a day,
112   But onward on his wey that nyght he lay,
And sente anon Ypolita the queene,
114   And Emelye, hir yonge suster sheene,
Unto the toun of Atthenes to dwelle,
116   And forth he rit; ther is namoore to telle.
117   The rede statue of Mars, with spere and targe,
So shyneth in his white baner large
119   That alle the feeldes gliteren up and doun,
120   And by his baner born is his penoun
121   Of gold ful riche, in which ther was ybete
122   The Mynotaur which that he slough in Crete.
Thus rit this duc, thus rit this conquerour,
124   And in his hoost of chivalrie the flour,
125   Til that he cam to Thebes, and alighte

~

102/ so ferforthly his myght = everything in his power. 103/ wreke = avenge. 107/ right
anoon = right away; abood = delay. 110/ neer = nearer. 112/ lay = continued. 114/ sheene
= bright. 116/ rit = rode. 117/ targe = shield. 119/ gliteren = glittered. 120/ penoun =
flag. 121/ ybete = embroidered. 122/ Mynotaur = monster with the head of a bull and the
body of a man. 124/ of chivalrie the flour = the flower of chivalry. 125/ alighte = stopped.

So he proudly agreed to put the town under siege,
And surrounded Thebes with all his men,
And pounded the city's walls, and when
Those towers were downfallen, then
His troops to dust demolished them.

Faire in a feeld, ther as he thoughte to fighte.
But shortly for to speken of this thyng
With Creon, which that was of Thebes kyng,
He faught, and slough hym manly as a knyght
In pleyn bataille, and putte the folk to flyght;
131   And by assaut he wan the citee after,
132   And rente adoun bothe wall and sparre and rafter;
And to the ladyes he restored agayn
The bones of hir freendes that weren slayn,
135   To doon obsequies, as was tho the gyse.
136   But it were al to longe for to devyse
137   The grete clamour and the waymentynge
That the ladyes made at the brennynge
Of the bodies, and the grete honour
That Theseus, the noble conquerour,
Dooth to the ladyes, whan they from hym wente;
But shortly for to telle is myn entente.
    Whan that this worthy duc, this Theseus,
Hath Creon slayn, and wonne Thebes thus,
Stille in that feeld he took al nyght his reste,
146   And dide with al the contree as hym leste.
147   To ransake in the taas of bodyes dede,
148   Hem for to strepe of harneys and of wede,
149   The pilours diden bisynesse and cure,
150   After the bataille and disconfiture;

⁓

131/ wan = conquered. 132/ rente adoun = tore down; sparre = beam. 135/ obsequies = funeral rites; gyse = custom. 136/ devyse = describe. 137/ waymentynge = grieving. 146/ as hym leste = as he liked. 147/ taas = pile. 148/ harneys = armour; wede = clothing. 149/ The pilours ... cure = The pillagers worked busily. 150/ disconfiture = defeat.

And when the brawl was ended he finally obtained
And returned to the Theban queen, for her pains,
The rest of her husband's majestic remains.

151   And so bifel that in the taas they founde
152   Thurgh-girt with many a grevous blody wounde,
153   Two yonge knyghtes liggynge by and by,
154   Bothe in oon armes, wroght ful richely,
155   Of whiche two Arcita highte that oon,
      And that oother knyght highte Palamon.
157   Nat fully quyke, ne fully dede they were,
158   But by hir cote-armures and by hir gere,
159   The heraudes knewe hem best in special
      As they that weren of the blood roial
161   Of Thebes, and of sustren two yborn.
      Out of the taas the pilours han hem torn,
163   And han hem caried softe unto the tente
      Of Theseus, and he ful soone hem sente
      To Atthenes, to dwellen in prisoun
166   Perpetuelly – he nolde no raunsoun.
      And whan this worthy duc hath thus ydon,
168   He took his hoost, and hoom he rit anon,
169   With laurer crowned as a conquerour;
      And ther he lyveth in joye and in honour
171   Terme of his lyf; what nedeth wordes mo?
172   And in a tour, in angwissh and in wo,
      This Palamon and his felawe Arcite
174   For evermoore, ther may no gold hem quite.

~

151/ taas = pile of bodies. 152/ Thurgh-girt = Pierced. 153/ liggynge by and by = lying
side by side. 154/ in oon armes = in matching armour. 155/ highte = was called.
157/ quyke = alive. 158/ cote-armures = embroidered tunics; gere = armour. 159/ heraudes
= heralds; in special = especially. 161/ of sustren two yborn = born of two sisters.
163/ softe = carefully. 166/ he nolde no raunsoun = with no bail allowed. 168/ rit anon =
rode soon. 169/ laurer = laurel leaves. 171/ Terme of his lyve = The rest of his life.
172/ tour = tower. 174/ hem quite = save them.

Deep in the wreckage the people were left with,

Two knights were detected, well-dressed and connected

By royal bloodlines, though it was expected

They would be dead soon from the head wounds inflicted.

But Theseus ordered that they be protected,

And sent them to Athens where they could be hidden,

And by his decision, the two knights were given

A prison to live in, though they were forbidden

To step from within 'til their ghosts had uprisen.

The names of these knights, in plain language:

Arcite and Palamon. Utterly thankless

That they were not hanged with the rest of the vanquished,

They were caged in a tower for ages to languish,

And waste away hours and days with their anguish.

This passeth yeer by yeer, and day by day,
176 Till it fil ones, in a morwe of May,
That Emelye, that fairer was to sene
Than is the lylie upon his stalke grene,
And fressher than the May with floures newe –
180 For with the rose colour stroof hir hewe,
181 I noot which was the fyner of hem two –
182 Er it were day, as was hir wone to do,
183 She was arisen, and al redy dight,
184 For May wole have no slogardie anyght;
185 The sesoun priketh every gentil herte,
And maketh hym out of his slepe to sterte,
And seith, "Arys and do thyn observaunce."
This maked Emelye have remembraunce
To doon honour to May, and for to ryse.
190 Yclothed was she fressh, for to devyse,
191 Hir yelow heer was broyded in a tresse
Bihynde hir bak, a yerde long, I gesse,
193 And in the gardyn, at the sonne upriste,
194 She walketh up and doun, and as hir liste
She gadereth floures, party white and rede,
To make a subtil gerland for hir hede,
And as an aungel hevenysshly she soong.

∾

176/ fil ones = happened; morwe = morning. 180/ stroof hir hewe = her face compared.
181/ noot = don't know. 182/ wone = habit. 183/ dight = prepared. 184/ slogardie
anyght = laziness at night. 185/ priketh = inspires. 190/ devyse = describe. 191/ broyded
in a tresse = twisted in a braid. 193/ the sonne upriste = sunrise. 194/ as hir liste = as
she pleased.

Years pass, 'til at last on a bright May morning,
Emelye rose, as dawn was just forming,
To walk in the garden, with flowers adorning
Her head as a tribute to spring, and her singing,
As soft as an angel's, rose up and just happened
To waft in a window and cause a distraction,

The grete tour, that was so thikke and stroong,
Which of the castel was the chief dongeoun,
(Ther as the knyghtes weren in prisoun,
Of whiche I tolde yow, and tellen shal),
202   Was evene joynant to the gardyn wal
203   Ther as this Emelye hadde hir pleyynge.
Bright was the sonne, and cleer that morwenynge,
And Palamoun, this woful prisoner,
206   As was his wone, by leve of his gayler,
Was risen, and romed in a chambre on heigh,
208   In which he al the noble citee seigh,
And eek the gardyn, ful of braunches grene,
210   Ther as this fresshe Emelye the shene
Was in hire walk, and romed up and doun.
This sorweful prisoner, this Palamoun,
Goth in the chambre romynge to and fro,
And to hym-self compleynynge of his wo.
That he was born, ful ofte he seyde, "allas!"
216   And so bifel, by aventure or cas,
That thurgh a wyndow, thikke of many a barre
218   Of iren greet, and square as any sparre,
He cast his eye upon Emelya,
220   And therwithal he bleynte, and cryede "A!"
As though he stongen were unto the herte.

∾

202/ joynant to = adjacent to. 203/ pleyynge = playing. 206/ wone = custom; by leve of his gayler = with his jailer's permission. 208/ seigh = saw. 210/ shene = bright. 216/ aventure or cas = accident or chance. 218/ sparre = beam. 220/ bleynte = turned pale.

And that's when the passionate noise then uprose
To where Palamon paced, giving voice to his woes.
   "Woe, woe is me, woe ... Whoah!"
   Palamon, struck to the quick by this vision,
In his heart knew his lust to conflict his religion.
She looked like a goddess, and he must be forgiven
If he thought she was Venus and asked for deliverance,
As he felt an upsurging of happiness in him,
A hope was emerging that perhaps she would give him
A premature evacuation from prison.

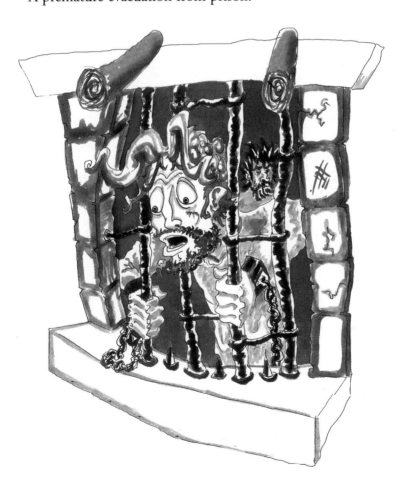

222   And with that cry Arcite anon up sterte

223   And seyde, "Cosyn myn, what eyleth thee,

That art so pale and deedly on to see?

225   Why cridestow? Who hath thee doon offence?

For Goddess love, taak al in pacience

Oure prisoun, for it may noon oother be;

Fortune hath yeven us this adversitee.

Som wikke aspect or disposicioun

Of Saturne, by som constellacioun

231   Hath yeven us this, al though we hadde it sworn;

232   So stood the hevene whan that we were born.

We moste endure; this is the short and playn."

234   This Palamon answerde and seyde agayn,

"Cosyn, for sothe, of this opinioun

236   Thow hast a veyn ymaginacioun.

This prison caused me nat for to crye,

238   But I was hurt right now thurgh myn ye

239   Into myn herte, that wol my bane be.

The fairnesse of that lady that I see

Yond in the gardyn romen to and fro,

Is cause of al my criyng and my wo.

243   I noot wher she be womman or goddesse,

But Venus is it soothly, as I gesse."

～

222/ up sterte = stood up. 223/ what eyleth thee = what's wrong with you. 225/ Why cridestow? = Why did you cry out? 231/ hadde it sworn = had denied it. 232/ So stood ... born = We were born under a bad sign. 234/ seyde agayn = replied. 236/ a veyn ymaginacioun = the wrong idea. 238/ ye = eye. 239/ bane = downfall. 243/ noot wher = don't know whether.

Meanwhile, Arcite had noticed the cracks in
His cousin's demeanour and focus, and asked him,
"Why are you looking so hopeless; what's happened?
What have you seen to provoke this reaction?"
      And Palamon sighed: "I'm choked with such passion
For her that I see down below, yet I'm trapped in
This prison, my station the lowest in Athens.
Until I escape, I'll have no satisfaction."

And therwithal on knees doun he fil,
And seyde, "Venus, if it be thy wil
Yow in this gardyn thus to transfigure
Bifore me, sorweful, wrecched creature,
249   Out of this prisoun helpe that we may scapen!
And if so be my destynee be shapen
By eterne word to dyen in prisoun,
252   Of oure lynage have som compassioun,
That is so lowe ybroght by tirannye."
And with that word Arcite gan espye
Wher as this lady romed to and fro,
And with that sighte hir beautee hurte hym so,
That, if that Palamon was wounded sore,
Arcite is hurt as moche as he, or moore.
And with a sigh he seyde pitously,
260   "The fresshe beautee sleeth me sodeynly
Of hire that rometh in the yonder place,
262   And but I have hir mercy and hir grace,
That I may seen hir atte leeste weye,
264   I nam but deed; ther is namoore to seye."
        This Palamon, whan he tho wordes herde,
266   Dispitously he looked and answerde,
267   "Wheither seistow this in ernest or in pley?"
268   "Nay," quod Arcite, "in ernest by my fey,
269   God helpe me so, me list ful yvele pleye."

～

249/ scapen = escape. 252/ lynage = royal birth. 260/ sleeth = slays. 262/ but = unless.
264/ I nam but deed = I'm as good as dead. 266/ Dispitously = Scornfully. 267/
Wheither seistow this = Do you say this. 268/ by my fey = by my faith. 269/ me list ful
yvele pleye = I'm not joking.

Palamon had gazed, and had paid the price,
And Arcite now bravely laid his eyes
Amazed upon the maiden guise
Of Emelye, and to his great surprise,
She made him sigh, and feel as sore
Inside as Palamon, and more.
Arcite fell to the stone and swore:
   "This fresh beauty and peerless grace
Has rescued me; it clears away
The sorrow of this dreary place.
If only she'd appear each day,
I'd cheerfully stay here just to see her face."
   Palamon's answer was close to delirious:
"Be clear with this, brother, are you joking or serious?"
Choking on tears, his emotions were furious.
   Arcite just sneered at this: "I would never say
Anything as heavyweight as this merely in clever play."

This Palamon gan knytte his browes tweye;
271 "It nere," quod he, "to thee no greet honour
For to be fals, ne for to be traitour
To me, that am thy cosyn and thy brother,
Ysworn ful depe, and ech of us til oother,
275 That nevere, for to dyen in the peyne,
Til that the deeth departe shal us tweyne,
Neither of us in love to hyndre other,
278 Ne in noon oother cas, my leeve brother,
279 But that thou sholdest trewely forthren me
In every cas, as I shal forthren thee –
This was thyn ooth, and myn also, certeyn,
I woot right wel thou darst it nat withseyn.
283 Thus artow of my conseil, out of doute,
And now thou woldest falsly been aboute
To love my lady, whom I love and serve
286 And evere shal, til that myn herte sterve.
Nay, certes, false Arcite, thow shalt nat so!
I loved hire first, and tolde thee my wo
As to my conseil and my brother sworn,
To forthre me, as I have toold biforn,
For which thou art ybounden as a knyght
To helpen me, if it lay in thy myght,
Or elles artow fals, I dar wel seyn."

～

271/ It nere = It is not. 275/ for to dyen ... peyne = even tortured to death. 278/ leeve = dear. 279/ forthren me = support me. 283/ of my conseil = in my trust. 286/ sterve = dies.

Palamon felt his pleasure fade:
  "Then you have betrayed me, and openly broken
Your oath to me, plainly by both of us spoken
So faithfully, traded to pose as a token
Of total devotion; we must put that above
Any quarrel we have over matters of love.
All we have is our blood, and that is a trust
Rather tough to just patch up after it's cut."

This Arcite ful proudly spak ageyn,

"Thow shalt," quod he, "be rather fals than I;

296   And thou art fals, I telle thee outrely,

297   For paramour I loved hir first er thow.

298   What wiltow seyn? Thou wistest nat yet now

Wheither she be a womman or goddesse!

300   Thyn is affeccioun of hoolynesse,

And myn is love as to a creature;

302   For which I tolde thee myn aventure

As to my cosyn and my brother sworn.

304   I pose that thow lovedest hir biforn;

Wostow nat wel the olde clerkes sawe,

That 'who shal yeve a lovere any lawe?'

307   Love is a gretter lawe, by my pan,

Than may be yeve of any erthely man.

309   And therfore positif lawe and swich decree

Is broken al day for love in ech degree.

311   A man moot nedes love, maugree his heed,

312   He may nat fleen it, thogh he sholde be deed,

313   Al be she mayde, or wydwe, or elles wyf.

And eek it is nat likly al thy lyf

315   To stonden in hir grace; namoore shal I;

316   For wel thou woost thyselven, verraily,

317   That thou and I be dampned to prisoun

318   Perpetuelly; us gayneth no raunsoun.

~

296/ outrely = outright. 297/ For paramour = Amorously. 298/ What wiltow seyn? = What will you say?; wistest = knew. 300/ affeccioun of hoolynesse = religious passion. 302/ aventure = situation. 304/ I pose = Suppose. 307/ by my pan = by my head. 309/ positif lawe = human law; swich decree = such rules. 311/ moot nedes love = must necessarily love; maugree his heed = despite resisting. 312/ fleen it = escape it. 313/ Al be she = Whether she be. 315/ stonden in hir grace = get her favour. 316/ verraily = truly. 317/ dampned = condemned. 318/ gayneth no raunsoun = with no hope of ransom.

Arcite laughed as if touched, with a covered smirk:
"In other words, since you loved her first,
I'm supposed to pretend that it doesn't hurt,
And I'm not even allowed to covet her,
When *I'm* the one who suffers worse?
Why should I thirst while my brother flirts?
It's enough to reverse one's trusted word."

"We stryven as dide the houndes for the boon;
320 They foughte al day, and yet hir part was noon.
321 Ther cam a kyte, whil they weren so wrothe,
And baar awey the boon bitwixe hem bothe.
And therfore at the kynges court, my brother,
Ech man for hymself, ther is noon oother.
325 Love if thee list, for I love and ay shal;
326 And soothly, leeve brother, this is al.
Heere in this prisoun moote we endure,
328 And everich of us take his aventure."
    Greet was the strif and long bitwix hem tweye,
330 If that I hadde leyser for to seye,
331 But to th'effect; it happed on a day,
To telle it yow as shortly as I may,
A worthy duc that highte Perotheus,
That felawe was unto duc Theseus
335 Syn thilke day that they were children lite,
Was come to Atthenes his felawe to visite,
And for to pleye as he was wont to do;
For in this world he loved no man so,
And he loved hym als tendrely agayn.
So wel they lovede, as olde bookes sayn,
That whan that oon was deed, soothly to telle,
His felawe wente and soughte hym doun in helle;

~

320/ hir part was noon = their reward was nothing. 321/ kyte = hawk; wrothe = angry.
325/ list = want; ay shal = always will. 326/ leeve = dear. 328/ everich = each. 330/ leyser
= leisure. 331/ th'effect = the point. 335/ Syn thilke = Since that; lite = little.

Their hate and need were great indeed,
And made them seethe impatiently,
But destiny soon gave them leave
Of one another's company,
When Arcite was released suddenly,
'Cause one of his friends did something to please
Theseus, who grudgingly agreed
To let Arcite run free.

But of that storie list me nat to write;
Duc Perotheus loved wel Arcite,
And hadde hym knowe at Thebes yeer by yere,
And finally, at requeste and preyere
Of Perotheus, withouten any raunsoun,
Duc Theseus hym leet out of prisoun
349   Frely to goon wher that hym liste overal,
350   In swich a gyse as I you tellen shal.
351   This was the forward, pleynly for t'endite,
Bitwixen Theseus and hym Arcite:
That if so were that Arcite were yfounde
354   Evere in his lif, by day or nyght or stounde,
In any contree of this Theseus,
And he were caught, it was acorded thus,
That with a swerd he sholde lese his heed;
358   Ther nas noon oother remedie ne reed,
But taketh his leve, and homward he him spedde;
360   Lat hym be war! His nekke lith to wedde!
How greet a sorwe suffreth now Arcite!
The deeth he feeleth thurgh his herte smyte;
He wepeth, wayleth, crieth pitously;
364   To sleen hymself he waiteth prively.

. . . .

∼

349/ wher that hym liste overal = anywhere he pleased. 350/ gyse = form. 351/ forward =
terms; t'endite = to write.   354/ stounde = moment.   358/ reed = course of action.
360/ lith to wedde = is on the line. 364/ sleen = kill; waiteth prively = planned secretly.

But the pardon came with one decree:
That, once released from his country,
If Arcite came within a hundred feet
Of Athens, he'd soon be underneath
The axe and be beheaded violently,
So he returned to abide in Thebes.

Upon that oother syde, Palamon,
Whan that he wiste Arcite was agon,
Swich sorwe he maketh that the grete tour
420   Resouneth of his youlyng and clamour.
421   The pure fettres on his shynes grete
Weren of his bittre salte teeres wete.

. . . .

The somer passeth, and the nyghtes longe
Encressen double wise the peynes stronge
Bothe of the lovere and the prisoner;
482   I noot which hath the wofuller mester.
For, shortly for to seyn, this Palamoun
Perpetuelly is dampned to prisoun,
In cheynes and in fettres to been deed,
486   And Arcite is exiled upon his heed,
487   For evere mo as out of that contree,
Ne nevere mo he shal his lady see.
Yow loveres axe I now this questioun:
Who hath the worse, Arcite or Palamoun?
That oon may seen his lady day by day,
But in prison he moot dwelle alway;
493   That oother wher hym list may ride or go,
But seen his lady shal he nevere mo.
495   Now demeth as yow liste, ye that kan,
For I wol telle forth as I bigan.

~

420/ Resouneth of his youlyng = Resounded with his yelling. 421/ The pure ... grete =
The great chains on his legs. 482/ wofuller mester = most urgent need. 486/ upon his
heed = on pain of death. 487/ as out of = banished from. 493/ wher hym list = where he
likes. 495/ demeth = decide; liste = like.

Now, try and see the irony.
Palamon was left in the tyrant's keep,
With shackled hands and ironed feet,
And every day his eyes could peek
At Emelye, in all her vibrancy,
While Arcite was unconfined, yet he
Was not allowed inside the city
Of Athens, and if he tried to sneak,
Or slyly creep by, it'd be
Like a deadly game of hide-and-seek,
So Emelye was outside his reach.
But it's up to you to decide which of these
Two knights' bleak lives was the highest defeat.

The Knight's Tale: Part Two

Whan that Arcite to Thebes comen was,

498 Ful ofte a day he swelte and seyde "Allas!"

For seen his lady shal he nevere mo;

And shortly to concluden al his wo,

So muche sorwe hadde nevere creature,

502 That is, or shal whil that the world may dure.

503 His slep, his mete, his drynke is hym biraft,

504 That lene he wex and drye as is a shaft.

Hise eyen holwe and grisly to biholde,

506 His hewe falow and pale as asshen colde;

And solitarie he was and evere allone

508 And waillynge al the nyght, makynge his mone.

And if he herde song or instrument,

510 Thanne wolde he wepe, he myghte nat be stent.

So feble eek were hise spiritz, and so lowe,

And chaunged so, that no man koude knowe

His speche nor his voys, though men it herde.

514 And in his geere for al the world he ferde

515 Nat oonly lik the loveris maladye

516 Of Hereos, but rather lyk manye

517 Engendred of humour malencolik

518 Biforen in his celle fantastik,

498/ swelte = grew faint. 502/ dure = endure. 503/ biraft = denied. 504/ lene he wex =
he grew lean; shaft = stick. 506/ hewe falow = colour yellow. 508/ makynge his mone =
moaning. 510/ stent = stopped. 514/ geere = behaviour; ferde = acted. 515/ loveris
maladye = lovesickness. 516/ manye = mania. 517/ humour malencolik = depression.
518/ Biforen in = In the front of; celle fantastik = delirious mind.

For two long years in the city of Thebes
Arcite remained, weeping piteously,
Until he was finally ready to leave.

519	And shortly turned was al up so doun
520	Bothe habit and eek disposicioun
521	Of hym, this woful lovere daun Arcite.
522	What sholde I al day of his wo endite?
	Whan he endured hadde a yeer or two
	This crueel torment and this peyne and wo,
	At Thebes in his contree, as I seyde,
	Upon a nyght in sleep as he hym leyde,
527	Hym thoughte how that the wynged god Mercurie
	Biforn hym stood, and bad hym to be murie.
529	His slepy yerde in hond he bar uprighte;
	An hat he werede upon hise heris brighte.
531	Arrayed was this god, as he took keep,
532	As he was whan that Argus took his sleep;
533	And seyde hym thus, "To Atthenes shaltou wende,
534	Ther is thee shapen of thy wo an ende."
	And with that word Arcite wook and sterte.
536	"Now trewely, how soore that me smerte,"
537	Quod he, "to Atthenes right now wol I fare,
538	Ne for the drede of deeth shal I nat spare
	To se my lady that I love and serve,
540	In hire presence I recche nat to sterve."
541	And with that word he caughte a greet mirour,
	And saugh that chaunged was al his colour,
543	And saugh his visage al in another kynde.

~

519/ up so doun = upside down. 520/ habit = appearance. 521/ daun = Sir. 522/ endite = write. 527/ Hym thoughte = He dreamed. 529/ slepy yerde = magic staff. 531/ he took keep = he noticed. 532/ Argus = mythological giant with a hundred eyes. 533/ wende = go. 534/ shapen = destined. 536/ how soore that me smerte = however much it hurts. 537/ fare = go. 538/ spare = give up. 540/ I recche nat to sterve = I don't care if I die. 541/ caughte = grabbed. 543/ visage = face; kynde = form.

And he looked in a mirror, and in it he could see
That his face had been altered so hideously
From grief that it seemed he had a deadly disease.

And right anon it ran hym in his mynde
545   That sith his face was so disfigured
546   Of maladye, the which he hadde endured,
547   He myghte wel, if that he bar hym lowe,
548   Lyve in Atthenes everemoore unknowe,
        And seen his lady wel ny day by day.
550   And right anon he chaunged his array,
        And cladde hym as a povre laborer,
        And al allone, save oonly a squier
553   That knew his privetee and al his cas,
554   Which was disgised povrely as he was,
555   To Atthenes is he goon the nexte way.
        And to the court he wente upon a day,
557   And at the gate he profreth his servyse,
558   To drugge and drawe, what so men wol devyse.
        And shortly of this matere for to seyn,
560   He fil in office with a chamberleyn,
        The which that dwellynge was with Emelye,
562   For he was wys and koude soone espye
        Of every servant which that serveth here.
564   Wel koude he hewen wode, and water bere,
        For he was yong and myghty for the nones,
        And therto he was strong and big of bones
567   To doon that any wight kan hym devyse.

~

545/ sith = since. 546/ Of maladye = By depression. 547/ bar hym lowe = kept a low
profile. 548/ everemoore unknowe = undetected. 550/ array = clothes. 553/ privetee =
secrets; cas = situation. 554/ povrely = poorly. 555/ nexte = nearest. 557/ profreth =
offered. 558/ drugge and drawe = manual labour; devyse = decide. 560/ fil in office = got
a job; chamberleyn = house servant. 562/ espye = observe. 564/ bere = carry. 567/ wight
= person.

He was so different to see that he wasn't turned away

When Arcite at last returned to stay

In Athens, and was fast to learn the ways

Of breaking his back for a servant's wage,

A yeer or two he was in this servyse,
569   Page of the chambre of Emelye the brighte,
570   And Philostrate he seyde that he highte.
       But half so wel biloved a man as he
       Ne was ther nevere in court, of his degree;
       He was so gentil of condicioun
       That thurghout al the court was his renoun.
       They seyden that it were a charitee
576   That Theseus wolde enhauncen his degree,
577   And putten hym in worshipful servyse
578   Ther as he myghte his vertu exercise.
579   And thus withinne a while his name is spronge,
       Bothe of hise dedes and his goode tonge,
       That Theseus hath taken hym so neer
       That of his chambre he made hym a squier,
       And gaf hym gold to mayntene his degree.
       And eek men broghte hym out of his contree
585   From yeer to yeer, ful pryvely his rente.
       But honestly and slyly he it spente,
       That no man wondred how that he it hadde.
588   And thre yeer in this wise his lif he ladde,
589   And bar hym so, in pees and eek in werre,
590   Ther was no man that Theseus hath derre.
591   And in this blisse lete I now Arcite,
       And speke I wole of Palamon a lite.

~

569/ Page of the chambre = Personal servant. 570/ highte = was called. 576/ enhauncen
his degree = promote him. 577/ worshipful servyse = respectable employment.
578/ vertu exercise = prove his worthiness. 579/ spronge = spread. 585/ ful pryvely his
rente = a secret income. 588/ wise = way; ladde = led. 589/ pees = peace. 590/ hath
derre = held dearer. 591/ lete = leave.

Making him act like an earnest page,
And gradually he earned the praise
Of everyone concerned, and made
Sure his plans were firmly laid;
For Emelye he yearned and prayed,
But never said a word, afraid.

        In derknesse and horrible and strong prisoun
        Thise seven yeer hath seten Palamoun,
595   Forpyned, what for wo and for distresse.
596   Who feeleth double soor and hevynesse
597   But Palamon, that love destreyneth so,
598   That wood out of his wit he goth for wo?
        And eek therto he is a prisoner,
        Perpetuelly, noght oonly for a yer.
         Who koude ryme in Englyssh proprely
        His martirdom? For sothe it am nat I;
        Therfore I passe as lightly as I may.
         It fel that in the seventhe yer, in May,
        The thridde nyght, (as olde bookes seyn,
        That al this storie tellen moore pleyn),
607   Were it by aventure or destynee –
608   As, whan a thyng is shapen, it shal be –
        That soone after the mydnyght Palamoun
        By helpyng of a freend, brak his prisoun
        And fleeth the citee faste as he may go;
612   For he hade yeve his gayler drynke so
613   Of a clarree maad of a certeyn wyn,
614   With nercotikes and opie of Thebes fyn,
        That al that nyght, thogh that men wolde him shake,
        The gayler sleep, he myghte nat awake.
        And thus he fleeth as faste as evere he may;

∽

595/ Forpyned = tormented. 596/ soor = pain. 597/ destreyneth = distresses. 598/ wood = insane. 607/ aventure or destynee = accident or fate. 608/ is shapen = happens. 612/ yeve his gayler = given his jailer. 613/ clarree maad = cocktail made. 614/ opie = opium.

Now, for seven long years, I aim to tell
How Palamon stayed, chained in his cell;
This wretched prisoner remained to dwell
In darkness, and felt the flames of hell,
Tortured and stretched, in pain, until
One fortunate night he came to fill
His jailer's drink with these strange pills,
So the guard became ill, since the dope was made
From local opiates, and so he escaped.

618   The nyght was short and faste by the day,
619   That nedes-cost he moot hymselven hyde;
620   And til a grove, faste ther bisyde,
621   With dredeful foot thanne stalketh Palamoun.
       For, shortly, this was his opinioun,
       That in that grove he wolde hym hyde al day,
       And in the nyght thanne wolde he take his way
       To Thebes-ward, his freendes for to preye
626   On Theseus to helpe hym to werreye;
       And shortly outher he wolde lese his lif,
       Or wynnen Emelye unto his wyf;
       This is th'effect and his entente pleyn.
           Now wol I turne to Arcite ageyn,
       That litel wiste how ny that was his care,
       Til that Fortune had broght him in the snare.
       The bisy larke, messager of day,
634   Salueth in hir song the morwe gray,
635   And firy Phebus riseth up so brighte
       That al the orient laugheth of the light,
637   And with hise stremes dryeth in the greves
       The silver dropes hangynge on the leves.
       And Arcita, that is in the court roial
       With Theseus, his squier principal,
       Is risen, and looketh on the myrie day.
       And for to doon his observaunce to May,

∽

618/ faste = close. 619/ nedes-cost he moot = necessarily he must. 620/ faste ther
bisyde = nearby. 621/ dredeful = fearful. 626/ werreye = wage war. 634/ Salueth =
Salutes. 635/ firy Phebus = the sun. 637/ stremes = rays; greves = groves.

He was sorely afraid, but slowly he made
His lonely way to a grove where he stayed
Unexposed in the shade and to lay low for a day.
    Arcite that morning made no delay,
And rode out from court so he could pay
Respect to the sport and frequent play
That people seek in May,

Remembrynge on the poynt of his desir,

644   He on a courser, startlynge as the fir,

Is riden into the feeldes hym to pleye,

Out of the court, were it a myle or tweye.

And to the grove of which that I yow tolde

648   By aventure his wey he gan to holde,

649   To maken hym a gerland of the greves,

Were it of wodebynde or hawethorn leves.

. . . .

667   Ful litel woot Arcite of his felawe,

668   That was so ny to herknen al his sawe,

For in the bussh he sitteth now ful stille.

Whan that Arcite hadde romed al his fille

671   And songen al the roundel lustily,

672   Into a studie he fil al sodeynly,

673   As doon thise loveres in hir queynte geres,

674   Now in the croppe, now doun in the breres,

Now up, now doun as boket in a welle.

Right as the Friday, soothly for to telle,

Now it shyneth, now it reyneth faste,

678   Right so kan geery Venus overcaste

The hertes of hir folk; right as hir day

680   Is gereful, right so chaungeth she array.

681   Selde is the Friday al the wowke ylike.

682   Whan that Arcite had songe, he gan to sike,

And sette hym doun withouten any moore;

~

644/ courser = horse; startlynge as the fir = leaping like fire. 648/ gan to holde = began to turn. 649/ greves = boughs. 667/ woot = knew. 668/ sawe = speech. 671/ roundel = song; lustily = energetically. 672/ studie = meditation. 673/ queynte geres = strange ways. 674/ croppe = canopy; breres = bushes. 678/ geery = fickle; overcaste = cloud over. 680/ gereful = unpredictable. 681/ Selde = Seldom; wowke = week. 682/ sike = sigh.

And he came by chance
To aim his lance into those same high stands of trees,
And began to complain on his hands and knees.

"Allas," quod he, "that day that I was bore!

How longe, Juno, thurgh thy crueltee,

686   Woltow werreyen Thebes the Citee?

Allas, ybroght is to confusioun

688   The blood roial of Cadme and Amphioun, –

Of Cadmus, which that was the firste man

That Thebes bulte, or first the toun bigan,

And of the citee first was crouned kyng,

Of his lynage am I, and his ofspryng

693   By verray ligne, as of the stok roial,

694   And now I am so caytyf and so thral

That he that is my mortal enemy,

696   I serve hym as his squier povrely.

And yet dooth Juno me wel moore shame,

698   For I dar noght biknowe myn owene name,

699   But theras I was wont to highte Arcite,

Now highte I Philostrate, noght worth a myte.

701   Allas, thou felle Mars! Allas, Juno!

702   Thus hath youre ire oure lynage al fordo,

Save oonly me and wrecched Palamoun,

That Theseus martireth in prisoun.

705   And over al this, to sleen me outrely,

706   Love hath his firy dart so brennyngly

Ystiked thurgh my trewe careful herte,

708   That shapen was my deeth erst than my sherte.

Ye sleen me with youre eyen, Emelye!

~

686/ werreyen = wage war on. 688/ Cadme and Amphioun = founders of Thebes.
693/ verray ligne = true ancestry; stok roial = royal blood. 694/ caytyf and so thral =
wretched and enslaved. 696/ squier povrely = lowly servant. 698/ biknowe = reveal.
699/ wont to highte = once called. 701/ felle = cruel. 702/ fordo = ruined. 705/ sleen
me outrely = slay me utterly. 706/ brennyngly = hotly. 708/ erst = sooner.

And said, "I can't believe I came from royalty,
And my family's name will be destroyed in me!
Emelye's to blame for spoiling me,
'Cause she's tempting me to shamefully toil and be
My enemy's page, and change my loyalty!"

"Ye been the cause wherfore that I dye.

Of al the remenant of myn oother care

712   Ne sette I nat the montance of a tare,

713   So that I koude doon aught to youre plesaunce."

And with that word he fil doun in a traunce

715   A longe tyme, and after he upsterte.

        This Palamoun, that thoughte that thurgh his herte

He felte a coold swerd sodeynliche glyde,

718   For ire he quook; no lenger wolde he byde.

And whan that he had herd Arcite's tale,

As he were wood, with face deed and pale,

He stirte hym up out of the buskes thikke,

722   And seide, "Arcite, false traytour wikke!

723   Now artow hent, that lovest my lady so,

For whom that I have al this peyne and wo,

And art my blood, and to my conseil sworn,

As I ful ofte have told thee heerbiforn,

727   And hast byjaped heere duc Theseus,

And falsly chaunged hast thy name thus.

I wol be deed, or elles thou shalt dye;

Thou shalt nat love my lady Emelye,

731   But I wol love hire oonly, and namo,

For I am Palamon, thy mortal foo!

712/ montance of a tare = value of a weed. 713/ doon ... plesaunce = do something
for your pleasure. 715/ upsterte = got up. 718/ For ire he quook = For anger he shook.
722/ wikke = wicked. 723/ hent = caught. 727/ byjaped = deceived. 731/ namo = no more.

Palamon's blood nearly boiled as he
Crouched and listened joylessly
To this pointless speech; so annoyed was he,
That he jumped up and uncoiled to speak:
  "I hate to spoil the deceit you've created in court,
And interrupt the life you betrayed me for,
But this is what I have been waiting for:
Waging war to decide who loves the lady more!"

"And though that I no wepene have in this place,

734   But out of prison am astert by grace,

735   I drede noght that outher thow shalt dye,

Or thow ne shalt nat loven Emelye.

Chees which thou wolt, for thou shalt nat asterte!"

738   This Arcite, with ful despitous herte,

Whan he hym knew, and hadde his tale herd,

As fiers as leoun pulled out his swerd,

And seyde thus: "By God that sit above,

742   Nere it that thou art sik and wood for love,

And eek that thow no wepne hast in this place,

Thou sholdest nevere out of this grove pace,

That thou ne sholdest dyen of myn hond.

746   For I defye the seurete and the bond

Which that thou seist that I have maad to thee.

What, verray fool, thynk wel that love is free,

749   And I wol love hir, maugree al thy myght!

But for as muche thou art a worthy knyght,

751   And wilnest to darreyne hire by bataille,

Have heer my trouthe; tomorwe I wol nat faille

753   Withoute wityng of any oother wight

That heere I wol be founden as a knyght,

755   And bryngen harneys right ynough for thee,

And ches the beste, and leef the worste for me.

734/ astert = escaped. 735/ drede = doubt; outher = either. 738/ despitous = spiteful.
742/ Nere it ... wood = If you weren't sick and insane. 746/ seurete = oath. 749/ maugree
= in spite of. 751/ wilnest to darreyne hire = wish to fight for her. 753/ wityng =
knowledge; wight = person. 755/ harneys = armour.

Arcite bared the blade of his sword,
And gravely gave his brave retort:
  "Has love so clouded your perception,
That without any sort of weapon
You would dare come forth and step in
To this place to make war and threaten?"

"And mete and drynke this nyght wol I brynge
Ynough for thee, and clothes for thy beddynge;
And if so be that thou my lady wynne,
And sle me in this wode ther I am inne,
Thow mayst wel have thy lady as for me."
　　This Palamon answerde, "I graunte it thee."
And thus they been departed til amorwe,
764　Whan ech of hem had leyd his feith to borwe.
　　O Cupide, out of alle charitee!
766　O regne, that wolt no felawe have with thee!
Ful sooth is seyd that love ne lordshipe
768　Wol noght, hir thankes, have no felaweshipe.
Wel fynden that Arcite and Palamoun.
Arcite is riden anon unto the toun,
And on the morwe, er it were dayes light,
772　Ful prively two harneys hath he dight,
773　Bothe suffisaunt and mete to darreyne
The bataille in the feeld bitwix hem tweyne.
And on his hors, allone as he was born,
He carieth al the harneys hym biforn,
And in the grove, at tyme and place yset,
This Arcite and this Palamon ben met.
To chaungen gan the colour in hir face,
Right as the hunters in the regne of Trace,
781　That stondeth at the gappe with a spere,
Whan hunted is the leoun and the bere,

～

764/ leyd ... borwe = promised on his faith to return. 766/ regne = power. 768/ Wol
noght ... felaweshipe = Will never willingly share. 772/ two harneys hath he dight =
he prepared two suits of armour. 773/ mete to darreyne = suitable to decide. 781/ gappe
= trap.

But Arcite was bound by his high honour,
To go back into town and provide armour
For his opponent, who would choose the best,
With clothes and food at his request,
And then rest for the night, since those were his dues
In the case of a feud, and his right,
And Arcite well knew he could never refuse
On the truth of his oath as a knight.

783   And hereth hym come russhyng in the greves,
       And breketh bothe bowes and the leves,
       And thynketh, "Heere cometh my mortal enemy!
       Withoute faille he moot be deed or I,
       For outher I moot sleen hym at the gappe,
788   Or he moot sleen me, if that me myshappe."
       So ferden they in chaungyng of hir hewe,
       As fer as everich of hem oother knewe.
791   Ther nas no 'good day' ne no saluyng,
792   But streight, withouten word or rehersyng,
       Everich of hem heelp for to armen oother,
       As freendly as he were his owene brother.
       And after that, with sharpe speres stronge,
796   They foynen ech at oother wonder longe.
797   Thou myghtest wene that this Palamoun
798   In his fightyng were a wood leon,
       And as a crueel tigre was Arcite.
       As wilde bores gonne they to smyte,
       That frothen white as foom for ire wood.
       Up to the ancle foghte they in hir blood.
       And in this wise I lete hem fightyng dwelle,
       And forth I wole of Theseus yow telle.
           The destinee, ministre general,
       That executeth in the world overal
807   The purveiaunce that God hath seyn biforn,

~

783/ greves = bushes. 788/ if that me myshappe = if I make a mistake. 791/ saluyng = greeting. 792/ rehersyng = small talk. 796/ foynen = thrust. 797/ wene = think. 798/ wood leon = mad lion. 807/ purveiaunce = providence.

Both awoke at first light and, the greetings refuted,

They helped one another to stand and get suited

Like brothers and, swords distributed,

They fought, 'til their guts were entangled

In knots, getting ruptured and mangled,

'Til it got where they stood up to their ankles

In pools of their blood,

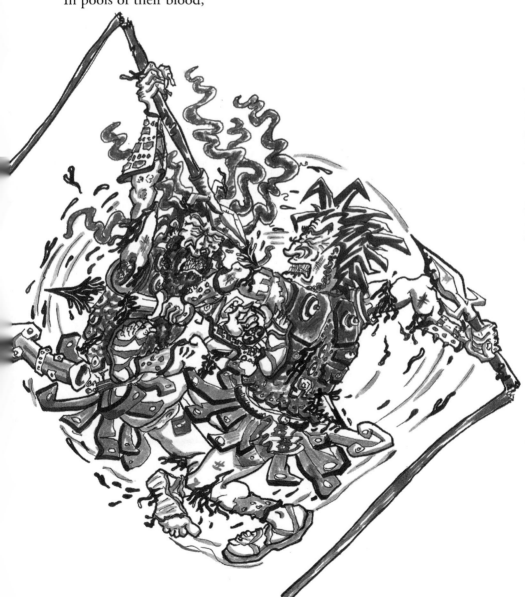

So strong it is, that though the world had sworn

The contrarie of a thyng, by ye or nay,

Yet somtyme it shal fallen on a day

811   That falleth nat eft withinne a thousand yeere.

For certeinly, oure appetites heere,

Be it of werre, or pees, or hate, or love,

814   Al is this reuled by the sighte above.

      This mene I now by myghty Theseus,

That for to hunten is so desirus,

817   And namely at the grete hert in May,

818   That in his bed ther daweth hym no day

819   That he nys clad, and redy for to ryde

820   With hunte and horn, and houndes hym bisyde.

For in his huntyng hath he swich delit

That it is al his joye and appetit

823   To been hymself the grete hertes bane –

824   For after Mars he serveth now Dyane.

Cleer was the day, as I have toold er this,

And Theseus, with alle joye and blis,

With his Ypolita, the faire quene,

And Emelye, clothed al in grene,

On huntyng be they riden roially,

830   And to the grove, that stood ful faste by,

In which ther was an hert, as men hym tolde,

832   Duc Theseus the streighte wey hath holde,

〜

811/ eft = again. 814/ the sighte above = destiny. 817/ grete hert = giant stag. 818/ daweth hym = dawns on him. 819/ nys = isn't. 820/ hunte = hunter. 823/ hertes bane = stag killer. 824/ Mars = god of war; Dyane = goddess of hunting (and chastity). 830/ faste by = nearby. 832/ the streighte wey hath holde = went straight there.

And they ought to've been thankful
That Theseus, hunting as he was accustomed,
Entered the grove and there came across them,
With all of his women arranged in procession;
Ypolita and Emelye were in his possession,

And to the launde he rideth hym ful right,
For thider was the hert wont have his flight,
And over a brook, and so forth in his weye.
836 This duc wol han a cours at hym or tweye
With houndes swiche as that hym list comaunde.
   And whan this duc was come unto the launde,
Under the sonne he looketh, and anon
He was war of Arcite and Palamon,
841 That foughten breme as it were bores two;
The brighte swerdes wenten to and fro
So hidously that with the leeste strook
It semed as it wolde felle an ook;
But what they were, nothyng he ne woot.
This duc his courser with his spores smoot,
847 And at a stert he was bitwix hem two,
848 And pulled out a swerd, and cride, "Hoo!
849 Namoore, up peyne of lesynge of youre heed!
850 By myghty Mars, he shal anon be deed
That smyteth any strook that I may seen.
852 But telleth me what myster men ye been,
853 That been so hardy for to fighten heere
Withouten juge or oother officere,
855 As it were in a lystes roially."

~

836/ cours = try. 841/ breme = ferociously; bores two = two wild boars. 847/ at a stert
= in a moment. 848/ Hoo! = Halt! 849/ up peyne of = on penalty of. 850/ anon = soon.
852/ myster men = sort of men. 853/ hardy = bold. 855/ lystes roially = official
tournament.

And seeing them, bravely he pulled out his weapon,
And rode safely forth on his horse to arrest them:
  "Throw down your swords, on pain of death!
You both will now be slain, unless
I find out who's to blame for this mess;
Now give me the two of your names and confess!"

This Palamon answerde hastily,
And seyde, "Sire, what nedeth wordes mo?
We have the deeth disserved bothe two.
859   Two woful wrecches been we, two caytyves,
860   That been encombred of oure owene lyves,
And as thou art a rightful lord and juge,
Ne yeve us neither mercy ne refuge,
863   But sle me first, for seinte charitee!
864   But sle my felawe eek as wel as me –
Or sle hym first, for though thow knowest it lite,
This is thy mortal foo, this is Arcite,
867   That fro thy lond is banysshed on his heed,
For which he hath deserved to be deed.
For this is he that cam unto thy gate,
870   And seyde that he highte Philostrate.
871   Thus hath he japed thee ful many a yer,
And thou hast maked hym thy chief squier,
And this is he that loveth Emelye.
For sith the day is come that I shal dye,
I make pleynly my confessioun
876   That I am thilke woful Palamoun,
That hath thy prisoun broken wikkedly.
I am thy mortal foo, and it am I
879   That loveth so hoote Emelye the brighte,
That I wol dye present in hir sighte;

~

859/ caytyves = outcasts. 860/ encombred of = burdened by. 863/ for seinte charitee = for God's sake. 864/ eek = also. 867/ on his heed = on punishment of losing his head. 870/ highte = was called. 871/ japed = deceived. 876/ thilke = that. 879/ hoote = passionately.

Palamon, with what remained of his breath,
Did his best to be plain and explain his distress:
    "I am Palamon, seeking your prison to flee,
And this is my brother, my sworn enemy,
Arcite, concealing his identity,
Who swears he's in love with the fair Emelye,
Who I love as well, so there's no remedy,
As she tenderly watches your sword rending me;
Since we both deserve condemned to be,
Kill him first, and turn your sword then to me!"

881 "Wherfore I axe deeth and my juwise –
   But sle my felawe in the same wise,
   For bothe han we deserved to be slayn."
     This worthy duc answered anon agayn,
   And seyde, "This is a short conclusioun,
   Youre owene mouth, by your confessioun;
887 Hath dampned yow, and I wol it recorde.
888 It nedeth noght to pyne yow with the corde;
   Ye shal be deed, by myghty Mars the rede!"
890   The queene anon, for verray wommanhede,
   Gan for to wepe, and so dide Emelye,
   And alle the ladyes in the compaignye.
   Greet pitee was it, as it thoughte hem alle,
   That evere swich a chaunce sholde falle.
   For gentil men they were of greet estaat,
   And no thyng but for love was this debaat,
   And saugh hir blody woundes wyde and soore,
   And alle crieden, both lasse and moore,
   "Have mercy, lord, upon us wommen alle!"
   And on hir bare knees adoun they falle,
   And wolde have kist his feet ther as he stood;
902 Til at the laste aslaked was his mood,
903 For pitee renneth soone in gentil herte.

~

881/ axe = ask for; juwise = justice. 887/ dampned = condemned; I wol it recorde = I'll
make note of it. 888/ pyne yow with the corde = torture you with rope. 890/ wommanhede
= female compassion. 902/ aslaked = satisfied. 903/ renneth = runs.

With wisdom, compassion, and great sympathy,
Theseus answered: "This makes sense to me,
And by your confession you must die instantly!"
    But the women began to cry and weep,
As blood in front of their eyes did seep
From the brothers' wounds both wide and deep;
They fell to pray beside his feet.
"Have mercy, lord, upon us all!"
The ladies whispered quietly,

904   And though he first for ire quook and sterte,
905   He hath considered shortly in a clause
      The trespas of hem bothe, and eek the cause,
      And although that his ire hir gilt accused,
      Yet in his resoun he hem bothe excused
      As thus: he thoghte wel that every man
      Wol helpe hymself in love, if that he kan,
911   And eek delivere hymself out of prisoun;
      And eek his herte hadde compassioun
913   Of wommen, for they wepen evere in oon;
      And in his gentil herte he thoughte anon,
      And softe unto hymself he seyde, "Fy
      Upon a lord that wol have no mercy,
      But been a leon, bothe in word and dede,
918   To hem that been in repentaunce and drede,
919   As wel as to a proud despitous man
920   That wol maynteyne that he first bigan.
921   That lord hath litel of discrecioun
922   That in swich cas kan no divisioun,
923   But weyeth pride and humblesse after oon."
      And shortly, whan his ire is thus agoon,
925   He gan to looken up with eyen lighte,
926   And spak thise same wordes al on highte:

～

904/ for ire quook = shook with anger; sterte = trembled. 905/ in a clause = in particular.
911/ eek = also. 913/ evere in oon = all together. 918/ repentaunce and drede = remorse
and fear. 919/ despitous = defiant. 920/ that he first began = the attitude he started with.
921/ discrecioun = good judgement. 922/ kan no divisioun = knows no difference.
923/ weyeth = values; after oon = the same. 925/ lighte = compassionate. 926/ al on
highte = out loud.

And when he heard their pious pleas,
Duke Theseus felt his pride appeased,
And forgave the knights their rivalry.

927   "The god of love, a benedicite!
         How myghty and how greet a lord is he!
929   Ayeyns his myght ther gayneth none obstacles;
930   He may be cleped a god for his myracles,
931   For he kan maken, at his owene gyse,
932   Of everich herte as that hym list divyse.
         Lo heere this Arcite and this Palamoun
934   That quitly weren out of my prisoun,
         And myghte han lyved in Thebes roially,
936   And witen I am hir mortal enemy,
         And that hir deth lith in my myght also,
938   And yet hath love, maugree hir eyen two,
         Broght hem hyder bothe for to dye.
940   Now looketh, is nat that an heigh folye?
941   Who may been a fole, but if he love?
         Bihoold, for Goddes sake that sit above,
943   Se how they blede! Be they noght wel arrayed?
         Thus hath hir lord, the god of Love, ypayed
         Hir wages and hir fees for hir servyse!
946   And yet they wenen for to been ful wyse
         That serven love, for aught that may bifalle;
948   But this is yet the beste game of alle,
949   That she for whom they han this jolitee,
950   Kan hem therfore as muche thank as me.
951   She woot namoore of al this hoote fare,
952   By God, than woot a cokkow or an hare!

∾

927/ benedicite! = bless you! 929/ gayneth none = can be no. 930/ cleped = called.
931/ at his owene gyse = in his own style. 932/ divyse = invent. 934/ quitly = freely.
936/ witen = know. 938/ maugree hir eyen two = despite their knowledge of the danger.
940/ is nat that an heigh folye? = isn't that stupid? 941/ fole = fool. 943/ wel arrayed =
attractive. 946/ wenen for to been = believe they are. 948/ beste game = biggest joke.
949/ jolitee = desire. 950/ Kan hem = knows them. 951/ hoote fare = passionate
struggle. 952/ cokkow = cuckoo bird.

So wise was he that he thus decreed:

"They must be freed," which was agreed

By all to be a just deed.

953 "But all moot ben assayed, hoot and coold;
     A man moot ben a fool, or yong or oold;
955 I woot it by myself ful yore agon,
956 For in my tyme a servant was I oon.
     And therfore, syn I knowe of loves peyne,
958 And woot how soore it kan a man distreyne,
959 As he that hath ben caught ofte in his laas,
960 I yow foryeve al hoolly this trespaas,
     At requeste of the queene that kneleth heere,
     And eek of Emelye, my suster deere.
     And ye shul bothe anon unto me swere
964 That nevere mo ye shal my contree dere,
     Ne make werre upon me, nyght ne day,
     But been my freendes in al that ye may.

     · · · · · · · · · · · ·

987   My wyl is this, for plat conclusioun,
988 Withouten any repplicacioun, –
     If that you liketh, take it for the beste,
     That everich of you shal goon where hym leste,
     Frely, withouten raunson or daunger,
992 And this day fifty wykes fer ne ner,
     Everich of you shal brynge an hundred knyghtes
994 Armed for lystes up at alle rightes,
995 Al redy to darreyne hire by bataille.

~

953/ assayed = tested. 955/ ful yore agon = long ago. 956/ servant = lover. 958/ distreyne
= distress. 959/ laas = snare. 960/ al hoolly = completely. 964/ dere = harm. 987/ for
plat conclusion = to tell it straight. 988/ repplicacioun = repetition. 992/ fer ne ner =
give or take. 994/ Armed for ... alle rightes = Armed for the tournament in every way.
995/ darreyne hire = fight for her.

Plus, the brothers' lust to please,
Theseus generously accorded
That one of them would be awarded
Emelye, once they had sorted
Out the victor of this sordid
Conflict, at the time afforded.

996   "And this bihote I yow withouten faille,
         Upon my trouthe, and as I am a knyght,
998   That wheither of yow bothe that hath myght—
         This is to seyn, that wheither he or thow
         May with his hundred, as I spak of now,
1001   Sleen his contrarie, or out of lystes dryve,
1002   Thanne shal I yeve Emelya to wyve
         To whom that Fortune yeveth so fair a grace.
         The lystes shal I maken in this place,
1005   And God so wisly on my soule rewe,
1006   As I shal evene juge been, and trewe.
         Ye shul noon oother ende with me maken,
         That oon of yow ne shal be deed or taken.
         And if yow thynketh this is weel ysayd,
1010   Seyeth youre avys and holdeth you apayd;
         This is youre ende and youre conclusioun."
1012   Who looketh lightly now but Palamoun?
         Who spryngeth up for joye but Arcite?
1014   Who kouthe telle, or who kouthe it endite,
         The joye that is maked in the place
1016   Whan Theseus hath doon so fair a grace?
         But doun on knees wente every maner wight,
         And thonken hym with al hir herte and myght,
1019   And namely the Thebans, often sithe.
1020   And thus with good hope and with herte blithe
         They taken hir leve, and homward gonne they ride
         To Thebes with hise olde walles wyde.

~

996/ bihote = promise. 998/ wheither = whichever. 1001/ Sleen his ... dryve = Kill
his enemy or knock him out of battle. 1002/ wyve = marry. 1005/ rewe = have mercy.
1006/ evene juge been = be a fair judge. 1010/ avys = opinion; apayd = satisfied.
1012/ lightly = happy. 1014/ endite = write. 1016/ doon so fair a grace = been so generous.
1019/ often sithe = often since. 1020/ blithe = joyful.

The duel was set for one year hence,
And each would bring for his defence
A hundred knights to guard against
His brother's vengeance and dispense
With justice, then home they went,
And each, received with welcome, spent
The year in Thebes, both well content.

I trowe men wolde deme it necligence
1024   If I foryete to tellen the dispence
Of Theseus, that gooth so bisily
1026   To maken up the lystes roially,
That swich a noble theatre as it was,
I dar wel seyen, in this world ther nas.
The circuit a myle was aboute,
1030   Walled of stoon, and dyched al withoute.
1031   Round was the shap, in manere of compas,
1032   Ful of degrees, the heighte of sixty pas,
That whan a man was set on o degree,
1034   He lette nat his felawe for to see.
Estward ther stood a gate of marbul whit,
Westward right swich another in the opposit;
And shortly to concluden, swich a place
1038   Was noon in erthe, as in so litel space.
For in the lond ther was no crafty man
1040   That geometrie or ars-metrike kan,
1041   Ne portreytour, ne kervere of ymages,
1042   That Theseus ne yaf him mete and wages,
1043   The theatre for to maken and devyse.

~

1024/ dispence = expenses. 1026/ lystes = tournament enclosure. 1030/ dyched al withoute = surrounded by a ditch. 1031/ in manere of compas = like a compass. 1032/ degrees = levels; pas = paces. 1034/ He lette nat ... see = He didn't block anyone's view. 1038/ space = time. 1040/ ars-metrike = arithmetic. 1041/ portreytour = painter; kervere of ymages = sculptor. 1042/ yaf him mete = gave him food. 1043/ devyse = design.

While the knights were gone away,
Theseus, to accommodate
Their combat, paid uncommon wages
To his most accomplished masons,
Who patiently went on to make
A theatre so strong and great,
With marble carvings on the gate,
That all who looked upon the place,
Did so with an astonished face,

And for to doon his ryte and sacrifise,

He estward hath upon the gate above,

In worshipe of Venus, goddesse of love,

1047   Doon make an auter and an oratorie.

And on the gate westward, in memorie

1049   Of Mars, he maked hath right swich another,

1050   That coste largely of gold a fother.

And northward, in a touret on the wal

1052   Of alabastre whit, and reed coral,

1053   An oratorie, riche for to see,

1054   In worshipe of Dyane, of chastitee,

1055   Hath Theseus doon wroght in noble wyse.

. . . .

The day approcheth of hir retournynge,

That everich sholde an hundred knyghtes brynge

1239   The bataille to darreyne, as I yow tolde.

And til Atthenes, hir covenantz for to holde,

Hath everich of hem broght an hundred knyghtes,

1242   Wel armed for the werre at alle rightes.

1243   And sikerly ther trowed many a man

1244   That nevere sithen that the world bigan,

1245   As for to speke of knyghthod of hir hond,

As fer as God hath maked see or lond,

1247   Nas of so fewe so noble a compaignye.

1047/ auter = altar; oratorie = temple. 1049/ Mars = god of war. 1050/ fother = cartload.
1052/ reed = red. 1053/ oratorie = temple. 1054/ Dyane, of chastitee = Diana, goddess
of chastity. 1055/ doon wroght = had made. 1239/ darreyne = decide. 1242/ at alle
rightes = in every way. 1243/ sikerly = truly; trowed = thought. 1244/ sithen = since.
1245/ knyghthod of hir hond = the deeds of knighthood. 1247/ Nas = Was never.

So much that structure shone with grace,
As did the Duke, whose honoured state
Demanded that he dominate.
   Now, on the long awaited day
That they'd agreed upon in May,
Arcite and Palamon did make
Their sombre way there to exonerate
Their honour and confront their fate.

1248   For every wight that lovede chivalrye,

1249   And wolde, his thankes, han a passant name,

Hath preyed that he myghte been of that game;

And wel was hym that therto chosen was.

For if ther fille tomorwe swich a cas

Ye knowen wel that every lusty knyght

1254   That loveth paramours and hath his myght,

Were it in Engelond or elles where,

1256   They wolde, hir thankes, wilnen to be there,

To fighte for a lady, benedicitee!

1258   It were a lusty sighte for to see.

· · · · · · · · · · · ·

The Sonday nyght, er day bigan to sprynge,

Whan Palamon the larke herde synge,

(Al though it nere nat day by houres two,

1354   Yet song the larke) and Palamon right tho,

With hooly herte and with an heigh corage

He roos to wenden on his pilgrymage

1357   Unto the blisful Citherea benigne –

1358   I mene Venus, honurable and digne.

1359   And in hir houre he walketh forth a pas

Unto the lystes, ther hire temple was,

1361   And doun he kneleth with ful humble cheere,

And herte soor, and seyde in this manere:

〜

1248/ every wight = everyone. 1249/ his thankes = gratefully; passant name = high
reputation. 1254/ paramours = passionately. 1256/ wilnen = want. 1258/ lusty = lovely.
1354/ tho = then. 1357/ Citherea = another name for Venus; benigne = benevolent.
1358/ digne = worthy. 1359/ hir houre = two hours before sunrise; a pas = slowly.
1361/ cheere = spirits.

Early Palamon did wake that day,
And went to pray and pay respects at
The statue of Venus they'd erected,
Standing in a temple decked with
Likenesses of all the reckless
Souls who love had misdirected.

"Faireste of faire, O lady myn, Venus,
Doughter to Jove and spouse of Vulcanus,
1365 Thow glader of the Mount of Citheron,
1366 For thilke love thow haddest to Adoon,
1367 Have pitee of my bittre teeris smerte,
And taak myn humble preyere at thyn herte.
Allas, I ne have no langage to telle
1370 Th'effectes ne the tormentz of myn helle!
1371 Myn herte may myne harmes nat biwreye;
I am so confus that I kan noght seye
But 'Mercy, lady bright, that knowest weele
My thought and seest what harmes that I feele!'
1375 Considere al this and rewe upon my soore,
1376 As wisly as I shal for everemoore,
1377 Emforth my myght, thy trewe servant be,
And holden werre alwey with chastitee.
1379 That make I myn avow, so ye me helpe;
1380 I kepe noght of armes for to yelpe,
1381 Ne I ne axe nat tomorwe to have victorie,
Ne renoun in this cas, ne veyne glorie
1383 Of pris of armes blowen up and doun,
But I wolde have fully possessioun
Of Emelye, and dye in thy servyse.

~

1365/ glader = bringer of joy. 1366/ Adoon = Adonis. 1367/ smerte = painful. 1370/ Th'effectes = The nature. 1371/ harmes nat biwreye = sorrows not reveal. 1375/ rewe upon my soore = have pity upon my pain. 1376/ wisly = surely. 1377/ Emforth my myght = As best I can. 1379/ so ye me helpe = if you help me. 1380/ I kepe ... yelpe = I'm not interested in strength or bragging rights. 1381/ Ne I ne = Neither do I. 1383/ pris of armes blowen = praise of my strength shouted.

Palamon's prayer to Venus:
    "Venus, I've come to ask if we
Might declare war on chastity!
My love is near capacity,
And Emelye just laughs at me.
Let me possess her passively,
Or let me die disastrously!"

"Fynd thow the manere how, and in what wyse –
1387   I recche nat, but it may bettre be
To have victorie of hem, or they of me –
So that I have my lady in myne armes.
For though so be that Mars is god of armes,
1391   Youre vertu is so greet in hevene above
1392   That if yow list, I shal wel have my love.
Thy temple wol I worshipe everemo,
And on thyn auter, where I ride or go,
1395   I wol doon sacrifice and fires beete.
And if ye wol nat so, my lady sweete,
Thanne preye I thee, tomorwe with a spere
1398   That Arcita me thurgh the herte bere.
1399   Thanne rekke I noght, whan I have lost my lyf,
Though that Arcita wynne hir to his wyf.
This is th'effect and ende of my preyere:
1402   Yif me my love, thow blisful lady deere!"
1403   Whan the orison was doon of Palamon,
His sacrifice he dide, and that anon,
1405   Ful pitously with alle circumstaunces,
1406   Al telle I noght as now his observaunces.
But atte laste the statue of Venus shook,
And made a signe wherby that he took
That his preyere accepted was that day.

~

1387/ I recche nat = I don't care. 1391/ vertu = influence. 1392/ if yow list = if it is
your will. 1395/ beete = burn. 1398/ bere = stab. 1399/ rekke I noght = I won't care. 1402/
Yif = Give. 1403/ orison = prayer. 1405/ pitously = piously; alle circumstaunces = due
diligence. 1406/ Al = Although.

After these fervent words he
Was assured that she had heard his plea,
For currently he was unnerved to see
The statue of her stir to re-
Assure him he deserved to be
Unburdened, free of urgency,

For thogh the signe shewed a delay,

1411 Yet wiste he wel that graunted was his boone,

And with glad herte he wente hym hoom ful soone.

1413   The thridde houre inequal that Palamon

Bigan to Venus temple for to gon,

Up roos the sonne, and up roos Emelye,

1416 And to the temple of Dyane gan hye.

1417 Hir maydens that she thider with hir ladde,

Ful redily with hem the fyr they hadde,

1419 Th'encens, the clothes, and the remenant al

1420 That to the sacrifice longen shal.

1421 The hornes fulle of meeth, as was the gyse,

Ther lakked noght to doon hir sacrifise,

Smokynge the temple, ful of clothes faire.

1424 This Emelye, with herte debonaire,

1425 Hir body wessh with water of a welle –

But how she dide hir ryte I dar nat telle,

But it be any thing in general;

1428 And yet it were a game to heeren al.

1429 To hym that meneth wel it were no charge,

1430 But it is good a man been at his large.

1431 Hir brighte heer was kembd, untressed al;

1432 A coroune of a grene ook cerial

1433 Upon hir heed was set ful fair and meete.

∾

1411/ wiste = knew; boone = wish. 1413/ The thridde houre inequal = Two hours after.
1416/ gan hye = hurried. 1417/ thider with hir ladde = led there with her. 1419/ remenant
al = all the rest. 1420/ longen shal = belonged. 1421/ meeth = mead; gyse = custom.
1424/ debonaire = gentle. 1425/ wessh = washed. 1428/ were a game = would be fun.
1429/ charge = problem. 1430/ been at his large = to be free. 1431/ kembd, untressed al
= combed loosely. 1432/ ook cerial = oak leaves. 1433/ meete = appropriate.

And as her faithful servant he
Inferred from these occurrences he
Was meant to be the first to see
His Emelye no virgin be.
Palamon returned with glee,
So sure was he that worthy Venus
Had averted the emergency.
     Emelye then went to see
Diane and prayed, and gave some words to
Try and save her maiden virtue.

1434   Two fyres on the auter gan she beete,

1435   And dide hir thynges, as men may biholde

1436   In Stace of Thebes and thise bookes olde.

       Whan kyndled was the fyr, with pitous cheere

       Unto Dyane she spak as ye may heere:

          "O chaste goddesse of the wodes grene,

1440   To whom bothe hevene and erthe and see is sene,

1441   Queene of the regne of Pluto derk and lowe,

       Goddesse of maydens, that myn herte hast knowe

       Ful many a yeer, and woost what I desire,

       As keep me fro thy vengeaunce and thyn ire,

1445   That Attheon aboughte cruelly.

1446   Chaste goddesse, wel wostow that I

1447   Desire to ben a mayden al my lyf,

1448   Ne nevere wol I be no love ne wyf.

       I am, thow woost, yet of thy compaignye,

1450   A mayde, and love huntynge and venerye,

       And for to walken in the wodes wilde,

       And noght to ben a wyf and be with childe.

1453   Noght wol I knowe the compaignye of man;

       Now helpe me, lady, sith ye may and kan,

       For tho thre formes that thou hast in thee.

~

1434/ beete = build. 1435/ thynges = rituals. 1436/ Stace of Thebes = *Thebaid*, a book about Thebes. 1440/ sene = visible. 1441/ Pluto = god of the underworld. 1445/ Attheon = Actaeon, one of Diana's victims; aboughte = suffered for. 1446/ wostow = you know. 1447/ mayden = virgin. 1448/ Ne nevere wol I be = I never want to be. 1450/ mayde = virgin; venerye = hunting-related activities. 1453/ wol = want; the compaignye of man = sex.

Emelye's prayer to Diane:

"Diane, you know that I am wild;
I have no wish to be defiled
By the hand of man, nor got with child,

"And Palamon, that hath swich love to me,
And eek Arcite, that loveth me so soore,
This grace I preye thee withoute moore,
As sende love and pees bitwixe hem two,
And fro me turne awey hir hertes so
That al hir hoote love and hir desir,
And al hir bisy torment and hir fir
1463　Be queynt, or turned in another place.
And if so be thou wolt do me no grace,
Or if my destynee be shapen so
1466　That I shal nedes have oon of hem two,
As sende me hym that moost desireth me.
Bihoold, goddesse of clene chastitee,
The bittre teeris that on my chekes falle.
Syn thou art mayde and kepere of us alle,
1471　My maydenhede thou kepe and wel conserve,
And whil I lyve a mayde, I wol thee serve."
1473　　The fires brenne upon the auter cleere,
Whil Emelye was thus in hir preyere;
1475　But sodeynly she saugh a sighte queynte,
1476　For right anon oon of the fyres queynte,
1477　And quyked agayn, and after that anon
1478　That oother fyr was queynt and al agon;
1479　And as it queynte it made a whistelynge,
1480　As doon thise wete brondes in hir brennynge;

~

1463/ queynt = quenched. 1466/ I shal nedes = I must. 1471/ maydenhede = virginity.
1473/ brenne = burned. 1475/ queynte = strange. 1476/ queynte = went out. 1477/
quyked = rekindled. 1478/ queynt = extinguished. 1479/ whistelynge = hissing. 1480/
wete brondes = wet branches.

"Therefore, I pray, be mild;
Don't let my honour be beguiled!"
   The altar fires burning, in plain English,
At her pious yearning were extinguished.

1481 And at the brondes ende out ran anon
       As it were blody dropes many oon;
1483 For which so soore agast was Emelye
1484 That she was wel ny mad, and gan to crye;
1485 For she ne wiste what it signyfied,
       But oonly for the feere thus hath she cried,
1487 And weep that it was pitee for to heere.
       And therwithal Dyane gan appeere,
       With bowe in honde, right as an hunteresse,
1490 And seyde, "Doghter, stynt thyn hevynesse.
       Among the goddes hye it is affermed,
       And by eterne word writen and confermed;
1493 Thou shalt ben wedded unto oon of tho
       That han for thee so muchel care and wo,
       But unto which of hem I may nat telle.
       Farwel, for I ne may no lenger dwelle.
       The fires whiche that on myn auter brenne
1498 Shule thee declaren, er that thou go henne,
       Thyn aventure of love, as in this cas."
       And with that word, the arwes in the caas
       Of the goddesse clateren faste and rynge,
       And forth she wente and made a vanysshynge;
1503 For which this Emelye astoned was,
       And seyde, "What amounteth this, allas?
       I putte me in thy proteccioun,
       Dyane, and in thy disposicioun!"

~

1481/ brondes = branches'. 1483/ agast = afraid. 1484/ wel ny = nearly. 1485/ ne wiste = didn't know. 1487/ weep = wept. 1490/ stynt = stop. 1493/ tho = those. 1498/ er that thou go henne = before you leave. 1503/ astoned = astonished.

Emelye, unsinged, just stared with dread,
As Diane reached out her hand, and there she bled
Upon her servant's weary head,
The blood of virgins, cherry-red.
    "Let it now be clearly said,
You will soon see your marriage bed!"
In response to this rejection,
Emelye asked a simple question:
    "Then what good is your protection,
If I fall prey to some erection?"

1507   And hoom she goth anon the nexte weye.
        This is th'effect; ther is namoore to seye.

1509   The nexte houre of Mars folwynge this,
        Arcite unto the temple walked is
        Of fierse Mars to doon his sacrifise,

1512   With alle the rytes of his payen wyse.
        With pitous herte and heigh devocioun,

1514   Right thus to Mars he seyde his orisoun:

1515   "O stronge god, that in the regnes colde
        Of Trace honoured art and lord yholde,
        And hast in every regne and every lond

1518   Of armes al the brydel in thyn hond,

1519   And hem fortunest as thee lyst devyse,

1520   Accepte of me my pitous sacrifise.
        If so be that my youthe may deserve,
        And that my myght be worthy for to serve

1523   Thy godhede, that I may been oon of thyne,

1524   Thanne preye I thee to rewe upon my pyne.
        For thilke peyne and thilke hoote fir

1526   In which thou whilom brendest for desir,

1527   Whan that thow usedest the greet beautee
        Of faire, yonge, fresshe Venus free,
        And haddest hir in armes at thy wille –

1530   Although thee ones on a tyme mysfille,

1531   Whan Vulcanus hadde caught thee in his las,

1532   And foond thee liggynge by his wyf, allas! –

1507/ nexte = nearest. 1509/ The nexte houre of Mars = Three hours later. 1512/ payen wyse = pagan ways. 1514/ orisoun = prayer. 1515/ regnes colde = cold land. 1518/ Of armes … hond = control over the outcome of battles. 1519/ hem fortunest = favour them; lyst devyse = decide as you like. 1520/ pitous = pious. 1523/ oon of thyne = one of your servants. 1524/ pyne = pain. 1526/ whilom brendest = once burned. 1527/ usedest = slept with. 1530/ mysfille = messed up. 1531/ Vulcanus = god of fire; las = snare. 1532/ liggynge = lying.

This was indeed a harsh defeat
For Emelye, both stark and bleak,
But rather let me start to speak
Of the brave-hearted Arcite,
Who laid himself so artfully
To pray for help at Mars's feet.
Arcite's prayer to Mars:

   "Strong God, in this degree,
I know you know the mysteries
Of love, and my sad history.

"For thilke sorwe that was in thyn herte,
1534   Have routhe as wel upon my peynes smerte!
1535   I am yong and unkonnynge, as thow woost,
        And, as I trowe, with love offended moost
1537   That evere was any lyves creature,
1538   For she that dooth me al this wo endure
1539   Ne reccheth nevere wher I synke or fleete.
1540   And wel I woot, er she me mercy heete,
1541   I moot with strengthe wynne hir in the place,
        And wel I woot, withouten help or grace
1543   Of thee ne may my strengthe noght availle.
        Thanne help me, lord, tomorwe in my bataille,
1545   For thilke fyr that whilom brente thee,
        As wel as thilke fyr now brenneth me,
1547   And do that I tomorwe have victorie.
1548   Myn be the travaille and thyn be the glorie!
1549   Thy sovereyn temple wol I moost honouren
        Of any place, and alwey moost labouren
1551   In thy plesaunce and in thy craftes stronge,
        And in thy temple I wol my baner honge,
        And alle the armes of my compaignye,
        And everemo, unto that day I dye,
1555   Eterne fir I wol biforn thee fynde.
        And eek to this avow I wol me bynde:

～

1534/ routhe = pity. 1535/ unkonnynge = inexperienced; woost = know. 1537/ lyves = living. 1538/ dooth = makes. 1539/ reccheth … fleete = doesn't care whether I sink or float. 1540/ heete = promise. 1541/ the place = the theatre. 1543/ noght availle = achieve nothing. 1545/ whilom brente = once burned. 1547/ do = make. 1548/ travaille = work. 1549/ sovereyn = peerless. 1551/ In thy plesaunce = to please you. 1555/ fynde = offer.

"In spite of all my misery,
My love no pity gives to me;
Therefore, if I am fit to be
Thy knight, grant me this victory!"

1557   "My beerd, myn heer, that hongeth long adoun,
1558   That nevere yet ne felte offensioun
1559   Of rasour nor of shere, I wol thee yeve,
        And ben thy trewe servant whil I lyve.
        Now lord, have routhe upon my sorwes soore;
1562   Yif me victorie; I aske thee namoore!"
1563   The preyere stynt of Arcita the stronge;
        The rynges on the temple dore that honge,
        And eek the dores, clatereden ful faste,
1566   Of which Arcita somwhat hym agaste.
1567   The fyres brenden upon the auter brighte,
        That it gan al the temple for to lighte;
1569   A sweete smel the ground anon up yaf,
1570   And Arcita anon his hand up haf,
        And moore encens into the fyr he caste,
        With othere rytes mo, and atte laste
1573   The statue of Mars bigan his hauberk rynge,
        And with that soun he herde a murmurynge,
        Ful lowe and dym, and seyde thus, "Victorie!"
        For which he yaf to Mars honour and glorie;
        And thus with joye and hope wel to fare,
1578   Arcite anon unto his in is fare,
1579   As fayn as fowel is of the brighte sonne.

∾

1557/ hongeth = hangs. 1558/ offensioun = offence. 1559/ rasour = razor; shere =
scissors; yeve = give. 1562/ Yif = Give. 1563/ stynt = ended. 1566/ hym agaste = was
afraid. 1567/ brenden = burned. 1569/ up yaf = gave out. 1570/ up haf = lifted up.
1573/ hauberk = chain mail coat. 1578/ unto his in is fare = went back to his room.
1579/ As fayn as fowel is = As happy as a bird.

At this, the statue ripped free
From its foundations viciously,
And said: "Since you give to me
Such devotion, it's agreed;
Soon I shall grant this to thee!"

    And right anon swich strif ther is bigonne

    For thilke grauntyng, in the hevene above

    Bitwixe Venus, the goddesse of love,

1583   And Mars the stierne god armypotente,

    That Jupiter was bisy it to stente;

    Til that the pale Saturnus the colde,

    That knew so manye of aventures olde,

1587   Foond in his olde experience an art

1588   That he ful soone hath plesed every part.

. . . .

    "My deere doghter Venus," quod Saturne,

. . . .

    "That Palamon, that is thyn owene knyght,

1614   Shal have his lady, as thou hast him hight.

1615   Though Mars shal helpe his knyght, yet nathelees

    Bitwixe yow ther moot be somtyme pees,

1617   Al be ye noght of o compleccioun,

    That causeth al day swich divisioun.

1619   I am thyn aiel, redy at thy wille;

1620   Weep now namoore; I wol thy lust fulfille."

1621   Now wol I stynten of the goddes above,

    Of Mars and of Venus, goddesse of love,

    And telle yow as pleynly as I kan

    The grete effect for which that I bygan.

1583/ stierne = stern; armypotente = powerful. 1587/ an art = a solution. 1588/ every part = everyone. 1614/ hight = promised. 1615/ nathelees = nevertheless. 1617/ o compleccioun = the same nature. 1619/ aiel = grandfather. 1620/ lust = wish. 1621/ stynten of = leave.

Now the gods, who must be honest,
Had in their wisdom justly promised
Arcite, here perhaps the strongest,
Triumph in the fight, along with
Palamon, no doubt the fondest,
True love, as we see in sonnets.
I now shall tell you straight how on this
Day in May it was accomplished.

The Knight's Tale: Part Four

. . . .

1719   Whan set was Theseus ful riche and hye,

         Ypolita the queene, and Emelye,

1721   And othere ladys in degrees aboute.

1722   Unto the seettes preesseth al the route,

         And westward thurgh the gates under Marte,

1724   Arcite, and eek the hondred of his parte,

         With baner reed is entred right anon;

1726   And in that selve moment Palamon

         Is under Venus estward in the place,

         With baner whyt, and hardy chiere and face.

. . . .

1736   And in two renges faire they hem dresse,

1737   Whan that hir names rad were everichon,

1738   That in hir nombre gyle were ther noon.

         Tho were the gates shet, and cried was loude,

1740   "Do now youre devoir, yonge knyghtes proude!"

1741   The heraudes lefte hir prikyng up and doun;

1742   Now ryngen trompes loude and clarioun.

         Ther is namoore to seyn, but west and est

1744   In goon the speres ful sadly in arrest;

1745   In gooth the sharpe spore into the syde.

         Ther seen men who kan juste and who kan ryde;

1747   Ther shyveren shaftes upon sheeldes thikke;

1748   He feeleth thurgh the herte-spoon the prikke.

~

1719/ riche and hye = prominent. 1721/ degrees = tiers of seats. 1722/ preesseth al the route = the crowd gathered. 1724/ parte = crew. 1726/ selve = same. 1736/ renges = ranks; hem dresse = arranged themselves. 1737/ rad were everichon = were all read. 1738/ gyle = fraud. 1740/ devoir = duty. 1741/ lefte hir prikyng = ceased their prancing. 1742/ clarioun = bugle. 1744/ ful sadly in arrest = firmly in their resting places. 1745/ spore into the syde = spur into the horse's side. 1747/ shyveren = shatter. 1748/ herte-spoon = spoon-shaped hollow in the breastbone.

Theseus, who was provider
Of the venue, and presided
Over it, was seated higher,
Where his queen by all was seen,
With Emelye beside her.

Up spryngen speres twenty foot on highte;

Out goon the swerdes as the silver brighte;

1751   The helmes they tohewen and toshrede;

1752   Out brest the blood with stierne stremes rede;

1753   With myghty maces the bones they tobreste.

1754   He thurgh the thikkeste of the throng gan threste;

Ther stomblen steedes stronge, and doun gooth al;

He rolleth under foot as dooth a bal;

1757   He foyneth on his feet with his tronchoun,

1758   And he hym hurtleth with his hors adoun;

1759   He thurgh the body is hurt and sithen ytake,

1760   Maugree his heed, and broght unto the stake;

1761   As forward was, right there he moste abyde;

Another lad is on that oother syde.

1763   And som tyme dooth hem Theseus to reste,

1764   Hem to refresshe, and drynken if hem leste.

Ful ofte a day han thise Thebanes two

1766   Togydre ymet, and wroght his felawe wo;

Unhorsed hath ech oother of hem tweye.

Ther nas no tygre in the vale of Galgopheye,

1769   Whan that hir whelp is stole whan it is lite,

So crueel on the hunte as is Arcite

For jelous herte upon this Palamon;

1772   Ne in Belmarye ther nys so fel leon

1773   That hunted is, or for his hunger wood,

Ne of his praye desireth so the blood,

1775   As Palamon to sleen his foo Arcite.

~

1751/ tohewen and toshrede = cut to pieces and shreds. 1752/ brest = burst; stierne = strong. 1753/ tobreste = smash. 1754/ He thurgh ... threste = He thrusts through the thickest of the crowd. 1757/ foyneth = stabs; tronchoun = spear shaft. 1758/ hurtleth = hurls. 1759/ sithen ytake = then taken. 1760/ Maugree his heed = Despite his efforts. 1761/ As forward was = As was agreed. 1763/ dooth hem Theseus to reste = Theseus made them rest. 1764/ if hem leste = if they like. 1766/ wroght his felawe wo = made his opponent suffer. 1769/ whelp = cub; lite = little. 1772/ fel leon = fierce lion. 1773/ wood = mad. 1775/ sleen his foo = kill his enemy.

Arcite, a worthy fighter,
Attacked his brother like a tiger,
And Palamon, alike a lion,
With equal fierceness did defy him.
The first, though not for lack of tryin',
Could no fatal blow get by him.

1776   The jelous strokes on hir helmes byte;
1777   Out renneth blood on bothe hir sydes rede.
      Som tyme an ende ther is of every dede.
    For er the sonne unto the reste wente,
1780   The stronge kyng Emetreus gan hente
    This Palamon, as he faught with Arcite,
    And made his swerd depe in his flessh to byte,
    And by the force of twenty is he take
1784   Unyolden, and ydrawe unto the stake.
1785   And in the rescus of this Palamoun
    The stronge kyng Lygurge is born adoun,
    And kyng Emetreus, for al his strengthe,
    Is born out of his sadel a swerdes lengthe,
    So hitte him Palamoun er he were take;
    But al for noght, he was broght to the stake.
    His hardy herte myghte hym helpe naught;
    He moste abyde, whan that he was caught,
1793   By force and eek by composicioun.
1794   Who sorweth now but woful Palamoun,
    That moot namoore goon agayn to fighte?
    And whan that Theseus hadde seyn this sighte,
1797   Unto the folk that foghten thus echon
1798   He cryde, "Hoo! namoore, for it is doon!
1799   I wol be trewe juge, and no partie;
    Arcite of Thebes shal have Emelie,
    That by his fortune hath hir faire ywonne!"

~

1776/ jelous = furious. 1777/ renneth = runs. 1780/ hente = grabbed. 1784/ Unyolden =
Without having surrendered. 1785/ rescus = rescue. 1793/ composicioun = according
to the rules. 1794/ sorweth = is sorry. 1797/ echon = each one. 1798/ Hoo! = Stop!
1799/ partie = partisan.

But then, to Palamon's poor luck,

Arcite's knight behind him snuck,

And stuck a spear into his gut;

Though far from mortal was the cut,

It was enough; Arcite struck,

And Palamon, too hurt to duck,

Was knocked down, and dropped in shock

Onto the rocky ground. Not a sound,

Nor any talk was found among the crowd,

'Til Theseus declared aloud:

"Arcite is the victor proud,

And Emelye, as I avowed,

To thee shall now be well endowed!"

Anon ther is a noyse of peple bigonne
For joye of this, so loude and heighe withalle
It semed that the lystes sholde falle.
    What kan now faire Venus doon above?
What seith she now? What dooth this queene of Love?
But wepeth so, for wantynge of hir wille,
Til that hir teeres in the lystes fille.
She seyde, "I am ashamed, doutelees."
    Saturnus seyde, "Doghter, hoold thy pees;

1811   Mars hath his wille, his knyght hath al his boone,
1812   And, by myn heed, thow shalt been esed soone."
    The trompes with the loude mynstralcie,
The heraudes that ful loude yolle and crie,
1815   Been in hir wele for joye of daun Arcite.
But herkneth me, and stynteth noyse a lite,
1817   Which a myracle ther bifel anon.
1818   This fierse Arcite hath of his helm ydon,
And on a courser for to shewe his face
1820   He priketh endelong the large place,
Lokynge upward upon this Emelye,
1822   And she agayn hym caste a freendlich eye,
1823   (For wommen, as to speken in comune,
Thei folwen alle the favour of Fortune)
1825   And was al his chiere, as in his herte.

~

1811/ boone = desire. 1812/ esed = eased. 1815/ in hir wele for joye = overjoyed; daun = Sir. 1817/ Which = What. 1818/ of his helm ydon = taken off his helmet. 1820/ priketh endelong = pranced from end to end. 1822/ agayn hym = in return. 1823/ in comune = in general. 1825/ al his chiere = his inspiration.

Arcite's happiness exploded
In him, and he rose and showed it,
As above his foe he gloated,
Crowed and boasted and showboated,

1826 Out of the ground a furie infernal sterte,

   From Pluto sent, at requeste of Saturne,

   For which his hors for fere gan to turne,

1829 And leep aside and foundred as he leep;

1830 And er that Arcite may taken keep,

1831 He pighte hym on the pomel of his heed,

   That in the place he lay as he were deed,

1833 His brest tobrosten with his sadel-bowe.

1834 As blak he lay as any cole or crowe,

   So was the blood yronnen in his face.

   Anon he was yborn out of the place,

   With herte soor, to Theseus paleys.

1838 Tho was he korven out of his harneys,

1839 And in a bed ybrought ful faire and blyve,

1840 For he was yet in memorie and alyve,

   And alwey criynge after Emelye.

   · · · · · · · · · · ·

1885 Swelleth the brest of Arcite, and the soore

   Encreesseth at his herte moore and moore.

1887 The clothered blood, for any lechecraft,

1888 Corrupteth, and is in his bouk ylaft,

1889 That neither veyne-blood, ne ventusynge,

   Ne drynke of herbes may ben his helpynge.

1891 The vertu expulsif, or animal,

   Fro thilke vertu cleped natural

1893 Ne may the venym voyden ne expelle.

∽

1826/ a furie infernal sterte = a jet of flame burst. 1829/ foundred = stumbled; leep = leapt. 1830/ taken keep = catch himself. 1831/ He pighte hym on the pomel = He landed on the crown. 1833/ brest tobrosten = chest shattered. 1834/ cole = coal. 1838/ Tho = Then; korven = cut; harneys = armour. 1839/ faire and blyve = carefully and quickly. 1840/ in memorie = conscious. 1885/ soore = pain. 1887/ clothered = clotted; for any lechecraft = despite any medicine. 1888/ Corrupteth ... ylaft = Got infected and was left in his body. 1889/ veyne-blood = bleeding; ventusynge = suction-cupping. 1891/ vertu expulsif = purgative. 1893/ the venym voyden = clear the poison.

'Til the gods were overloaded
With his pride, and so they smote it;
Arcite, with a blow demoted,
Fell onto his dome and broke it.

The pipes of his longes gonne to swelle,

1895   And every lacerte in his brest adoun

1896   Is shent with venym and corrupcioun.

1897   Hym gayneth neither for to gete his lif,

Vomyt upward, ne dounward laxatif;

1899   Al is tobrosten thilke regioun;

Nature hath now no dominacioun.

1901   And certeinly, ther Nature wol nat wirche,

1902   Fare wel phisik! Go ber the man to chirche!

1903   This al and som, that Arcita moot dye;

For which he sendeth after Emelye,

And Palamon, that was his cosyn deere.

Thanne seyde he thus, as ye shal after heere:

"Naught may the woful spirit in myn herte

1908   Declare o point of alle my sorwes smerte

To yow, my lady, that I love moost;

1910   But I biquethe the servyce of my goost

To yow aboven every creature,

1912   Syn that my lyf may no lenger dure.

Allas, the wo! Allas, the peynes stronge,

That I for yow have suffred, and so longe!

Allas, the deeth! Allas, myn Emelye!

Allas, departynge of our compaignye!

Allas, myn hertes queene! Allas, my wyf!

Myn hertes lady, endere of my lyf!

1919   What is this world? What asketh men to have?

Now with his love, now in his colde grave,

Allone, withouten any compaignye.

~

1895/ lacerte = muscle. 1896/ shent = ruined; corrupcioun = decay. 1897/ Hym gayneth = It helped him; gete = save. 1899/ Al is ... regioun = Everything in that area was broken. 1901/ wirche = work. 1902/ phisik = medicine. 1903/ This al and som = This is the long and short. 1908/ o point = one bit; sorwes smerte = painful sorrows. 1910/ biquethe = leave you. 1912/ dure = endure. 1919/ asketh men = do men ask.

His sorrow overflowed there; dying,
He pronounced his woes, where crying
Showed he'd go with no denying
That his soul was slowly rising.

"Farewel, my swete foo, myn Emelye!

1923   And softe taak me in youre armes tweye,

For love of God, and herkneth what I seye.

   "I have heer with my cosyn Palamon

Had strif and rancour many a day agon

For love of yow, and for my jalousye.

1928   And Juppiter so wys my soule gye,

To speken of a servaunt proprely,

With alle circumstances trewely –

That is to seyen, trouthe, honour, knyghthede,

1932   Wysdom, humblesse, estaat, and heigh kynrede,

1933   Fredom, and al that longeth to that art –

So Juppiter have of my soule part,

As in this world right now ne knowe I non

So worthy to ben loved as Palamon,

That serveth yow, and wol doon al his lyf;

And if that evere ye shul ben a wyf,

Foryet nat Palamon, the gentil man."

1940   And with that word his speche faille gan,

And from his herte up to his brest was come

The coold of deeth, that hadde hym overcome;

And yet moreover, for in hise armes two

1944   The vital strengthe is lost and al ago.

Oonly the intellect, withouten moore,

That dwelled in his herte syk and soore

Gan faillen, when the herte felte deeth.

1948   Dusked hise eyen two, and failled breeth,

But on his lady yet caste he his eye.

His laste word was "Mercy, Emelye!"

~

1923/ softe = gently. 1928/ gye = guide. 1932/ heigh kynrede = noble birth. 1933/ longeth
= belongs. 1940/ faille gan = began to fail. 1944/ ago = gone. 1948/ Dusked = Darkened.

And he left, while still professing
Love, and gave them both his blessing,
While requesting Emelye to be accepting—
Since he would in death be resting—
Of Palamon, the next best thing.

Then back his broken head he laid,
And gave his final spoken praise:

"Mercy, Emelye!"

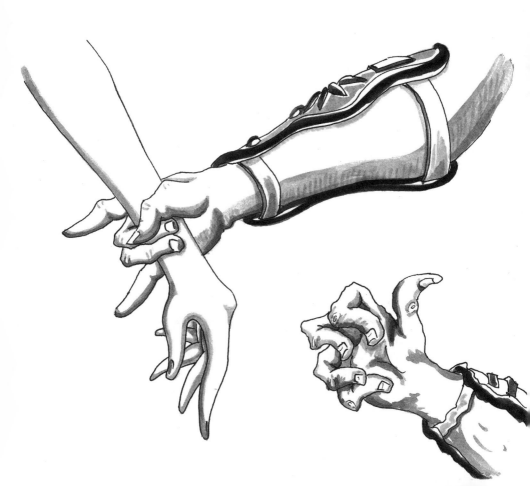

His spirit chaunged hous, and wente ther
1952   As I cam nevere, I kan nat tellen wher.
1953   Therfore I stynte; I nam no divinistre;
1954   Of soules fynde I nat in this registre,
1955   Ne me ne list thilke opinions to telle
Of hem, though that they writen wher they dwelle.
1957   Arcite is coold, ther Mars his soule gye!

· · · · · · · · · · · · · ·

And after that cam woful Emelye,
2053   With fyr in honde, as was that tyme the gyse,
To do the office of funeral servyse.
2055   Heigh labour and ful greet apparaillynge
Was at the service and the fyr-makynge,
2057   That with his grene top the heven raughte,
2058   And twenty fadme of brede the armes straughte;
2059   This is to seyn, the bowes weren so brode.
2060   Of stree first ther was leyd ful many a lode,
But how the fyr was maked upon highte,
Ne eek the names that the trees highte;

· · · · · · · · · · · · · ·

Ne how Arcite lay among al this;
Ne what richesse aboute his body is;
2083   Ne how that Emelye, as was the gyse,
Putte in the fyr of funeral servyse;

· · · · · · · · · · · · · ·

~

1952/ I cam nevere = I've never been. 1953/ stynte= stop; I nam no divinistre = I am no theologian. 1954/ registre = record. 1955/ thilke = those. 1957/ ther Mars his soule gye = may Mars guide his soul. 2053/ gyse = custom. 2055/ apparaillynge = preparation. 2057/ raughte = reached. 2058/ fadme of brede = fathoms wide (one fathom equals six feet); armes straughte = straight sides. 2059/ brode = broad. 2060/ stree = straw; lode = load. 2083/ gyse = custom.

The gentle maid then, in the ways

Of Athens, set the corpse ablaze,

And scorched away the source that makes

A mortal shape, and prayed his soul

Its course through heaven's portal take.

Ne how Arcite is brent to asshen colde;
2100   Ne how that lyche-wake was yholde
Al thilke nyght, ne how the Grekes pleye
2102   The wake-pleyes; ne kepe I nat to seye
Who wrastleth best naked with oille enoynt,
2104   Ne who that baar hym best in no disjoynt;
I wol nat tellen eek how that they goon
Hoom til Atthenes, whan the pley is doon;
But shortly to the point thanne wol I wende,
And maken of my longe tale an ende.
2109   By processe and by lengthe of certeyn yeres,
Al stynted is the moornynge and the teres
Of Grekes, by oon general assent.
Thanne semed me ther was a parlement
2113   At Atthenes, upon certein pointz and caas,
Among the whiche pointz yspoken was
To have with certein contrees alliaunce,
2116   And have fully of Thebans obeisaunce;
For which this noble Theseus anon
Leet senden after gentil Palamon,
2119   Unwist of hym what was the cause and why;
But in hise blake clothes sorwefully
2121   He cam at his comandement in hye;
2122   Tho sente Theseus for Emelye.
2123   Whan they were set, and hust was al the place,
2124   And Theseus abiden hadde a space
Er any word cam fram his wise brest,
2126   Hise eyen sette he ther as was his lest,
2127   And with a sad visage he siked stille,
2128   And after that right thus he seyde his wille:

∽

2100/ lyche-wake = wake. 2102/ wake-pleyes = funeral games. 2104/ disjoynt = difficulty. 2109/ processe = this process. 2113/ caas = cases. 2116/ obeisaunce = obedience. 2119/ Unwist of = Unknown to. 2121/ in hye = in haste. 2122/ Tho = Then. 2123/ hust = hushed. 2124/ abiden = paused; space = moment. 2126/ lest = wish. 2127/ visage = face; siked = sighed. 2128/ seyde his wille = announced his decision.

In order to at least dispel
The sorrow which in Greece did swell
The moment that Arcite fell,
Theseus released his will:

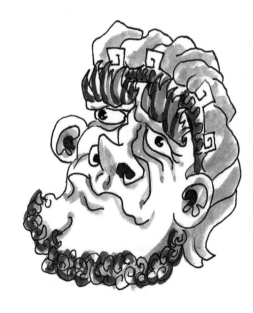

. . . .

2200	"Why grucchen we, why have we hevynesse,
	That goode Arcite, of chivalrie flour,
2202	Departed is with duetee and honour
	Out of this foule prisoun of this lyf?
	Why grucchen heere his cosyn and his wyf
	Of his welfare, that loved hem so weel?
2206	Kan he hem thank? Nay, God woot, never a deel,
	That bothe his soule and eek hemself offende,
2208	And yet they mowe hir lustes nat amende.
2209	 "What may I concluden of this longe serye,
2210	But after wo I rede us to be merye,
	And thanken Juppiter of al his grace?
	And er that we departen from this place
	I rede that we make of sorwes two
2214	O parfit joye lastyng everemo.
2215	And looketh now, wher moost sorwe is her inne,
2216	Ther wol we first amenden and bigynne.
2217	 "Suster," quod he, "this is my fulle assent,
2218	With all th'avys heere of my parlement,
	That gentil Palamon thyn owene knyght,
	That serveth yow with wille, herte, and myght,
	And evere hath doon, syn that ye first hym knewe,
2222	That ye shul of your grace upon hym rewe,
	And taken hym for housbonde and for lord.
	Lene me youre hond, for this is oure accord.

~

2200/ grucchen we = do we complain. 2202/ duetee and honour = due honour. 2206/ Kan he hem thank? = Can he thank them?; never a deel = not a bit. 2208/ lustes nat amende = desires not fulfill. 2209/ serye = sermon. 2210/ rede = advise. 2214/ O = One. 2215/ her inne = herein. 2216/ amenden = address. 2217/ assent = opinion. 2218/ th'avys = the advice. 2222/ rewe = pity.

"Why should his wife and cousin grieve?
Arcite is gone, yet doesn't he
Deserve to see his love in thee,
Alive, from up above in peace?
Thus Palamon and Emelye
Shall wed, if they my judgement heed!"

"Lat se now of youre wommanly pitee;

2226   He is a kynges brother sone, pardee,

And though he were a povre bacheler,

Syn he hath served yow so many a yeer,

And had for yow so greet adversitee,

2230   It moste been considered, leeveth me,

2231   For gentil mercy oghte to passen right."

Thanne seyde he thus to Palamon the knyght:

2233   "I trowe ther nedeth litel sermonyng

To make yow assente to this thyng.

Com neer, and taak youre lady by the hond."

Bitwixen hem was maad anon the bond

2237   That highte matrimoigne or mariage,

2238   By al the conseil and the baronage.

And thus with alle blisse and melodye

Hath Palamon ywedded Emelye;

And God, that al this wyde world hath wroght,

2242   Sende hym his love that hath it deere aboght;

2243   For now is Palamon in alle wele,

2244   Lyvynge in blisse, in richesse, and in heele,

And Emelye hym loveth so tendrely,

And he hir serveth so gentilly,

That nevere was ther no word hem bitwene

2248   Of jalousie or any oother teene.

Thus endeth Palamon and Emelye,

And God save al this faire compaignye! Amen.

Heere is ended the Knyghtes Tale.

﹏

2226/ pardee = indeed. 2230/ leeveth me = believe me. 2231/ passen right = overcome justice. 2233/ sermonyng = persuasion. 2237/ highte = is called. 2238/ baronage = nobles. 2242/ hath it deere aboght = has paid dearly for it. 2243/ alle wele = complete happiness. 2244/ heele = health. 2248/ teene = problem.

And since his wishes carried weight,
The two, with kisses, married straight,
And Palamon, though very late,
Did wear his bliss with a merry face,
'Cause he could barely wait
To take away her cherry state;
And Emelye took care she made
A loving wife, and rarely gave
Advice and, looking fair, obeyed;
And nothing more is there to say
About this strange affair, good day!

The End.

✝HE MILLER'S ✝ALE

The Miller's entry into the storytelling contest is as unorthodox as his personality and the tale he tells. When *The Knight's Tale* ends, the pilgrims applaud it as a "noble storie," and the response is especially positive from the "gentils everichon" (the upper class). Since the Knight has the highest social status among the pilgrims, and his *Tale* is the longest and the most elaborate in content, the storytelling competition at first seems to be organized according to the class hierarchy that dominated medieval society. Once the Knight is finished, the Host chooses the Monk as the next speaker, another of the "gentils" among the pilgrims. However, any hope of propriety is shattered when the Miller interrupts drunkenly, cursing and declaring that he will go next: "I kan a noble tale for the nones, / With which I will now quite the Knyghtes tale" (I know a good story for the occasion, with which I will now respond to the Knight's tale). The Host, seeing that the Miller is drunk, tries to talk him out of telling his tale, but the Miller threatens to quit the pilgrimage if he isn't allowed to speak, and the Host finally gives up: "Tel on, a devel wey! / Thou art a fool; thy wit is overcome." Once he has free range, the Miller goes on to trumpet his drunkenness, telling the pilgrims to blame the booze if they don't like his story, and then taunts the Reeve, who believes he is the Miller's target. The Miller is a bull deliberately set loose in a literary china shop, a device Chaucer uses to level the social scene and shake up the order of the competition. The Reeve "quites" the Miller, followed by the Cook, three of the lowest pilgrims in the medieval class hierarchy, and after that it is anyone's game.

Chaucer's portrait of the Miller in the *General Prologue* describes him as short-shouldered, broad, thick, and brawny, with a wide red beard and a large wart on his nose, wide black nostrils and a mouth like "a greet forneys" (a great furnace). Anyone who has seen the diameter of Busta Rhymes's mouth fully dilated can picture the Miller's orifice (Woo-hah!!). The Miller also has a violent streak, both in his penchant for wrestling and also in his treatment of doors, which resembles his treatment of social conventions: "Ther was no dore that he nolde heve of harre, / Or breke it at a rennyng with his heed" (There was no door that he wouldn't knock from its hinges, or break it at a running with his head). Chaucer also describes him as a "janglere and a goliardeys, / And that was moost of synne and harlotries" (a clown and a teller of rude stories, mostly about sex and sin). Between this and the Miller's drunkenness and belligerence in the *Prologue* to his tale, Chaucer takes great care to prepare the reader for the depravity to come, and to justify the very presence of the tale in his magnum opus. The Miller's black sheep personality puts him at odds with the intended literary pedigree of *The Canterbury Tales*. He is like the late Old Dirty Bastard ("Ooh baby, I like it raw!") or R. A. the Rugged Man rampaging at a conscious hip-hop showcase, reminding anyone who takes the occasion too seriously that the point is to have a good time.

Chaucer's alibi for this outburst of profanity is that he is just the messenger, so his readers shouldn't blame him if they get offended, "for I moot reherce / Hir tales alle, be they better or werse, / Or elles falsen som of my mateere" (Because I have to report all of their tales, good and bad, or else falsify my material). He cleverly sets up the sin of false witness against the sin of vulgarity, arguing that it is better to tell the truth in all of its gruesome detail than lie to protect sensitive ears. Of course, this is an ironic posture on Chaucer's part, since the Miller and his *Tale* are both fictional and deliberate. I have generally taken this same tack in my adaptation process, leaving all of the rude details intact without concealing or adding anything to the story, so that Chaucer can keep both the blame and the credit for the result. The one exception is the phrase "he caught her by the queynte," which I translated as: "he reached beneath her skirt with perverted intentions." Partially this was necessary to follow my rhyme scheme, but it was also because the word has a much more explicit meaning today than it did six hundred years ago. In Chaucer's day "queynte" was still ambiguous enough a term to pun on the adjective "strange" and the verbs "quench" and "extinguish." It wasn't used as a misogynist slur ("She's acting like a total queynte") and no drunkards would be heard shouting it as a curse word ("You stupid queynte!") as with its linguistic descendent. If I had used the literal translation it would retain none of the subtlety and wit that Chaucer infuses it with, so I opted for circumlocution. Ironically, this tiny detail has become one of the main points of contention in the critical response to "The Rap Canterbury Tales." A few news agencies (known in Chaucer's time as "janglers") picked up on the euphemism and chastised me for daring to censor Chaucer, as if modern audiences were more sensitive than medieval ones (or aren't they?). However, no publication that has criticized me over this omission has deigned to actually print the offending word in the article. The closest was *Rolling Stone*, which suggested I turn in a version with more of that "C U Next Tuesday vibe."

After all of his build-up and foreshadowing of the story's lewdness, Chaucer offers the reader one final chance to opt out of *The Miller's Tale*: "And therefore, whoso list it nat yheere, / Turne over the leef and chese another tale" (And therefore, whoever doesn't want to hear this, turn the page and choose another tale). This kind of warning can be found occasionally in hip-hop lyrics as well, as in Jay-Z's declaration: "Where the demons live, / My scene is vivid; / Squeamish kids, y'all get the fuck outa this verse / 'Cause it's about to get so obscene in a minute; / I've seen, and live it." However, the effect is usually the opposite, since squeamish kids (like everyone else) are inherently fascinated by obscenity, and nothing attracts attention like a warning that someone might be offended. Chaucer was perfectly aware of this, and his ironic invitation to turn the page is actually more of a teaser, provoking the reader's curiosity. Fortunately for rappers this wisdom has been lost on the conservative crusaders who devised the Parental Advisory labels on hip-hop albums, which have helped to boost rap music sales exponentially, especially among young people. Chaucer often addresses this species of irony in *The Canterbury Tales*, creating situations where a character's efforts produce the opposite of their intended outcome. He offers a solution of sorts in the final couplet of the Miller's *Prologue*, advising us all to look within, rather than vainly finger-pointing: "Avyseth yow, and put me out of blame; / And eek men shal nat maken ernest of game" (Check yourself, and don't blame me; and don't take playfulness seriously).

The Miller's Tale

1   **W**hilom ther was dwellynge at Oxenford

2   A riche gnof, that gestes heeld to bord,

    And of his craft he was a carpenter.

4   With hym ther was dwellynge a poure scoler,

5   Hadde lerned art, but al his fantasye

    Was turned for to lerne astrologye,

7   And koude a certeyn of conclusiouns,

8   To demen by interrogaciouns,

    If that men asked hym in certain houres

    Whan that men sholde have droghte or elles shoures,

    Or if men asked hym what sholde bifalle

12   Of every thyng; I may nat rekene hem alle.

13   This clerk was cleped hende Nicholas.

14   Of deerne love he koude and of solas;

15   And therto he was sleigh and ful privee,

    And lyk a mayden meke for to see.

    A chambre hadde he in that hostelrye

    Allone, withouten any compaignye,

19   Ful fetisly ydight with herbes swoote;

    And he hymself as sweete as is the roote

21   Of lycorys, or any cetewale.

22   His Almageste, and bookes grete and smale,

23   His astrelabie, longynge for his art,

24   His augrym stones layen faire apart,

25   On shelves couched at his beddes heed;

~

1/ Whilom = Once. 2/ gnof = commoner; gestes heeld to bord = rented rooms to lodgers.
4/ poure scoler = poor student. 5/ art = humanities; fantasye = desire. 7/ koude = knew;
conclusiouns = processes. 8/ demen = discover; interrogaciouns = calculations. 12/
rekene hem alle = recite them all. 13/ cleped hende = called gentle. 14/ deerne = secret;
koude = knew; solas = pleasure. 15/ sleigh = sly; privee = secretive. 19/ fetisly ... swoote
= carefully hung with sweet herbs. 21/ lycorys = licorice; cetewale = ginger-like root.
22/ Almageste = astrology book. 23/ astrelabie = astrology instrument; longynge for =
belonging to. 24/ augrym stones = counting stones (abacus). 25/ couched = set.

Listen to this tune: it's about a rich man
Licking a silver spoon, who lived in a mansion,
And rented a room to this young scholar kid,
Who'd been to the two most respected colleges
For logic and philosophy; he got scholarships,
But he still lived in poverty due to the preposterous
Cost of living; without a dollar he lived as an astrologist
And followed his dreams; his name was Nicholas,
And when it came to women his game was limitless.
The ladies he visited became libidinous
When he played his instruments; he'd just lick his lips
And sing a melody as sweet as licorice.

26   His presse ycovered with a faldyng reed;
27   And al above ther lay a gay sautrie,
      On which he made a-nyghtes melodie
      So swetely that all the chambre rong;
30   And *Angelus ad virginem* he song;
31   And after that he song the Kynges Noote.
      Ful often blessed was his myrie throte.
      And thus this sweete clerk his tyme spente
34   After his freendes fyndyng and his rente.
          This carpenter hadde wedded newe a wyf,
      Which that he lovede moore than his lyf;
      Of eighteteene yeer she was of age.
38   Jalous he was, and heeld hire narwe in cage,
      For she was wylde and yong, and he was old,
40   And demed hymself been lik a cokewold.
41   He knew nat Catoun, for his wit was rude,
42   That bad man sholde wedde his simylitude.
43   Men sholde wedden after hire estaat,
      For youth and elde is often at debaat.
      But sith that he was fallen in the snare,
      He moste endure, as oother folk, his care.
47   Fair was this yonge wyf, and therwithal
48   As any wezele hir body gent and smal.
49   A ceynt she werede, barred al of silk,
50   A barmclooth as whit as morne milk

~

26/ presse = linen chest; faldyng reed = red cloth. 27/ sautrie = stringed instrument.
30–31/ *Angelus ad virginum*; the Kynges Noote = songs. 34/ After his freendes fyndyng =
Supported by his friends. 38/ heeld hire narwe in cage = kept her narrowly caged.
40/ demed = feared; cokewold = cuckold (a betrayed husband). 41/ Catoun = writer of
school textbooks; rude = untaught. 42/ bad = commanded; simylitude = equal. 43/
after hire estaat = according to their place in life. 47/ therwithal = in this way. 48/
wezele = weasel; gent = petite; smal = slender. 49/ ceynt = belt; barred = striped. 50/
barmclooth = apron; morne = morning.

His virility eclipsed the man he was living with,

A rich, elderly fella whose name was John;

His flame was gone, and still he'd married a young filly

Who was really beyond his ability to satisfy,

'Cause in the sack this guy was on disability.

He was prone to senility, pride, and jealousy,

And slept with open eyes, terrified of infidelity.

His wife brought humility to life; in the village she

Liked to shop, wearing her husband's ring,

With her cheeks painted up a slutty pink.

Her name was Alison, and she had a naughty stink;

Her mouth was said to be as sweet as bubbly drink,

And if you saw her on the street, you'd probably think

She was a hottie, and had the body of a mink.

51   Upon her lendes, ful of many a goore.

52   Whit was hir smok, and broyden al bifoore
         And eek bihynde, on hir coler aboute,
         Of col-blak silk, withinne and eek withoute.

55   The tapes of hir white voluper

56   Were of the same suyte of hir coler;

57   Hir filet brood of silk, and set ful hye.

58   And sikerly she hadde a likerous ye;

59   Ful smale ypulled were hire browes two,

60   And tho were bent and blake as any sloo.
         She was ful moore blisful on to see

62   Than is the newe pere-jonette tree,

63   And softer than the wolle is of a wether.

64   And by hir girdel heeng a purs of lether,

65   Tasseled with silk and perled with latoun.
         In al this world, to seken up and doun,

67   There nys no man so wys that koude thenche

68   So gay a popelote or swich a wenche.
         Ful brighter was the shynyng of hir hewe

70   Than in the Tour the noble yforged newe.

71   But of hir song, it was as loude and yerne
         As any swalwe sittynge on a berne.

73   Therto she koude skippe and make game,
         As any kyde or calf folwynge his dame.

~

51/ lendes = loins; many a goore = frills. 52/ broyden al bifoore = embroidered in
the front. 55/ tapes = ribbons; voluper = hat. 56/ suyte = style. 57/ filet brood =
broad headwrap. 58/ sikerly = truly; likerous ye = flirtatious eye. 59/ ypulled = plucked.
60/ sloo = dark-coloured fruit. 62/ pere-jonette tree = pear tree. 63/ wolle is of a wether
= sheep's wool. 64/ girdel = belt. 65/ perled = adorned; latoun = brass-coloured metal.
67/ thenche = imagine. 68/ So gay a popelote = Such a pretty doll. 70/ the Tour = the
Tower of London; noble = gold coin. 71/ yerne = spirited. 73/ make game = play.

You'd probably think a lot of things, and start grovelling,
Especially if she dropped a wink, heart-softening,
With flirting glances that often fling a person's senses
Off the brink, and begin work against us.

75   Hir mouth was sweete as bragot or the meeth,

76   Or hoord of apples leyd in hey or heeth.

77   Wynsynge she was, as is a joly colt,

      Long as a mast, and upright as a bolt.

      A brooch she baar upon hir lowe coler,

80   As brood as is the boos of a bokeler.

      Hir shoes were laced on hir legges hye.

82   She was a prymerole, a piggesnye,

83   For any lord to leggen in his bedde,

84   Or yet for any good yeman to wedde.

85   Now, sire, and eft, sire, so bifel the cas

      That on a day this hende Nicholas

87   Fil with this yonge wyf to rage and pleye,

88   Whil that her housbonde was at Oseneye,

89   As clerkes ben ful subtile and ful queynte;

90   And prively he caughte hire by the queynte,

91   And seyde, "Ywis, but if ich have my wille,

92   For deerne love of thee, lemman, I spille."

93   And heeld hire harde by the haunchebones,

94   And seyde, "Lemman, love me al atones,

      Or I wol dyen, also God me save!"

96   And she sproong as a colt dooth in the trave,

97   And with hir heed she wryed faste awey,

98   And seyde, "I wol nat kisse thee, by my fey!

      Why, lat be," quod she, "lat be, Nicholas,

100   Or I wol crie 'out harrow' and 'allas'!

      Do wey youre handes, for youre curteisye!"

~

75/ bragot = wine; meeth = mead. 76/ heeth = bushes. 77/ Wynsyng = Excitable. 80/ the boos of a bokeler = the hub of a shield. 82/ prymerole ... piggesnye = flowers. 83/ leggen = lay. 84/ yeman = commoner. 85/ eft = again; so bifel the cas = it so happened. 87/ rage = flirt. 88/ at Oseneye = in town. 89/ queynte = clever. 90/ prively = discreetly; queynte = cunt. 91/ Ywis = I swear. 92/ deerne = secret; lemman = lover; spille = die. 93/ haunchebones = hips. 94/ al atones = all at once. 96/ sproong = jumped; trave = holding pen. 97/ wryed = twisted. 98/ by my fey = by my faith. 100/ out harrow = help.

Nicholas waited for the right circumstances,
And eventually he managed to catch her defenceless,
And he reached beneath her skirt with perverted intentions.
It was beneath her to stand such utter disrespect,
And she refused this would-be lover's kiss with threats
That she would scream bloody murder, and risk his neck.

This Nicholas gan mercy for to crye,
103   And spak so faire, and profred him so faste,
That she hir love hym graunted atte laste,
And swoor hir ooth, by Seint Thomas of Kent,
That she wol been at his comandement,
107   Whan that she may hir leyser wel espie.
"Myn housbonde is so ful of jalousie
109   That but ye wayte wel and been privee,
110   I woot right wel I nam but deed," quod she.
111   "Ye moste been ful deerne, as in this cas."
    "Nay, therof care thee noght," quod Nicholas.
113   "A clerk hadde litherly biset his whyle,
114   But if he koude a carpenter bigyle."
And thus they been accorded and ysworn
To wayte a tyme, as I have told biforn.
117   Whan Nicholas had doon thus everideel,
118   And thakked hire aboute the lendes weel,
119   He kiste hire sweete and taketh his sawtrie,
And pleyeth faste, and maketh melodie.
    Thanne fil it thus, that to the paryssh chirche,
Cristes owene werkes for to wirche,
This goode wyf went on an haliday.
Hir forheed shoon as bright as any day,
125   So was it wasshen whan she leet hir werk.

∿

103/ profred him = pressed his suit. 107/ hir leyser wel espie = see their chance.
109/ privee = secretive. 110/ I nam but deed = I'm as good as dead. 111/ deerne = discreet.
113/ litherly biset his whyle = wasted his time. 114/ bigyle = deceive. 117/ doon thus
everideel = arranged everything. 118/ thakked = patted; lendes = loins. 119/ sawtrie =
stringed instrument. 125/ leet = left.

But to him it seemed like just a twisted test,
And Nicholas persisted until her lips were set,
And dripping wet, as lips are quick to get
If caressed into bliss by gifted breath,
And Nicholas pressed her with his best
Tricks, until at last she just said yes
To the gist of his request for elicit sex,
Except she explicitly told him this, direct:
"My husband is jealous, as well as overzealous;
He's a menace when it comes to me lookin' at other fellas;
You can tell his love is hellish, so while this develops
We need to keep it secret, so that he doesn't kill us!"
Nicholas wasn't filled with fear—he was cool;
He said, "You think I've spent all these years at school
Without preparing the tools to make married men fools?
I'm aware of the rules; just watch the master at work!"
And with these brash words, he patted her curves,
Grabbed at her, kissed her, and had his last flirt,
Before she gathered her skirts and went to mass at her church.

Now was ther of that chirche a parissh clerk,

127   The which that was ycleped Absolon.

128   Crul was his heer, and as the gold it shoon,

129   And strouted as a fanne large and brode;

130   Ful streight and evene lay his joly shode;

131   His rode was reed, his eyen greye as goos.

132   With Poules wyndow corven on his shoos,

133   In hoses rede he wente fetisly.

134   Yclad he was ful smal and proprely

135   Al in a kirtel of a lyght waget;

136   Ful faire and thikke been the poyntes set.

137   And therupon he hadde a gay surplys

138   As whit as is the blosme upon the rys.

A myrie child he was, so God me save.

140   Wel koude he laten blood and clippe and shave,

141   And maken a chartre of lond or acquitaunce.

In twenty manere koude he trippe and daunce

143   After the scole of Oxenforde tho,

And with his legges casten to and fro,

145   And pleyen songes on a smal rubible;

146   Therto he song som tyme a loud quynyble;

147   And as wel koude he pleye on a giterne.

In al the toun nas brewhous ne taverne

149   That he ne visited with his solas,

150   Ther any gaylard tappestere was.

~

127/ ycleped = called. 128/ Crul was his heer = His hair was curled. 129/ strouted = spread; brode = broad. 130/ shode = locks. 131/ His rode was reed = His complexion was red. 132/ Poules wyndow corven = The window of St. Paul's carved. 133/ hoses = stockings; fetisly = elegantly. 134/ smal = tight. 135/ kirtel = coat; lyght waget = light blue. 136/ poyntes = laces. 137/ surplys = gown. 138/ rys = branch. 140/ clippe = cut hair. 141/ chartre of lond or acquitaunce = deeds of property. 143/ After the scole = In the style. 145/ rubible = fiddle. 146/ quynyble = high treble. 147/ giterne = stringed instrument. 149/ solas = pleasure-seeking. 150/ gaylard tappestere = cheerful barmaid.

This church had a clerk whose name was Absalon,
A romantic, emasculate man who had this long
Hair that was blond and brushed so that it shone.
His back was not strong, but what he lacked in brawn,
He made up with his passion when he played and practised on
His fiddle, dancing drunk at taverns 'til his cash was gone.

151 But sooth to seyn, he was somdeel squaymous
152 Of fartyng, and of speche daungerous.
153   This Absolon, that jolif was and gay,
154 Gooth with a sencer on the haliday,
155 Sensynge the wyves of the parisshe faste;
     And many a lovely look on hem he caste,
     And namely on this carpenteris wyf.
     To looke on hire hym thoughte a myrie lyf,
159 She was so propre and sweete and likerous.
     I dar wel seyn, if she hadde been a mous,
161 And he a cat, he wolde hire hente anon.
     This parissh clerk, this joly Absolon,
     Hath in his herte swich a love-longynge
     That of no wyf took he noon offrynge;
     For curteisie, he seyde, he wolde noon.
     The moone, whan it was nyght, ful brighte shoon,
167 And Absolon his gyterne hath ytake;
168 For paramours he thoghte for to wake.
     And forth he gooth, jolif and amorous,
     Til he cam to the carpenters hous
     A litel after cokkes hadde ycrowe,
172 And dressed hym up by a shot-wyndowe
     That was upon the carpenteris wall.
     He syngeth in his voys gentil and smal,
     "Now, deere lady, if thy wille be,
176 I praye yow that ye wole rewe on me,"

~

151/ somdeel squaymous = somewhat squeamish.   152/ speche daungerous = rude
language. 153/ jolif = jolly. 154/ sencer = incense-holder. 155/ faste = close-up. 159/
likerous = alluring. 161/ hire hente anon = quickly catch her. 167/ gyterne = stringed
instrument. 168/ For paramours ... wake = He stayed awake for love. 172/ dressed hym =
positioned himself; shot-wyndowe = window with shutters. 176/ rewe on = pity.

Now it happened that Absalon's fancy chanced upon
Alison, and he began to romance and fawn,
And prance on her lawn at the crack of dawn,
Panting fondly, chanting pansy songs,

177   Ful wel acordaunt to his gyternynge.
       This carpenter awook, and herde him synge,
       And spak unto his wyf, and seyde anon,
180   "What! Alison! Herestow nat Absolon,
181   That chaunteth thus under oure boures wal?"
       Ans she answerde hir housbonde therwithal,
183   "Yis, God woot, John, I heere it every deel."
184   This passeth forth; what wol ye bet than weel?
       Fro day to day this joly Absolon
186   So woweth hire that hym is wo bigon.
       He waketh al the nyght and al the day;
188   He kembeth his lokkes brode, and made hym gay;
189   He woweth hire by meenes and brocage,
190   And swoor he wolde been hir owene page;
191   He syngeth, brokkynge as a nyghtyngale;
192   He sente hire pyment, meeth, and spiced ale,
193   And wafres, pipyng hoot out of the gleede;
194   And, for she was of towne, he profred meede.
       For som folk wol ben wonnen for richesse,
196   And somme for strokes, and somme for gentillesse.
197   Somtyme, to shewe his lightnesse and maistrye,
198   He pleyeth Herodes upon a scaffold hye.
       But what availleth hym as in the cas?
       She loveth so this hende Nicholas
201   That Absolon may blowe the bukkes horn;
       He ne hadde for his labour but a scorn.

177/ acordaunt to = in tune with; gyternynge = music. 180/ Herestow nat = Don't you hear. 181/ chaunteth = sings; boures wal = bedroom wall. 183/ Yis = Yes; every deel = every bit. 184/ what wol ye bet than weel? = how else would you have it? 186/ woweth hire = woos her; wo bigon = hopeless. 188/ kembeth = combs. 189/ meenes and brocage = messengers. 190/ page = servant. 191/ brokkynge = warbling. 192/ pyment, meeth = wine, mead. 193/ wafres = cakes; gleede = oven. 194/ meede = money. 196/ strokes = flattery. 197/ lightnesse and maistrye = agility and skill. 198/ Herodes = Herod (in a play); scaffold hye = high stage. 201/ blowe the bukkes horn = blow his horn.

But her husband wasn't jealous; he would laugh, catching on,
And ask, "What's wrong, honey, can't you hear Absalon,
Prattling on?" And she would stretch and yawn:
"He won't take no for an answer, John."
So Absalon kept his pants on—his hopes were slim—
He was a joke to them, and Alison hardly noticed him,
'Cause her devotion went instead to Nicholas,

203   And thus she maketh Absolon hire ape,
204   And al his ernest turneth til a jape.
       Ful sooth is this proverbe, it is no lye,
206   Men seyn right thus: 'Alwey the nye slye
207   Maketh the ferre leeve to be looth.'
208   For though that Absolon be wood or wrooth,
       By cause that he fer was from hire sight,
       This nye Nicholas stood in his light.
          Now ber thee wel, thou hende Nicholas,
       For Absolon may waille and synge 'allas.'
       And so bifel it on a Saturday,
       This carpenter was goon til Osenay;
       And hende Nicholas and Alison
       Acorded been to this conclusioun,
217   That Nicholas shal shapen hym a wyle
218   This sely jalous housbonde to bigyle;
       And if so be the game wente aright,
       She sholde slepen in his arm al nyght,
       For this was his desir and hire also.
       And right anon, withouten wordes mo,
       This Nicholas no lenger wolde tarie,
       But dooth ful softe unto his chambre carie
       Bothe mete and drynke for a day or tweye,
       And to hire housbonde bad hire for to seye,
       If that he axed after Nicholas,
       She sholde seye she nyste where he was,

~

203/ ape = fool. 204/ jape = joke. 206/ the nye slye = the one who is close and clever.
207/ ferre leeve to be looth = the absent lover to be forgotten. 208/ wood or wrooth =
crazy or angry. 217/ shapen hym a wyle = cook up a scheme. 218/ sely = silly; bigyle =
deceive.

Whose wits were spent in a wicked attempt
To trick her husband into giving them
A chance to get busy in original sin.

Now, this is what Nicholas did to begin:
He went to his bedroom on the top floor,
And he stayed there with a locked door

Of al that day she saugh hym nat with ye;
230   She trowed that he was in maladye,
For, for no cry hir mayde koude hym calle,
232   He nolde answere for thyng that myghte falle.
233   This passeth forth al thilke Saterday,
That Nicholas stille in his chambre lay,
235   And eet and sleep, or dide what hym leste,
Til Sonday, that the sonne gooth to reste.
237   This sely carpenter hath greet merveyle
238   Of Nicholas, or what thyng myghte hym eyle,
And seyde, "I am adrad, by Seint Thomas,
It stondeth nat aright with Nicholas.
241   God shilde that he deyde sodeynly!
242   This world is now ful tikel, sikerly.
243   I saugh today a cors yborn to chirche
244   That now, on Monday last, I saugh hym wirche.
245   "Go up," quod he unto his knave anoon,
246   "Clepe at his dore, or knokke with a stoon.
Looke how it is, and tel me boldely."
248   This knave gooth hym up ful sturdily,
And at the chambre dore whil that he stood,
He cride and knokked as that he were wood,
"What! how! What do ye, maister Nicholay?
How may ye slepen al the longe day?"
But al for noghte; he herde nat a word.

~

230/ She trowed … in maladye = She thought he was sick. 232/ nolde = would not; thyng that myghte falle = anything. 233/ thilke = that. 235/ hym leste = he wanted. 237/ greet merveyle = great wonder. 238/ eyle = ail. 241/ God shilde = God forbid; deyde sodeynly = died suddenly. 242/ tikel, sikerly = unpredictable, certainly. 243/ cors yborn = corpse carried. 244/ wirche = work. 245/ knave = servant. 246/ Clepe = Call. 248/ sturdily = bravely.

For three days, inquisitive knocks ignored,
And he gazed at the stars, lost and absorbed,
And he played with his astrology charts,

An hole he foond, ful lowe upon a bord,

Ther as the cat was wont in for to crepe,

And at that hole he looked in ful depe,

And at the laste he hadde of hym a sight.

258   This Nicholas sat evere capyng upright,

259   As he had kiked on the newe moone.

Adoun he gooth, and tolde his maister soone

In what array he saugh this ilke man.

  This carpenter to blessen hym bigan,

And seyde, "Help us, Seinte Frydeswyde!

264   A man woot litel what hym shal bityde.

This man is falle, with his astromye,

266   In som woodnesse or in som agonye,

I thoghte ay wel how that it sholde be!

268   Men sholde nat knowe of Goddes pryvetee.

269   Ye, blessed be alwey a lewed man

270   That noght but oonly his bileve kan!

So ferde another clerk with astromye;

He walked in the feeldes for to prye

Upon the sterres, what ther sholde bifalle,

274   Til he was in a marle-pit yfalle;

He saugh nat that. But yet, by Seint Thomas,

276   Me reweth soore of hende Nicholas.

277   He shal be rated of his studiyng,

If that I may, by Jhesus, hevene kyng!

~

258/ capyng upright = gazing upward. 259/ kiked on = stared at. 264/ woot = knows;
hym shal bityde = will happen to him. 266/ woodnesse = madness; agonye = passion.
268/ Goddes pryvetee = God's secrets. 269/ lewed man = simple man. 270/ That nought
... kan = Who only knows what he believes. 274/ marle-pit yfalle = fell into a clay pit.
276/ Me reweth soore of = I feel sorry for. 277/ rated of = liberated from.

And since John had no knowledge of these arts,
When he broke in, he saw what he thought
Was a man possessed, caught in a sleepwalk,
And never suspected it was all a cheap fraud.

279   "Get me a staf, that I may underspore,
      Whil that thou, Robyn, hevest up the dore.
281   He shal out of his studiyng, as I gesse"
282   And to the chambre dore he gan hym dresse.
283   His knave was a strong carl for the nones,
284   And by the haspe he haaf it of atones;
      Into the floor the dore fil anon.
      This Nicholas sat ay as stille as stoon,
287   And evere caped upward into the eir.
288   This carpenter wende he were in despeir,
289   And hente hym by the sholdres myghtily
290   And shook him harde, and cride spitously,
      "What! Nicholay! What, how! What, looke adoun!
      Awak, and thenk on Christes passioun!
293   I crouche thee from elves and fro wightes."
294   Therwith the nyght-spel seyde he anon-rightes
      On foure halves of the hous aboute,
      And on the tresshfold of the dore withoute:
      "Jhesu Crist and Seinte Benedight,
      Blesse this hous from every wikked wight,
299   For nyghtes verye, the white *pater-noster*!
300   Where wentestow, Seinte Petres soster?"
          And atte laste this hende Nicholas
302   Gan for to sike soore, and seyde, "Allas!
303   Shal al the world be lost eftsoones now?"

～

279/ underspore = pry up. 281/ shal out = shall be brought out. 282/ gan hym dresse = went. 283/ carl for the nones = man for the job. 284/ by the haspe he haaf it of atones = by the hinges he heaved it off all at once. 287/ caped = gazed. 288/ wende = thought. 289/ hente = grabbed. 290/ spitously = urgently. 293/ crouche = protect; wightes = spirits. 294/ nyght-spel = a protective charm; anon-rightes = immediately. 299/ white pater-noster = a charm. 300/ Where wentestow ... soster? = Where did you go, St. Peter's sister? 302/ sike soore = sigh pitifully. 303/ eftsoones now = so soon as now.

He said, "Nicholas, what's wrong—have you lost your mind?
You've been watching the skies for an awful long time,
Clouding your eyes with astrological signs;
This is not wise!"

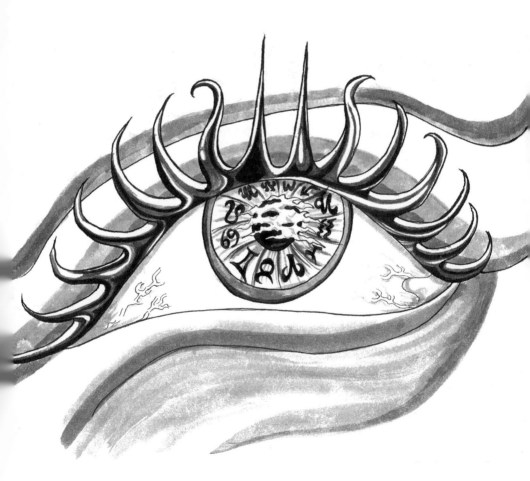

304   This carpenter answerde, "What seystow?

305   What! Thynk on God, as we doon, men that swynke."

        This Nicholas answerde, "Fecche me drynke,

307   And after wol I speke in pryvetee

308   Of certeyn thyng that toucheth me and thee.

        I wol telle it noon oother man, certeyn."

        This carpenter gooth doun, and comth ageyn,

311   And broghte of myghty ale a large quart;

        And whan that ech of hem had dronke his part,

313   This Nicholas his dore faste shette,

        And doun the carpenter by hym he sette.

315   He seyde "John, myn hooste, lief and deere,

        Thou shalt upon thy trouthe swere me heere

317   That to no wight thou shalt this conseil wreye;

        For it is Cristes conseil that I seye,

319   And if thou telle it man, thou art forlore;

        For this vengeaunce thou shalt han therfore,

        That if thou wreye me, thou shalt be wood."

        "Nay, Crist forbede it, for his hooly blood!"

323   Quod tho this sely man, "I nam no labbe,

324   Ne, though I seye, I nam nat lief to gabbe.

        Sey what thou wolt; I shal it nevere telle

326   To child ne wyf, by hym that harwed helle!"

        "Now John," quod Nicholas, "I wol nat lye;

        I have yfounde in myn astrologye,

⌇

304/ What seystow? = What did you say? 305/ swynke = work. 307/ in pryvetee = privately. 308/ toucheth = concerns. 311/ myghty ale = strong ale. 313/ shette = shut. 315/ lief = beloved. 317/ wreye = reveal. 319/ forlore = lost. 323/ sely = silly; labbe = gossip. 324/ I nam nat lief to gabbe = I don't like to gab. 326/ by hym that harwed helle = by Christ.

Nicholas thought of a lie that would leave John blind.
He dropped to his knees and said, "You will not believe
What I've seen with my astrology! In all honesty,
It's a prophecy, a vision from God!

"As I have looked in the moone bright,
330   That now a Monday next, at quarter nyght,
331   Shal falle a reyn, and that so wilde and wood,
That half so greet was nevere Noes flood.
This world," he seyde, "in lasse than an hour
334   Shal al be dreynt, so hidous is the shour.
335   Thus shal mankynde drenche, and lese hir lyf."
    This carpenter answerde, "Allas, my wyf!
And shal she drenche? Allas, myn Alisoun!"
For sorwe of this he fil almoost adoun,
And seyde, "Is ther no remedie in this cas?"
    "Why, yis, for Gode," quod hende Nicholas,
341   "If thou wolt werken after loore and reed.
342   Thou mayst nat werken after thyn owene heed;
For thus seith Salomon, that was ful trewe:
344   'Werk al by conseil, and thou shalt not rewe.'
And if thou werken wolt by good conseil,
346   I undertake, withouten mast and seyl,
Yet shal I saven hire and thee and me.
Hastow nat herd hou saved was Noe,
Whan that oure Lord hadde warned hym biforn
350   That al the world with water sholde be lorn?"
351   "Yis," quod this Carpenter, "ful yoore ago."
    "Hastou nat herd," quod Nicholas, "also
The sorwe of Noe with his felawshipe,

~

330/ at quarter nyght = after midnight. 331/ wood = crazy. 334/ dreynt = drowned.
335/ drenche = drown. 341/ loore and reed = learning and counsel. 342/ heed = head.
344/ rewe = regret. 346/ I undertake = I am certain. 350/ lorn = lost. 351/ ful yoore
ago = long ago.

"Man's hypocrisy is really pissin' Him off,
And makin' a mockery of all the wisdom and love
He's offering. John, this isn't a bluff!
He's not pleased, and now it's His decision to flood
The earth with rough seas, and drown the wicked in blood.

"Er that he myghte gete his wyf to shipe?
355 Hym hadde be levere, I dar wel undertake,
356 At thilke tyme, than alle his wetheres blake
357 That she hadde had a ship hirself allone.
358 And therfore, woostou what is best to doone?
This asketh haste, and of an hastif thyng
Men may nat preche or maken tariyng.
361   "Anon go gete us faste into this in
362 A knedyng-trogh, or ellis a kymelyn,
For ech of us, but looke that they be large,
364 In which we mowe swymme as in a barge,
365 And han therinne vitaille suffisant
366 But for a day – fy on the remenant!
367 The water shal aslake and goon away
368 Aboute pryme upon the nexte day.
But Robyn may nat wite of this, thy knave,
Ne eek thy mayde Gille I may nat save;
Axe nat why, for though thou aske me,
I wol nat tellen Goddes pryvetee.
373 Suffiseth thee, but if thy wittes madde,
To han as greet a grace as Noe hadde.
Thy wyf shal I wel saven, out of doute.
376 Go now thy wey, and speed thee heer-aboute.
    "But whan thou hast, for hire and thee and me,
Ygeten us thise knedyng-tubbes three,

~

355/ Hym hadde be levere = He would have preferred; undertake = say. 356/ thilke =
that; than alle his wetheres blake = to trade all his black sheep. 357/ That = So that.
358/ woostou = do you know. 361/ in = house. 362/ knedyng-trogh = trough for kneading
dough; kymelyn = brewing vat. 364/ swymme = float; barge = ship. 365/ vitaille suffisant
= enough food. 366/ fy on the remenant = forget about the rest. 367/ aslake = subside.
368/ pryme = 9 a.m. 373/ but if thy wittes madde = unless you are crazy. 376/ speed thee
heer-aboute = hurry up with it.

"But you and your wife, plus me, will be lifted above
The slaughter. Us three can just drift in a tub
Until the waters recede and He's given it up.

"Thanne shaltow hange hem in the roof ful hye,
380   That no man of oure purveiaunce espye.
        And whan thou thus hast doon as I have seyd,
382   And hast oure vitaille faire in hem yleyd,
383   And eek an ax to smyte the corde atwo,
        Whan that the water comth, that we may go
385   And breke an hole an heigh, upon the gable,
386   Unto the gardyn-ward, over the stable,
        That we may frely passen forth oure way,
        Whan that the grete shour is goon away.
        Thanne shaltou swymme as myrie, I undertake,
        As dooth the white doke after hire drake.
        Thanne wol I clepe, 'How, Alison! How, John!
        Be myrie, for the flood wol passe anon.'
        And thou wolt seyn, 'Hayl, maister Nicholay!
        Good morwe, I see thee wel, for it is day.'
        And thanne shul we be lordes al oure lyf
        Of al the world, as Noe and his wyf.
            "But of o thyng I warne thee ful right:
398   Be wel avysed on that ilke nyght
399   That we ben entred into shippes bord,
        That noon of us ne speke nat a word,
401   Ne clepe, ne crie, but be in his preyere;
402   For it is Goddes owene heeste deere.

~

380/ of oure purveiaunce espye = discover our plans. 382/ vitaille = food. 383/ smyte the
corde atwo = cut the rope in two. 385/ an heigh = on high; gable = upper wall. 386/ Unto
the gardyn-ward = On the garden side. 398/ ilke = specific. 399/ into shippes bord =
aboard the ships. 401/ clepe = call. 402/ heeste = commandment.

"But we've gotta prepare, and I solemnly swear
That God declared we're supposed to hang this tub up in the air,
At the top of the house, and when the flood gets there,
We can cut the ropes and float out, with nothin' to fear!"

403   "Thy wyf and thou moote hange fer atwynne;
For that bitwixe yow shal be no synne,
Namoore in lookyng than ther shal in deede,
406   This ordinance is seyd. Go, God thee speede!
Tomorwe at nyght, whan men ben alle aslepe,
Into oure knedyng-tubbes wol we crepe,
And sitten there, abidyng Goddes grace.
Go now thy wey; I have no lenger space
To make of this no lenger sermonyng.
Men seyn thus, 'sende the wise, and sey no thing.'
Thou art so wys, it needeth thee nat teche.
Go, save oure lyf, and that I the biseche."
    This sely carpenter goth forth his wey.
Ful ofte he seide 'Allas' and 'weylawey,'
417   And to his wyf he tolde his pryvetee,
418   And she was war, and knew it bet than he,
419   What al this queynte cast was for to seye.
420   But natheless she ferde as she wolde deye,
And seyde, "Allas! go forth thy wey anon,
422   Help us to scape, or we been dede echon!
I am thy trewe, verray wedded wyf;
Go, deere spouse, and help to save oure lyf."
425   Lo, which a greet thyng is affeccioun!
Men may dyen of ymaginacioun,
So depe may impressioun be take.
428   This sely carpenter bigynneth quake;

~

403/ atwynne = apart. 406/ ordinance = order. 417/ pryvetee = secret. 418/ bet = better.
419/ queynte cast = strange plot; seye = mean. 420/ ferde as she wolde deye = acted
afraid. 422/ scape = escape; echon = each one. 425/ which = what; affeccioun =
emotion. 428/ bigynneth quake: began to tremble.

Now this foolish man just threw his hands up in despair,
Flustered and scared, and cried, "It just isn't fair!"
But he had to put his trust in God's justice and care;
He was thankful, at least, that his instructions were clear.

Hym thynketh verraily that he may see
430   Noees flood come walwynge as the see
To drenchen Alisoun, his hony deere.
432   He wepeth, weyleth, maketh sory cheere;
433   He siketh with ful many a sory swogh;
He gooth and geteth hym a knedyng-trogh,
435   And after that a tubbe and a kymelyn,
And pryvely he sente hem to his in,
And heng hem in the roof in pryvetee.
His owene hand he made laddres thre,
439   To clymben by the ronges and the stalkes
440   Unto the tubbes hangynge in the balkes,
441   And hem vitailled, bothe trogh and tubbe,
442   With breed and chese, and good ale in a jubbe,
Suffisynge right ynogh as for a day.
444   But er that he hadde maad al this array,
445   He sente his knave, and eek his wenche also,
Upon his nede to London for to go.
And on the Monday, whan it drow to nyght,
He shette his dore withoute candel-lyght,
449   And dressed alle thyng as it sholde be.
And shortly, up they clomben alle thre;
451   They seten stille wel a furlong way.
452   "Now, *Pater-noster*, clom!" seyde Nicholay,
And "Clom!" quod John, and "Clom!" seyde Alisoun.

~

430/ walwynge as the see = swelling like the sea. 432/ maketh sory cheere = looked miserable. 433/ siketh = sighed; swogh = groan. 435/ kymelyn = brewing vat. 439/ stalkes = uprights. 440/ balkes = rafters. 441/ hem vitailled = filled them with food. 442/ jubbe = jug. 444/ array = arrangements. 445/ wenche = servant girl. 449/ dressed alle thyng = set everything. 451/ furlong way = short time. 452/ Pater-noster = the Lord's prayer; Clom! = Hush!

He spent the day in his workshop, with dust in his hair,

Building this tub; first he constructed it there,

Then he dragged it to his house, and he lugged it upstairs,

And suspended it so that it hung up in the air,

And could be cut free if the "flood" should appear.

This carpenter seyde his devocioun,
455 And stille he sit, and biddeth his preyere,
Awaitynge on the reyn, if he it heere.
457 The dede sleep, for wery bisynesse,
Fil on this carpenter right, as I gesse,
459 Aboute corfew-tyme, or litel moore;
460 For travaille of his goost he groneth soore,
461 And eft he routeth, for his heed myslay.
Doun of the laddre stalketh Nicholay,
And Alisoun ful softe adoun she spedde;
Withouten wordes mo they goon to bedde,
465 Ther as the carpenter is wont to lye.
Ther was the revel and the melodye;
And thus lith Alison and Nicholas,
468 In bisynesse of myrthe and of solas,
469 Til that the belle of laudes gan to rynge,
470 And freres in the chauncel gonne synge.
This parissh clerk, this amorous Absolon,
472 That is for love alwey so wo bigon,
Upon the Monday was at Oseneye
474 With compaignye, hym to disporte and pleye,
475 And axed upon cas a cloisterer
Ful prively after John the carpenter;
477 And he drough hym apart out of the chirche,
478 And seyde, "I noot, I saugh hym heere nat wirche

~

455/ biddeth his preyere = said his prayers. 457/ wery bisynesse = work-weariness.
459/ corfew-tyme = dusk. 460/ travaille of his goost = exhaustion of spirit. 461/ eft =
also; routeth = snored; myslay = lay wrong. 465/ Ther as = There where; is wont to lye =
normally would lie. 468/ In bisynesse … of solas = In the business of pleasure. 469/ belle
of laudes = pre-dawn church service bell. 470/ freres = friars. 472/ wo bigon = miserable.
474/ disporte = socialize. 475/ upon cas = by chance. 477/ drough hym apart = drew him
aside. 478/ noot = don't know.

Once he'd gotten prepared, John offered a prayer
To comfort his spirit, and fell asleep in the tub,
Exhausted, and there we'll leave him, above
Where Nicholas and Alison conduct their secret love.
    Blushing, the two of them rushed to the very place
John was usually tucked, and there they laid,
And crudely made lust, and while the pair played
In the night's dark shade, Absalon came,

"Syn Saterday; I trowe that he be went
For tymber, ther oure abott hath hym sent;
For he is wont for tymber for to go
482   And dwellen at the grange a day or two;
Or elles he is at his hous, certeyn.
Where that he be, I kan nat soothly seyn."
      This Absolon ful joly was and light,
And thoghte, "Now is tyme to wake al nyght;
487   For sikirly I saugh hym nat stirynge
Aboute his dore, syn day bigan to sprynge.
489   "So moot I thryve, I shal, at cokkes crowe,
Ful pryvely knokken at his wyndowe
491   That stant ful lowe upon his boures wal.
To Alison now wol I tellen al
493   My love-longynge, for yet I shal nat mysse
494   That at the leeste wey I shal hire kisse.
495   Som maner confort shal I have, parfay.
496   My mouth hath icched al this longe day;
That is a signe of kissyng atte leeste.
498   Al nyght me mette eek I was at a feeste.
Therfore I wol go slepe an houre or tweye,
And al the nyght thanne wol I wake and pleye."
      Whan that the firste cok hathe crowe, anon
502   Up rist this joly lovere Absolon,
503   And hym arraieth gay, at poynt-devys.

~

482/ the grange = outlying farm. 487/ sikirly = truly. 489/ So moot I thryve = So that I
succeed. 491/ stant = stands; boures wal = bedroom wall. 493/ mysse = fail. 494/ at the
leeste wey = at least. 495/ parfay = I swear. 496/ icched = itched. 498/ me mette = I
dreamed. 502/ Up rist = Up rose. 503/ hym arraieth ... point-devys = groomed himself
meticulously.

Beneath the window pane, calling Alison's name,

With the flame of love alive in his brain,

Which he tried to explain by describing his pain.

504   But first he cheweth greyn and lycorys,
       To smellen sweete, er he hadde kembd his heer.
506   Under his tonge a trewe-love he beer,
507   For therby wende he to ben gracious.
       He rometh to the carpenteres hous,
       And stille he stant under the shot-wyndowe –
510   Unto his brest it raughte, it was so lowe –
511   And softe he cougheth with a semy soun:
       "What do ye, hony-comb, sweete Alisoun,
513   My faire bryd, my sweete cynamome?
514   Awaketh, lemman myn, and speketh to me!
       Wel lithel thynken ye upon my wo,
       That for youre love I swete ther I go.
517   No wonder is thogh that I swelte and swete;
518   I moorne as dooth a lamb after the tete.
519   Ywis, lemman, I have swich love-longynge,
520   That lik a turtel trewe is my moornynge.
       I may nat ete na moore than a mayde."
522   "Go fro the wyndow, Jakke fool," she sayde;
523   "As help me God, it wol not be 'com pa me.'
       I love another – and elles I were to blame –
       Wel bet than thee, by Jhesu, Absolon.
       Go forth thy wey, or I wol caste a ston,
527   And lat me slepe, a twenty devel wey!"

504/ greyn and lycorys = breath-fresheners. 506/ trewe-love he beer = he put a sprig of
herbs. 507/ wende = hoped; gracious = attractive. 510/ raughte = reached. 511/ semy
soun = gentle sound. 513/ bryd = bird. 514/ lemman myn = my love. 517/ swelte and
swete = faint and sweat. 518/ moorne = yearn. 519/ Ywis, lemman = I swear, lover.
520/ turtel = turtledove; moornynge = grieving. 522/ Jakke fool = you idiot. 523/ com
pa me = come kiss me. 527/ a twenty devel wey = twenty devils take you.

He sighed, "The way you act is a crying shame!
Forsaken and sad, I strive in vain,
Wasting my breath on sacred pacts,
Patiently waiting for you to pay them back!"
Alison sat up, raging mad,
And laughed in his face with disdainful wrath:
"Take that 'sacred pact' heartbreak crap
Away from this place, you disgraceful rat!"

528 "Allas," quod Absolon, "and weylawey,

529 That trewe love was evere so yvel biset!

530 Thanne kysse me, syn it may be no bet,

For Jhesus love, and for the love of me."

"Wiltow thanne go thy wey therwith?" quod she.

"Ye, certes, lemman," quod this Absolon.

"Thanne make thee redy," quod she, "I come anon."

And unto Nicholas she seyde stille,

536 "Now hust, and thou shalt laughen al thy fille."

This Absolon doun sette hym on his knees

538 And seyde, "I am a lord at alle degrees;

For after this I hope ther cometh moore.

540 Lemman, thy grace, and sweete bryd, thyn oore!"

541 The wyndow she undoth, and that in haste.

542 "Have do," quod she, "com of, and speed the faste,

Lest that oure neighebores thee espie."

This Absolon gan wype his mouth ful drie.

545 Derk was the nyght as pich, or as a cole,

And at the wyndow out she putte hir hole,

547 And Absolon, hym fil no bet ne wers,

But with his mouth he kiste hir naked ers

549 Ful savorly, er he were war of this.

~

528/ weylawey = woe is me. 529/ so yvel biset = so unfortunate. 530/ no bet = no better. 536/ hust = hush. 538/ at alle degrees = in every way. 540/ oore = mercy. 541/ undoth = opened. 542/ Have do = Let's go; com of = come on. 545/ pich = pitch. 547/ no bet ne wers = neither better nor worse. 549/ Ful savorly = Savouringly; er he were war = before he knew.

"But wait," she said, "I take it back;
You can have a kiss, if you wish, but make it fast!"
The night was slate-black as she raised the glass,
And displayed her backside and waited, relaxed,
As Absalon reached out his lips and gave it his best,
And proudly kissed the middle of her naked ass.

Abak he stirte, and thoughte it was amys,

For wel he wiste a womman hath no berd.

552   He felte a thyng al rough and long yherd,

And seyde, "Fy! allas! what have I do?"

"Tehee!" quod she, and clapte the wyndow to,

555   And Absolon gooth forth a sory pas.

556   "A berd! A berd!" quod hende Nicholas,

557   "By Goddes corpus, this goth faire and weel."

558   This sely Absolon herde every deel,

And on his lippe he gan for anger byte,

560   And to hymself he seyde, "I shall thee quyte."

561   Who rubbeth now, who froteth now his lippes

With dust, with sond, with straw, with clooth, with chippes,

But Absolon, that seith ful ofte, "Allas!"

564   "My soule bitake I unto Sathanas,

565   But me were levere than al this toun," quod he,

566   "Of this despit awroken for to be.

567   Allas," quod he, "allas, I ne hadde ybleynt!"

568   His hoote love was coold and al yqueynt;

For fro that tyme that he hadde kist her ers,

570   Of paramours he sette nat a kers,

For he was heeled of his maladie.

572   Ful ofte paramours he gan deffie,

And weep as dooth a child that is ybete.

574   A softe paas he wente over the strete

∾

552/ long yherd = long-haired. 555/ a sory pas = unhappily. 556/ A berd = A trick.
557/ corpus = body. 558/ sely = silly; every deel = every word. 560/ quyte = pay back.
561/ froteth = scrubs. 564/ bitake = commit. 565/ me were ... toun = I would rather get
revenge than own this whole town. 566/ despit awroken = insult avenged. 567/ ybleynt
= turned away. 568/ yqueynt = extinguished. 570/ paramours = romance; sette nat a kers
= didn't give a damn. 572/ deffie = defy. 574/ softe paas = short way.

But something was weird: it tasted bad,
And had a beard of long, rough hairs.
Absalon's fears were given a nudge
When Alison giggled and slammed the window shut.
He didn't blow up, but he did hold a grudge.
　When he realized the ass-kiss was true,
Absalon knew what he just had to do.

575   Until a smyth men cleped daun Gerveys,
576   That in his forge smythed plough harneys;
577   He sharpeth shaar and kultour bisily.
578   This Absolon knokketh al esily,
579   And seyde, "Undo, Gerveys, and that anon."
        "What, who artow?" "It am I, Absolon."
581   "What, Absolon! For Cristes sweete tree,
582   Why rise ye so rathe? Ey, benedicitee!
        What eyleth yow? Som gay gerl, God it woot,
584   Hath broght yow thus upon the viritoot.
        By Seinte Note, ye woot wel what I mene."
586   This Absolon ne roghte nat a bene
        Of all his pley; no word agayn he yaf;
588   He hadde moore tow on his distaf
        Than Gerveys knew, and seyde, "Freend so deere,
590   That hoote kultour in the chymenee heere,
591   As lene it me; I have therwith to doone,
        And I wol brynge it thee agayn ful soone."
        Gerveys answerde, "Certes, were it gold,
594   Or in a poke nobles alle untold,
        Thou sholdest have, as I am trewe smyth.
596   Ey, Cristes foo! What wol ye do therwith?"
597   "Therof," quod Absolon, "be as be may.
        I shal wel telle it thee to-morwe day" –
        And caughte the kultour by the colde stele,
600   Ful softe out at the dore he gan to stele,
        And wente unto the carpenteris wal.

575/ Until = To; daun = Sir. 576/ harneys = equipment. 577/ sharpeth shaar = sharpened blades; kultour = vertical plow blade. 578/ esily = casually. 579/ Undo = Open up. 581/ Cristes sweete tree = the Cross. 582/ rathe = early; benedicitee = good God. 584/ upon the viritoot = on the prowl. 586/ roghte nat a bene = didn't care. 588/ moore tow on his distaf = bigger things on his mind. 590/ hoote kultour = hot steel blade; chymenee = furnace. 591/ As lene it me = Lend it to me. 594/ in a poke ... untold = a bag of gold coins. 596/ Cristes foo = the devil. 597/ be as be may = whatever may be. 600/ stele = sneak.

He ran quickly to this blacksmith he knew,
And asked if he'd do a favour, as a friend's requirement,
Inquiring if he could borrow the man's branding iron,
Which happened to be standing in the fire he was fanning
Higher to get it heated. When he had what he needed,
Absalon proceeded back to the scene at
The mansion, where he'd been mistreated,

He cogheth first, and knokketh therwithal

603 Upon the wyndowe, right as he dide er.

This Alison answerde, "Who is ther

605 That knokketh so? I warante it a theef."

606   "Why, nay," quod he, "God woot, my sweete leef,

607 I am thyn Absolon, my deerelyng.

Of gold," quod he, "I have thee broght a ryng.

My mooder yaf it me, so God me save;

610 Ful fyn it is, and therto wel ygrave.

This wol I yeve thee, if thou me kisse."

This Nicholas was risen for to pisse,

613 And thoughte he wolde amenden al the jape;

He sholde kisse his ers er that he scape.

And up the wyndowe dide he hastily,

And out his ers he putteth pryvely

617 Over the buttok, to the haunche-bon;

And therwith spak this clerk, this Absolon,

619 "Spek, sweete bryd, I noot nat where thou art."

620   This Nicholas anon leet fle a fart,

621 As greet as it had been a thonder-dent,

622 That with the strook he was almoost yblent;

And he was redy with his iren hoot,

And Nicholas amydde the ers he smoot.

625   Of gooth the skyn an hande brede aboute,

626 The hoote kultour brende so his toute,

～

603/ dide er = did before. 605/ I warante it = I swear it's. 606/ leef = love.
607/ deerelyng = darling. 610/ ygrave = engraved. 613/ amenden al the jape = improve
the joke. 617/ haunche-bon = hips. 619/ I noot nat = I don't know. 620/ leet fle = let
fly. 621/ thonder-dent = thunderclap. 622/ yblent = blinded. 625/ Of gooth = Off goes;
an hande brede aboute = the width of a hand. 626/ toute = ass.

And in his sweetest voice he pleaded,
"Oh, Lover Lips, it would be utter bliss
If you could see fit to give me another kiss!"
Above, Nicholas had gotten up to piss,
And he muttered in a muffled whisper under his breath,
"What a glutton for punishment this sucker is!"
So he slid *his* butt out the window up to his hips,
Sensing nothing amiss, with his grip to hold him steady,
But Absalon couldn't guess where to strike, so instead he
Cried, "Say something, Miss!" and Nicholas broke wind heavy,
The sound thunderous, like a motor revving.
For Absalon there was no forgetting; he knew this joke already,
But this time he had his red-hot poker ready,
And he reached overhead and scalded his ass badly.

627   And for the smert he wende for to dye.
       As he were wood, for wo he gan to crye,
       "Help! Water! Water! Help for Goddes herte!"
       This carpenter out of his slomber sterte,
631   And herde oon crien 'water!' as he were wood,
       And thoughte, "Allas, now comth Nowelis flood!"
       He sit hym up withouten wordes mo,
       And with his ax he smoot the corde atwo,
635   And doun gooth al; he foond neither to selle
636   Ne breed ne ale, til he cam to the celle
637   Upon the floor, and ther aswowne he lay.
       Up stirte hire Alison and Nicholay,
       And criden "Out" and "Harrow" in the strete.
640   The neighebores, bothe smale and grete,
641   In ronnen for to gauren on this man,
       That yet aswowne lay, bothe pale and wan,
643   For with the fal he brosten hadde his arm.
644   But stonde he moste unto his owene harm;
645   For whan he spak, he was anon bore doun
       With hende Nicholas and Alisoun.
647   They tolden every man that he was wood;
648   He was agast so of Nowelis flood
649   Thurgh fantasie that of his vanytee
       He hadde yboght hym knedyng-tubbes thre,
       And hadde hem hanged in the roof above;

~

627/ for the smert ... dye = he thought he would die from the pain. 631/ as he were wood = like he was crazy. 635/ he foond neither to selle = he didn't stop to sell. 636/ Ne breed ne ale = neither bread nor ale; celle = boards. 637/ aswowne = unconscious. 640/ smale and grete = small and large. 641/ In ronnen = Ran in; gauren on = stare at. 643/ brosten = burst. 644/ stonde he moste ... harm= things got worse when he stood up. 645/ bore doun = shouted down. 647/ wood = nuts. 648/ agast so = so afraid. 649/ vanytee = foolishness.

With the hole in his flesh expanding, Nicholas ran
Through the house, cauterized, screaming, "Water! Water!"
Cries of "Water!" started to rise up and surprised
John, who thought his cries were because he saw the flood
Waters arrive. Suddenly, he shot upright,
And before he'd even got his eyes opened well,
John reached out with his pocketknife, cut the rope, and fell
From up on high, without a hope in hell,
And broke his elbow when he smoked the windowsill.
But the greatest shame of all was when the neighbours came
To investigate the screams, 'cause the others made it seem
Like John was plain insane, raving about Noah,
Roped up in a boat, waiting for the flood to show up.

652   And that he preyed hem, for Goddes love,

653   To sitten in the roof, par compaignye.

      The folk gan laughen at his fantasye;

655   Into the roof they kiken and they cape,

656   And turned al his harm unto a jape.

      For what so that this carpenter answerde,

      It was for noght, no man his reson herde.

659   With othes grete he was so sworn adoun

      That he was holde wood in al the toun;

661   For every clerk anonright heeld with oother.

662   They seyde, "The man is wood, my leeve brother";

      And every wight gan laughen at this stryf.

664   Thus swyved was this carpenteris wyf,

      For al his kepyng and his jalousye;

666   And Absolon hath kist hir nether ye;

667   And Nicholas is scalded in the towte.

668   This tale is doon, and God save al the rowte!

Heere endeth the Millere his Tale.

~

652/ preyed hem = begged them. 653/ par compaignye = for company. 655/ kiken = stared; cape = gaped. 656/ jape = joke. 659/ othes grete = great oaths; sworn adoun = shouted down. 661/ anonright heeld = immediately agreed. 662/ wood = crazy; leeve = dear. 664/ swyved = screwed. 666/ nether ye = lower eye. 667/ towte = ass. 668/ rowte = group.

They all had a good laugh at these three sad saps:

John with his fractured arm, flat on his back;

And Absalon's kiss, smack dab in the crack;

And Nicholas with the flesh of his ass scabbed black;

And Alison sat back, relaxed, and laughed,

The only one left with her rep intact;

And that's the end of that, as a matter of fact!

The End.

THE PARDONER'S TALE

The Pardoner is Chaucer's most unapologetically corrupt character, and also one of his most keenly intelligent. As his title implies, the Pardoner is an agent of the Church whose job is to pardon sins in exchange for money, and he uses this official sanction for protection while committing every imaginable sin himself. Besides perpetrating the notorious sale of indulgences that helped bring the medieval Catholic Church to disgrace, Chaucer's Pardoner is also a peddler of fake religious relics and a mercenary preacher who terrorizes parishioners into filling both church coffers and his own pockets. The Pardoner's self-serving medieval televangelism is offered in contrast to the honest work of the "povre person" (poor parson) who is a true spiritual minister and not concerned about profit:

> But with thise relikes, whan that he fond
> A povre person dewellynge upon lond,
> Upon a day he gat hym moore moneye
> Than that the person gat in monthes tweye;

> (But with these relics, when he found
> A poor parson living on the land,
> In one day he got more money
> Than the parson got in two months.)

The patent message of the Pardoner's character is that crime pays, and there is no natural reason to associate strength and intelligence with virtue, and no reason to expect worldly justice for calculated misdeeds. This "cruel world" theme is also flaunted in rap lyrics that explore criminal activities and gangsterism, in which the person with the least compassion often achieves the greatest wealth (C.R.E.A.M. = Cash Rules Everything Around Me). The Pardoner's ratio of two months' honest pay for a day of hustling relics resembles Wyclef's parable in "Street Jeopardy" when he raps, "The professor says, 'Whatcha wanna do, sell drugs or get a degree?' / I looked at him and smiled with thirty-two gold teeth / And said, 'what you make in a year, I make it in a week.'"

Chaucer's Pardoner is similarly ostentatious with his wealth, and his appearance foreshadows his unsavoury character. His "heer as yelow as wex" (hair as yellow as wax) hangs in long greasy strands over his shoulders, like Kid Rock on the cover of his *Devil Without a Cause* album. The Pardoner dresses in the latest fashions and speaks to the pilgrims in a "voys … as smal as hath a goot" (a voice as high as a goat's), and pierces them with his gaze: "Swiche glarynge eyen hadde he as an hare" (He had glaring eyes like a hare). However, his most striking feature is his effeminacy: "No berd hadde he, ne nevere sholde have; / As smothe it was as it were late shave" (He had no beard, nor ever would; his cheeks were as smooth as if they were just shaved). Chaucer's parting shot is as close as he comes to being snide or judgmental in the *General Prologue*: "I trowe he were a gelding or a mare" (I thought he was either castrated or female). This has provoked endless critical speculation on the Pardoner's sexuality, and he has variously been declared impotent or sterile; or a eunuch, a homosexual, a hermaphrodite, or simply an effeminate heterosexual like Absolon in *The Miller's Tale*. However, only this last claim can be backed up within the text, since the Pardoner later asks the Wife of Bath for advice in getting married, and makes other references to female company.

The most remarkable thing about the Pardoner is not that he embodies religious hypocrisy in every possible way, but that he brags openly about it in the *Prologue* to his *Tale*, laying his corruption bare to impress the other pilgrims. Speaking with the confidence of a villain who knows he is above the law, the Pardoner explains:

> I peyne me to han an hauteyn speche,
> And rynge it out as round as gooth a belle,
> For I kan al by rote that I telle.
> My theme is alwey oon, and evere was –
> *Radix malorum est Cupiditas.*
>
> (I make sure to have a proud voice,
> And ring it out as loud as a bell,
> For I have memorized everything I say.
> My theme is always the same—
> *Greed is the root of all evil.*)

The Pardoner preaches against the sin of avarice explicitly for the purpose of loosening his victims' purse strings: "For to make hem free / To yeven hir pens, and namely unto me" (To make them free to give me their money). This would seem to make him the ultimate hypocrite, save for the fact that he is so open and honest about his hypocrisy, which complicates his character. He is the most deceptive and at the same time the most forthcoming of all the pilgrims, casually admitting, "Myn entente is nat but for to wynne, / And nothing for correccioun of synne" (My intent is only to get paid, and never for correcting sins). The Pardoner's moral corruption is so complete that he has grown comfortable with exploitation as a way of life, and the examples he gives are stark:

> I wol have moneie, wolle, chese, and whete,
> Al were it yeven of the povereste page,
> Or of the povereste wydwe in a village,
> Al sholde hir children sterve for famyne.
>
> (I will have money, wool, cheese, and wheat,
> Even given by the poorest servant,
> Or the poorest widow in the village,
> Even if her children starve for hunger.)

The Pardoner's relationship with society is entirely parasitic; he is a spiritual crack dealer preying on the paranoia and weakness of the poor, living a life of luxury without excuse or apology. In his boasting over material wealth, the Pardoner strikes the same tone as gangsta rap's ubiquitous pimp persona, which is also designed to provoke both indignation and envy. The Notorious B.I.G. claims to "pop bottles with models," while the Pardoner declares, "I wol drynke licour of the vyne, / And have a joly wenche in every toun." Ludacris updates this boast for the twenty-first century in the form of a chorus: "I got hos in different area codes."

For his *Tale* the Pardoner offers the pilgrims an example of his mercenary morality: a story of three drunken thugs who hear about someone dying of the plague and decide to go on a quest to try and kill Death, with gruesome results. Unlike the Pardoner himself, the characters in his story are harshly punished for their pride and immorality, as they must be in order to empower their creator. The story opens in a tavern where the three friends (called "the rioters") are drinking, but it soon digresses into a lengthy religious sermon on the seven deadly sins. There is nothing in the sermon or the rest of *The Pardoner's Tale* that explicitly reveals the corruption of its narrator, but our foreknowledge of his character lends extra weight to every word. The story is one of the most exquisite in *The Canterbury Tales*, as told by one of Chaucer's most dangerous and ingenious characters. The Pardoner uses language as a weapon to achieve wealth and power, and to exercise influence over people. He warns the pilgrims in his *Prologue* that anyone who "[h]ath trespased to my bretheren or to me" (has offended me or my people) will be punished: "Thanne wol I stynge hym with my tonge smerte / In prechyng." The *Tale* is not aimed at any of the pilgrims explicitly; instead it is meant to showcase the Pardoner's mastery of the art of oratory, demonstrating what he is capable of if provoked: "Thus spitte I out my venym under hewe / Of hoolynesse" (I spit out my venom under the pretense of holiness).

In a bizarre twist, when the Pardoner finishes telling his tale he immediately tries to sell his relics to the pilgrims, apparently forgetting that he has already exposed himself as a fraud, or perhaps he is so supremely confident in his persuasive powers that he doesn't think it will matter. The Host proceeds to insult and humiliate him merrily, undeterred by the Pardoner's menacing. I didn't include this epilogue in the rap version since it is external to the narrative of the tale, but it is printed here because it provides comic relief and also because of how effectively it wraps the scene, taking the sinister edge off of the Pardoner's entire episode.

The Pardoner's Tale

1   In Flaundres whilom was a compaignye
2   Of yonge folk that haunteden folye,
3   As riot, hasard, stywes, and tavernes,
4   Wher as with harpes, lutes, and gyternes
5   They daunce and pleyen at dees bothe day and nyght,
     And eten also and drynken over hir myght,
     Thurgh which they doon the devel sacrifise
     Withinne that develes temple in cursed wise,
9   By superfluytee abhomynable.
     Hir othes been so grete and so dampnable
     That it is grisly for to heere hem swere.
12   Oure blissed Lordes body they totere –
     Hem thoughte that Jewes rente hym noght ynough –
14   And ech of hem at otheres synne lough.
15   And right anon thanne comen tombesteres,
16   Fetys and smale, and yonge frutesteres,
17   Syngeres with harpes, baudes, wafereres,
     Whiche been the verray develes officeres
     To kyndle and blowe the fyr of lecherye,
20   That is annexed unto glotonye.
     The hooly writ take I to my witnesse
22   That luxurie is in wyn and dronkenesse.
23   Lo, how that dronken Looth, unkyndely
     Lay by hise doghtres two, unwityngly;
25   So dronke he was, he nyste what he wroghte.

~

1/ whilom = once. 2/ haunteden folye = were prone to recklessness. 3/ riot = rowdiness; hasard = gambling; stywes = whoring. 4/ lutes, and gyternes = stringed instruments. 5/ dees = dice. 9/ superfluytee abhomynable = terrible wastefulness. 12/ totere = tear up. 14/ lough = laughed. 15/ tombesteres = dancers. 16/ Fetys and smale = Pretty and petite; frutesteres = fruit-sellers. 17/ baudes = clowns; wafereres = sweets-sellers. 20/ annexed unto = connected to. 22/ luxurie = lust. 23/ Looth = Lot; unkyndely = unnaturally. 25/ he nyste what he wroghte = he didn't know what he did.

My story begins at a bar, where three friends
Drink cheap gin and party hard all weekend.
These men were riot-starter types,
Who spent the better part of their money on cards and dice,

26　　　Herodes, whoso wel the stories soghte,

27　　Whan he of wyn was repleet at his feeste,

28　　Right at his owene table he yaf his heeste

　　　To sleen the Baptist John, ful giltelees.

30　　Senec seith a good word, doutelees;

　　　He seith he kan no difference fynde

　　　Bitwix a man that is out of his mynde

33　　And a man which that is dronkelewe,

34　　But that woodnesse, fallen in a shrewe,

　　　Persevereth lenger than dooth dronkenesse.

　　　O glotonye, ful of cursednesse!

　　　O cause first of oure confusioun!

38　　O original of oure dampnacioun,

　　　Til Crist hadde boght us with his blood agayn!

40　　Lo how deere, shortly for to sayn,

41　　Aboght was thilke cursed vileynye!

　　　Corrupt was al this world for glotonye!

　　　　Adam oure fader, and his wyf also,

　　　Fro Paradys to labour and to wo

45　　Were dryven for that vice, it is no drede.

　　　For whil that Adam fasted, as I rede,

　　　He was in Paradys, and whan that he

48　　Eet of the fruyt deffended on the tree,

　　　Anon he was out cast to wo and peyne.

50　　O glotonye, on thee wel oghte us pleyne!

~

26/ Herodes = Herod. 27/ repleet = saturated. 28/ yaf his heeste = commanded. 30/ Senec = Seneca. 33/ dronkelewe = an alcoholic. 34/ woodnesse = madness; shrewe = scoundrel. 38/ original = first cause. 40/ deere = costly. 41/ Aboght = Paid for; thilke = that. 45/ it is no drede = there is no doubt. 48/ deffended = forbidden. 50/ pleyne = complain.

Livin' the life of loose women and vice,

Pickin' fights, seduced by all seven different types

Of sins, a feeding frenzy of Vengeance,

Vanity, Lust, Greed, and Envy.

51   O, wiste a man how manye maladyes
        Folwen of excesse and of goltonyes,
        He wolde been the moore mesurable
        Of his diete, sittynge at his table.
        Allas, the shorte throte, the tendre mouth,
        Maketh that est and west and north and south,
57   In erthe, in eir, in water, man to swynke
        To gete a glotoun deyntee mete and drynke!
59   Of this matiere, O Paul, wel kanstow trete:
60   "Mete unto wombe, and wombe eek unto mete,
        Shal God destroyen bothe," as Paulus seith.
        Allas, a foul thyng is it, by my feith,
        To seye this word, and fouler is the dede,
64   Whan man so drynketh of the white and rede
65   That of his throte he maketh his pryvee
66   Thurgh thilke cursed superfluitee.
67   The apostel, wepying, seith ful pitously,
        "Ther walken manye of whiche yow toold have I –
        I seye it now wepyng, with pitous voys –
        They been enemys of Cristes croys,
71   Of whiche the ende is deeth; wombe is hir god!"
72   O wombe! O bely! O stynkyng cod,
        Fulfilled of donge and of corrupcioun!
74   At either ende of thee foul is the soun;
75   How greet labour and cost is thee to fynde!
        Thise cookes, how they stampe, and streyne, and grynde,

~

51/ wiste a man = if a man knew; maladyes = health problems. 57/ swynke = work. 59/ Paul = St. Paul; trete = illustrate. 60/ wombe = stomach. 64/ white and rede = wines. 65/ pryvee = toilet. 66/ superfluitee = excess. 67/ The apostel = St. Paul. 71/ wombe = appetite. 72/ cod = bag. 74/ soun = sound. 75/ fynde = satisfy.

Devious energy left them half-insane,

Laughing deranged like hyenas at their bastard games;

As each glass was drained and each bet was placed,

They set the pace and left space for their next mistakes,

77   And turnen substaunce into accident

78   To fulfillen al thy likerous talent!

     Out of the harde bones knokke they

80   The mary, for they caste noght awey

81   That may go thurgh the golet softe and swoote;

     Of spicerie of leef, and bark, and roote

     Shal been his sauce ymaked by delit,

     To make hym yet a newer appetit.

85   But, certes, he that haunteth swiche delices

     Is deed, whil that he lyveth in tho vices.

       A lecherous thyng is wyn, and dronkenesse

88   Is ful of stryvyng and of wrecchednesse.

     O dronke man, disfigured is thy face,

90   Sour is thy breeth, foul artow to embrace,

     And thurgh thy dronke nose semeth the soun

92   As though thow seydest ay, "Sampsoun! Sampsoun!"

     And yet, God woot, Sampsoun drank nevere no wyn.

94   Thou fallest as it were a styked swyn;

95   Thy tonge is lost, and al thyn honeste cure,

96   For dronkenesse is verray sepulture

97   Of mannes wit and his discrecioun,

     In whom that drynke hath dominacioun,

99   He kan no conseil kepe; it is no drede.

     Now kepe yow fro the white and fro the rede,

~

77/ substaunce into accident = potential into waste. 78/ likerous talent = greedy appetite. 80/ mary = marrow. 81/ golet = gullet; swoote = sweet. 85/ haunteth = is prone to; delices = delights. 88/ stryvyng = violence. 90/ foul artow = you are foul. 92/ Sampsoun = Samson. 94/ styked swyn = stuck pig. 95/ honeste cure = sense of decency. 96/ sepulture = tomb. 97/ discrecioun = judgment. 99/ conseil = secret.

All excessive waste and drunken rambling,

With eager hands trembling; eventually gambling

Leads to panhandling,

101 And namely fro the white wyn of Lepe

102 That is to selle in Fysshstrete or in Chepe.

This wyn of Spaigne crepeth subtilly

In othere wynes, growynge faste by,

Of which ther ryseth swich fumositee

That whan a man hath dronken draughtes thre,

107 And weneth that he be at hoom in Chepe,

He is in Spaigne, right at the toune of Lepe,

109 Nat at the Rochele, ne at Burdeux toun;

And thanne wol he seye "Sampsoun, Sampsoun!"

 But herkneth, lordynges, o word I yow preye,

That alle the sovereyn actes, dar I seye,

Of victories in the Olde Testament,

Thurgh verray God that is omnipotent

Were doon in abstinence and in preyere.

Looketh the Bible, and ther ye may it leere.

 Looke, Attilla, the grete conquerour,

Deyde in his sleepe, with shame and dishonour,

Bledynge ay at his nose in dronkenesse.

A capitayn sholde lyve in sobrenesse;

And over al this avyseth yow right wel

122 What was comaunded unto Lamuel –

Nat Samuel, but Lamuel, seye I –

Redeth the Bible and fynde it expresly,

125 Of wyn yevyng to hem that han justise.

Namoore of this, for it may wel suffise.

⁓

101/ Lepe = area in Spain. 102/ Fysshstrete ... Chepe = areas in London. 107/ weneth that = believes that. 109/ Rochele ... Burdeux = areas in France. 122/ Lamuel = Lemuel, a biblical king. 125/ yevyng = giving; justise = authority.

But that's the price
You pay to cast the dice, and other appetites
Pay the same sacrifice, while the false assumption
Is they help us function, when really it's just a dungeon
Of self-consumption.

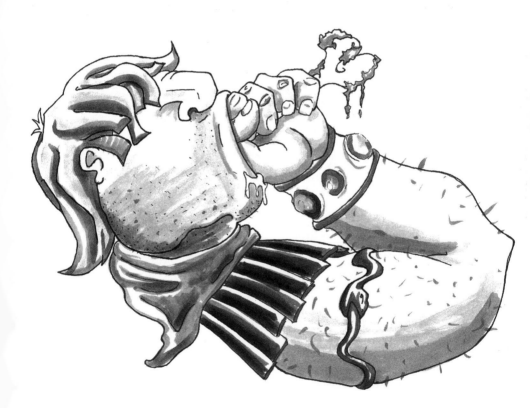

And now that I have spoken of glotonye,
128 Now wol I yow deffenden hasardrye.
129 Hasard is verray mooder of lesynges,
130 And of deceite and cursed forswerynges,
Blaspheme of Crist, manslaughtre, and wast also
132 Of catel and of tyme, and forthermo
133 It is repreeve and contrarie of honour
134 For to ben holde a commune hasardour.
And ever the hyer he is of estaat,
The moore is he holden desolaat;
If that a prynce useth hasardrye,
In all governaunce and policye
He is, as by commune opinioun,
Yholde the lasse in reputacioun.
141 Stilboun, that was a wys embassadour,
142 Was sent to Corynthe in ful greet honour,
143 Fro Lacidomye to maken hire alliaunce.
And whan he cam, hym happede par chaunce
That alle the gretteste that were of that lond
Pleyynge atte hasard he hem fond.
For which, as soone as it myghte be,
148 He stal hym hoom agayn to his contree,
And seyde, "Ther wol I nat lese my name,
Ne I wol nat take on me so greet defame,
Yow for to allie unto none hasardours.

∼

128/ deffenden hasardrye = discuss gambling. 129/ Hasard = Gambling; mooder of lesynges = mother of lies. 130/ forswerynges = false witness. 132/ catel = property. 133/ repreeve = shameful. 134/ hasardour = gambler. 141/ Stilboun = Greek philosopher. 142–43/ Corynthe … Lacidomye = Greek cities. 148/ stal = stole.

In other words, it's not worth it;
This world is not perfect, but it gets worse if
Flesh is the only god you worship.

"Sendeth othere wise embassadours;
153 For, by my trouthe, me were levere dye
Than I yow sholde to hasardours allye.
For ye that been so glorious in honours
156 Shul nat allyen yow with hasardours
As by my wyl, ne as by my tretee."
This wise philosophre, thus seyde hee.
    Looke eek that to the kyng Demetrius
160 The kyng of Parthes, as the book seith us,
161 Sente him a paire of dees of gold, in scorn,
For he hadde used hasard ther-biforn;
For which he heeld his glorie or his renoun
At no value or reputacioun.
165 Lordes may fynden oother maner pley
Honeste ynough to dryve the day awey.
167   Now wol I speke of othes false and grete
A word or two, as olde bookes trete.
Gret sweryng is a thyng abhominable,
And fals sweryng is yet moore reprevable.
The heighe God forbad sweryng at al,
Witnesse on Mathew; but in special
173 Of sweryng seith the hooly Jeremye,
174 "Thou shalt swere sooth thyne othes, and nat lye,
175 And swere in doom and eek in rightwisnesse";
But ydel sweryng is a cursednesse.

∽

153/ me were levere dye = I would rather die. 156/ hasardours = gamblers. 160/ Parthes
= Persia. 161/ dees = dice. 165/ oother maner pley = other diversions. 167/ othes = oaths.
173/ Jeremye = Jeremiah. 174/ sooth = truthfully. 175/ in doom = discriminatingly; in
rightwisnesse = righteously.

As mortal men, you
Need more than the sinews in your corpse to defend you.

Bihoold and se that in the firste table
178   Of heighe Goddes heestes honurable,
How that the seconde heeste of hym is this:
"Take nat my name in ydel or amys."
Lo, rather he forbedeth swich sweryng
182   Than homycide or many a cursed thyng;
I seye that as by ordre thus it stondeth;
This knoweth that hise heestes understondeth
How that the seconde heeste of God is that.
186   And forther-over I wol thee telle al plat
That vengeance shal nat parten from his hous
That of hise othes is to outrageous.
"By Goddes precious herte," and "By his nayles,"
190   And "By the blood of Crist that is in Hayles,
191   Sevene is my chaunce, and thyn is cynk and treye!"
"By Goddes armes, if thou falsly pleye,
This daggere shal thurghout thyn herte go!"
194   This fruyt cometh of the bicched bones two:
Forsweryng, ire, falsnesse, homycide!
Now, for the love of Crist, that for us dyde,
197   Lete youre othes bothe grete and smale.
But, sires, now wol I telle forth my tale.
    Thise riotoures thre, of whiche I telle,
200   Longe erst er prime rong of any belle,
Were set hem in a taverne for to drynke,

~

178/ heestes = commandments. 182/ Than = More than. 186/ forther-over = moreover; al plat = plainly. 190/ Hayles = Hales Abbey. 191/ chaunce = roll; cynk and treye = five and three. 194/ bicched bones = cursed dice. 197/ Lete = Cease. 200/ Longe erst er prime = Long before 9 a.m.

But let the story continue, the same as before,
Where these three hard-core men drink at the bar.

And as they sat, they herde a belle clynke
203   Biforn a cors, was caried to his grave.
204   That oon of hem gan callen to his knave,
205   "Go bet," quod he, "and axe redily
       What cors is this that passeth heer forby;
       And looke that thou reporte his name weel."
208   "Sire," quod this boy, "it nedeth never a deel;
       It was me toold er ye cam heer two houres.
210   He was, pardee, an old felawe of youres,
       And sodeynly he was yslayn to-nyght,
       Fordronke, as he sat on his bench upright.
213   Ther cam a privee theef men clepeth Deeth,
214   That in this contree al the peple sleeth,
215   And with his spere he smoot his herte atwo,
       And wente his wey withouten wordes mo.
217   He hath a thousand slayn, this pestilence.
       And, maister, er ye come in his presence,
       Me thynketh that it were necessarie
       For to be war of swich an adversarie.
       Beth redy for to meete hym everemoore;
222   Thus taughte me my dame; I sey namoore."
       "By Seinte Marie!" seyde this taverner,
       "The child seith sooth, for he hath slayn this yeer,
225   Henne over a mile, withinne a greet village,
226   Bothe man and womman, child, and hyne, and page;
       I trowe his habitacioun be there.

203/ cors = corpse. 204/ knave = servant. 205/ bet = quick. 208/ it nedeth never a deel
= there's no need. 210/ pardee = by God. 213/ privee = secret; clepeth = call. 214/ sleeth
= kills. 215/ smoot = split. 217/ pestilence = plague. 222/ dame = mother. 225/ Henne
over a mile = A mile from here. 226/ hyne = worker; page = servant.

Someone came in the door and ordered a beer,
And told a sad story they were sorry to hear;
Choking on tears, he said, "Death is a thief!
My friend was asleep and his breath just ceased.
May he rest in peace, and never be stressed;
I guess people ever need to be ready to meet Death!"

228   "To been avysed, greet wysdom it were,
       Er that he dide a man a dishonour."
          "Ye, Goddes armes!" quod this riotour,
       "Is it swich peril with hym for to meete?
       I shal hym seke, by wey and eek by strete;
       I make avow to Goddes digne bones!

234   Herkneth, felawes, we thre been al ones;
       Lat ech of us holde up his hand til oother,
       And ech of us bicomen otheres brother,

237   And we wol sleen this false traytour Deeth.
       He shal be slayn, which that so manye sleeth,
       By Goddes dignitee, er it be nyght!"

240   Togidres han thise thre hir trouthes plight
       To lyve and dyen ech of hem for oother,
       As though he were his owene ybore brother;
       And up they stirte, al dronken in this rage,
       And forth they goon towardes that village,
       Of which the taverner hadde spoke biforn.
       And many a grisly ooth thanne han they sworn,

247   And Cristes blessed body they torente –

248   Deeth shal be deed, if that they may hym hente!
       Whan they han goon nat fully half a mile,

250   Right as they wolde han troden over a stile,

251   An oold man and a povre with hem mette.
       This olde man ful mekely hem grette,

253   And seyde thus, "Now, lordes, God yow see!"

∼

228/ avysed = forewarned. 234/ Herkneth = Listen; been al ones = are united. 237/ sleen = kill. 240/ hir trouthes plight = pledged their word. 247/ torente = ripped. 248/ hente = catch. 250/ stile = steps over a fence. 251/ An oold man and a povre = a poor old man. 253/ God yow see = God bless you.

Disrespectfully, the three inebriated rioters
Proceeded to curse and debated the guy's words:
"I've heard," stated the first, "enough about Death!
Every town is gripped in his clutches without rest.
What is it about this foe that's so scary? Please!
If an adversary bleeds and breathes the same air as me,
I can bury it! See, fellas, what I'm tellin'
You is: Death is a villain, and the rest is irrelevant,
So let's go kill him!" When he'd said his piece,
The rest agreed, and the three friends hit the streets,
And went to seek their destiny, and provoke a confrontation,
In a drunken rage, hoping Death would come and face them.
Their intoxication made them sure of their purpose,
And fed the infernal furnace of their courage, a kernel
Nourished by these three murderous wretches in denial.

 Less than a mile into their quest to put Death on trial,
They met this guy all wrapped in bandages,
An old handicapped man, with disadvantages,

The proudeste of thise riotoures three
255   Answerde agayn, "What, carl, with sory grace,
256   Why artow al forwrapped save thy face?
Why lyvestow so longe in so greet age?"
258   This olde man gan looke in his visage,
And seyde thus: "For I ne kan nat fynde
260   A man, though that I walked into Ynde,
Neither in citee ne in no village,
That wolde chaunge his youthe for myn age;
263   And therfore moot I han myn age stille,
As longe tyme as it is Goddes wille.
Ne Deeth, allas, ne wol nat han my lyf.
266   Thus walke I lyk a resteles kaityf,
And on the ground, which is my moodres gate,
I knokke with my staf bothe erly and late,
269   And seye, 'Leeve mooder, leet me in!
Lo how I vanysshe, flessh and blood and skyn!
Allas, whan shul my bones been at reste?
272   Mooder, with yow wolde I chaunge my cheste,
That in my chambre longe tyme hath be,
274   Ye, for an heyre-clowt to wrappe me.'
275   But yet to me she wol nat do that grace,
276   For which ful pale and welked is my face.
But, sires, to yow it is no curteisye
To speken to an old man vileynye,
279   But he trespasse in word, or elles in dede.

~

255/ carl = fellow; sory grace = bad luck. 256/ forwrapped = wrapped up. 258/ visage =
face. 260/ Ynde = India. 263/ moot = must. 266/ kaityf = wretch. 269/ Leeve = Dear.
272/ cheste = fortune. 274/ heyre-clowt = hair-cloth. 275/ grace = favour. 276/ welked
= wrinkled. 279/ But = Unless.

And the three friends examined his bleeding flesh,
And demanded he tell them how he was cheating Death.
Seeming perplexed, the old man responded with soft words,
And said, "I walk the earth like a creature God has cursed!
My lot is the worst and most desperate place to be;
I pray faithfully every day for Death to take me,
Waiting patiently, and someday he will arrive,
But in the meantime, until I die, I'm still alive."

"In Hooly Writ ye may yourself wel rede:

281 'Agayns an oold man, hoor upon his heed,

282 Ye sholde arise;' wherfore I yeve yow reed,

Ne dooth unto an oold man noon harm now,

Namoore than that ye wolde men did to yow

In age, if that ye so longe abyde.

And God be with yow where ye go or ryde.

I moote go thider, as I have to go."

288   "Nay, olde cherl, by God, thou shalt nat so,"

Seyde this oother hasardour anon;

"Thou partest nat so lightly, by Seint John!

291 Thou spak right now of thilke traytour Deeth,

That in this contree alle oure freendes sleeth.

Have heer my trouthe, as thou art his espye,

294 Telle where he is, or thou shalt it abye,

By God and by the hooly sacrament!

296 For soothly thou art oon of his assent

To sleen us yonge folk, thou false theef!"

298   "Now, sires," quod he, "if that ye be so leef

To fynde Deeth, turne up this croked wey,

For in that grove I lafte hym, by my fey,

Under a tree, and there he wole abyde;

302 Noght for your boost he wole him no thyng hyde.

303 Se ye that ook? Right ther ye shal hym fynde.

God save yow that boghte agayn mankynde,

And yow amende!" Thus seyde this olde man;

∼

281/ hoor = hoarfrost (wispy white hair.) 282/ I yeve yow reed = I advise you. 288/ cherl = fool. 291/ thilke = that. 294/ it abye = be punished for it. 296/ oon of his assent = one of his henchmen. 298/ leef = eager. 302/ boost = boast. 303/ ook = oak tree.

In a burst of ill-advised pride, the first
Of the three rioters replied, "This guy
Is a spy, or worse! I guess Death is his master,
And gives him everlasting life forever after,
A benevolent benefactor, perhaps, to have protecting you,
But nothing gets a confession faster than weapons do!"
And stepping to this old man with mindless threats,
They demanded he tell them where they could find Death.
"Find Death?" laughed the old man, "Perhaps you will;
He lives under that tree on that grassy hill."

And everich of thise riotoures ran
Til he cam to that tree, and ther they founde
308 Of floryns fyne of gold ycoyned rounde
309 Wel ny an eighte busshels, as hem thoughte.
No lenger thanne after Deeth they soughte,
But ech of hem so glad was of that sighte,
For that the floryns been so faire and brighte,
That doun they sette hem by this precious hoord.
The worste of hem, he spak the firste word.
  "Bretheren," quod he, "taak kepe what I seye;
316 My wit is greet, though that I bourde and pleye.
317 This tresor hath Fortune unto us yeven,
In myrthe and joliftee oure lyf to lyven,
And lightly as it comth, so wol we spende.
320 Ey, Goddes precious dignitee! Who wende
To-day that we sholde han so fair a grace?
But myghte this gold be caried fro this place
Hoom to myn hous, or elles unto youres –
For wel ye woot that al this gold is oures –
325 Thanne were we in heigh felicitee.
But trewely, by daye it may nat bee;
Men wolde seyn that we were theves stronge,
328 And for oure owene tresor doon us honge.
This tresor moste ycaried be by nyghte
As wisely and as slyly as it myghte.

∿

308/ floryns = gold coins. 309/ eighte busshels = eight bushels (one bushel equals 36.4 litres). 316/ bourde = joke. 317/ tresor = treasure; yeven = given. 320/ Who wende = Who knew. 325/ heigh felicitee = great happiness. 328/ doon us honge = have us hanged.

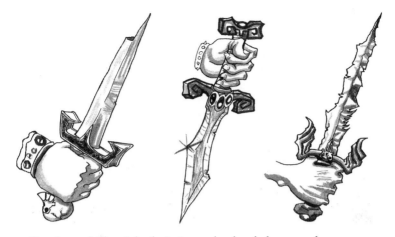

Ready to kill, with their jagged-edged daggers drawn,

The three aggravated braggarts staggered up the lawn,

And without dragging on while the story is told,

Beneath the tree they found a bag filled with glorious gold.

The hoard was more than forty-fold their wildest dreams,

And they smiled like demons, hatching violent schemes,

While the steam from their previous plan was dissipated;

They were so fixated on the gold, it just abated,

And the search for death was traded for work of greater urgency.

Now the worst of the three had the first words to speak,

And said, "Certainly it seems Fortune gave us this gold

To save us from having to work and slave in the cold;

But Fortune favours the bold, and to spend this treasure

On endless pleasures, to begin we'd better

Take preventative measures, 'cause if the switch from poor to rich

Is too disproportionate, then law enforcement will get

Suspicious of how we afforded it, and then we'll pay the price,

So let's sit tight and play this right:

See, we'll wait 'til late at night, and if all is not lost,

Under the cover of darkness we can haul this all off;

331   "Wherfore I rede that cut among us alle
       Be drawe, and lat se wher the cut wol falle,
333   And he that hath the cut, with herte blithe
334   Shal renne to the towne, and that ful swithe,
335   And brynge us breed and wyn ful prively;
       And two of us shul kepen subtilly
       This tresor wel; and if he wol nat tarie,
       Whan it is nyght, we wol this tresor carie,
       By oon assent, where as us thynketh best."
       That oon of hem the cut broghte in his fest,
       And bad hem drawe and looke where it wol falle;
       And it fil on the yongeste of hem alle,
       And forth toward the toun he wente anon.
       And al so soone as that he was gon,
       That oon of hem spak thus unto that oother,
       "Thou knowest wel thou art my sworen brother;
       Thy profit wol I telle thee anon.
       Thou woost wel that oure felawe is agon,
       And heere is gold, and that ful greet plentee,
350   That shal departed been among us thre.
       But nathelees, if I kan shape it so
       That it departed were among us two,
353   Hadde I nat doon a freendes torn to thee?"
       That oother answerde, "I noot hou that may be;
       He woot how that the gold is with us tweye;
       What shal we doon? What shal we to hym seye?"

∾

331/ I rede that cut among us alle = I suggest we draw lots. 333/ blithe = carefree. 334/ swithe = swift. 335/ prively = secretly. 350/ departed been = be divided. 353/ freendes torn = friend's turn.

"But for now we'll draw straws, since we've got a lot of time,
And one of us can run off and buy a bottle of wine."
  The others thought the plot was fine, and trusted its wit,
And the youngest among them drew the cut stick,
And rushed to get booze so this could be celebrated,
As the other two plotted and whispered while they waited.
The worst delegated again and said, "Listen friend,
Let's invent a way to get paid a greater dividend.
In the end we can each have half this treasure,
If we get our acts together now and take drastic measures."
The other asked incredulously, "How can this be,
When right now we're bound to split the treasure by three?"

357   "Shal it be conseil?" seyde the firste shrewe,
        "And I shal tellen in a wordes fewe
        What we shal doon, and bryngen it wel aboute."
        "I graunte," quod that oother, "out of doute,
361   That by my trouthe I shal thee nat biwreye."
        "Now," quod the firste, "thou woost wel we be tweye,
        And two of us shul strenger be than oon.
        Looke whan that he is set, that right anoon
365   Arys as though thou woldest with hym pleye,
366   And I shal ryve hym thurgh the sydes tweye,
        Whil that thou strogelest with hym as in game,
        And with thy daggere looke thou do the same;
369   And thanne shal al this gold departed be,
        My deere freend, bitwixen me and thee.
        Thanne may we bothe oure lustes all fulfille,
        And pleye at dees right at oure owene wille."
373   And thus acorded been thise shrewes tweye
        To sleen the thridde, as ye han herd me seye.
            This yongeste, which that wente unto the toun,
376   Ful ofte in herte he rolleth up and doun
        The beautee of thise floryns newe and brighte.
        "O lorde," quod he, "if so were that I myghte
        Have al this tresor to my-self allone,
380   Ther is no man that lyveth under the trone
        Of God that sholde lyve so murye as I."

⁓

357/ conseil = agreed. 361/ biwreye = betray. 365/ Arys = Arise. 366/ ryve = stab. 369/ departed be = be divided. 373/ shrewes = villains. 376/ rolleth up and doun = turns over in his mind. 380/ trone = throne.

"Let's see," said the first with a savage laugh,

"Just imagine the third man gets stabbed in the back.

Now, I'm bad at math, addition and subtraction,

But don't we get to split the treasure in half then?

You distract him when he comes back with the wine,

And I'll make sure our young friend gets stabbed in the spine.

The first attack is mine, then you back me up;

Just slash his gut, and add the last cut

To our friend's bad luck." And because of his greed,

The other agreed to this covetous deed.

By the trunk of this tree they waited to pounce,

While the youngest of the three made his way into town,

Weighted down by the thought of a whole lotta gold,

Which inaudibly caught ahold of him and gnawed at his soul.

382   And atte laste the feend, oure enemy,
383   Putte in his thought that he sholde poyson beye,
      With which he myghte sleen hise felawes tweye;
      For-why, the feend foond hym in swich lyvynge
386   That he hadde leve hem to sorwe brynge.
387   For this was outrely his fulle entente,
      To sleen hem bothe, and nevere to repente.
      And forth he gooth, no lenger wolde he tarie,
390   Into the toun unto a pothecarie,
      And preyde hym that he hym wolde selle
392   Som poysoun, that he myghte hise rattes quelle;
393   And eek ther was a polcat in his hawe,
394   That, as he seyde, hise capouns hadde yslawe;
395   And fayn he wolde wreke hym, if he myghte,
      On vermyn that destroyed hym by nyghte.
           The pothecarie answerde, "And thou shalt have
      A thyng that, al so God my soule save,
      In al this world ther is no creature
400   That eten or dronken hath of this confiture
401   Noght but the montance of a corn of whete,
402   That he ne shal his lif anon forlete;
403   Ye, sterve he shal, and that in lasse while
404   Than thou wolt goon a paas nat but a mile,
      This poysoun is so strong and violent."

~

382/ the feend = the devil. 383/ beye = buy. 386/ hadde leve = was free. 387/ outrely =
utterly. 390/ pothecarie = pharmacist. 392/ quelle = kill. 393/ polcat = weasel; hawe =
yard. 394/ capouns = chickens; yslawe = killed. 395/ fayn = gladly; wreke hym = avenge
himself. 400/ confiture = concoction. 401/ montance = amount; corn of whete = grain
of wheat. 402/ forlete = forfeit. 403/ sterve = die; lasse while = less time. 404/ a paas =
to walk.

He wanted it so bad he could taste it;
Any part of it shared was like a part of it wasted,
And he harboured a hatred in his heart, and decided
Never to let this precious treasure get divided;
And guided by the shine of carnal greed,
He went to buy the wine, and then to the pharmacy,
And, sounding harmless, he asked for this black ointment
That he'd seen used in the past as rat poison,

406   This cursed man hath in his hond yhent
407   This poysoun in a box, and sith he ran
        Into the nexte strete unto a man,
        And borwed of hym large botels thre;
        And in the two his poyson poured he;
        The thridde he kepte clene for his drynke.
412   For al the nyght he shoop hym for to swynke
        In cariynge of the gold out of that place.
        And whan this riotour, with sory grace,
        Hadde filed with wyn his grete botels thre,
        To hise felawes agayn repaireth he.
            What nedeth it to sermone of it moore?
        For right as they hadde cast his deeth bifoore,
        Right so they han him slayn, and that anon.
        And whan that this was doon, thus spak that oon:
        "Now lat us sitte and drynke, and make us merie,
        And afterward we wol his body berie."
423   And with that word it happed hym, par cas,
        To take the botel ther the poysoun was,
        And drank, and yaf his felawe drynke also,
426   For which anon they storven bothe two.
427   But certes, I suppose that Avycen
428   Wroot nevere in no canoun, ne in no fen,
429   Mo wonder signes of empoisonyng
        Than hadde thise wrecches two, er hir endyng.

~

406/ yhent = taken. 407/ sith = swift. 412/ shoop hym for to swynke = intended to work.
423/ par cas = by chance. 426/ storven = died. 427/ Avycen = Arabic medical writer.
428/ canoun = book; fen = chapter. 429/ Mo wonder signes = More incredible symptoms.

Meaning to trap his boys into drinking tainted wine,

While at the same time thinking, "The game is mine!"

Another famous line that became his last words,

'Cause when he got back the others acted first,

And stabbed him mercilessly with vicious blows,

And since the kid was quick to give up the ghost,

They proposed a victory toast to the crime,

And both enjoyed a glass of the poisoned wine,

And collapsed, going blind, in a fit of convulsions,

Which halted their pulses and ultimately resulted in

Their spirits' expulsions,

Thus ended been thise homycides two,
And eek the false empoysoner also.

    O cursed synne of alle cursednesse!
O traytours homycide, O wikkednesse!
O glotonye, luxurie, and hasardrye!
Thou blasphemour of Crist with vileynye
437   And othes grete, of usage and of pride!
Allas, mankynde, how may it bitide
That to thy Creatour which that the wroghte,
And with His precious herte-blood thee boghte,
Thou art so fals and so unkynde, allas?
Now, goode men, God foryeve yow youre trespas,
443   And ware yow fro the synne of avarice!
444   Myn hooly pardoun may yow alle warice,
445   So that ye offre nobles or sterlynges,
Or elles silver broches, spoones, rynges;
Boweth youre heed under this hooly bulle!
Cometh up, ye wyves, offreth of youre wolle!
Youre names I entre heer in my rolle anon;
Into the blisse of hevene shul ye gon.
451   I yow assoille by myn heigh power,
Yow that wol offre, as clene and eek as cleer
As ye were born. – And lo, sires, thus I preche.
454   And Jesu Crist, that is oure soules leche,
So graunte yow his pardoun to receyve,
For that is best, I wol yow nat deceyve.

~

437/ usage = habit. 443/ ware yow fro = protect you from. 444/ warice = absolve.
445/ nobles or sterlynges = gold or silver. 451/ assoille = pardon. 454/ leche = healer.

And because of their greed,
They did indeed find Death under the tree.

The End.

AFTERWARD

"But sires, o word forgat I in my tale:

458   I have relikes and pardoun in my male,

As faire as any man in Engelond,

460   Whiche were me yeven by the popes hond.

If any of yow wole of devocioun

Offren, and han myn absolucioun,

Com forth anon, and kneleth heere adoun,

And mekely receyveth my pardoun;

465   Or elles taketh pardoun as ye wende,

Al newe and fressh at every miles ende,

So that ye offren alwey newe, and newe

468   Nobles or pens, whiche that be goode and trewe.

It is an honour to everich that is heer

470   That ye mowe have a suffisant pardoneer

471   T'assoille yow in contree as ye ryde,

For aventures whiche that may bityde.

473   Paraventure ther may fallen oon or two

Doun of his hors and breke his nekke atwo.

475   Look which a seuretee is it to yow alle

That I am in youre felaweship yfalle,

That may assoille yow, bothe moore and lasse,

Whan that the soule shal fro the body passe.

479   I rede that oure Hoost heere shal bigynne,

For he is moost envoluped in synne.

Com forth, sire Hoost, and offre first anon,

≈

458/ male = bag.   460/ me yeven = given to me.   465/ as ye wende = as you ride. 468/ Nobles or pens = Gold or copper coins.   470/ suffisant = capable.   471/ T'assoille yow = To pardon your sins.   473/ Paraventure = Perhaps.   475/ seuretee = safeguard. 479/ rede = say.

482 And thou shalt kisse my relikes everychon,

483 Ye, for a grote! Unbokele anon thy purs."

   "Nay, nay," quod he, "thanne have I Cristes curs!

485 Lat be," quod he, "it shal nat be, so theech!

486 Thou woldest make me kisse thyn olde breech,

   And swere it were a relyk of a seint,

488 Though it were with thy fundement depeint!

489 But by the croys which that Seint Eleyne fond,

490 I wolde I hadde thy coillons in myn hond

491 In stide of relikes or of seintuarie.

   Lat kutte hem of, I wol thee helpe hem carie;

493 They shul be shryned in an hogges toord!"

   This Pardoner answerde nat a word;

495 So wrooth he was, no word ne wolde he seye.

   "Now," quod oure Hoost, "I wol no lenger pleye

   With thee, ne with noon oother angry man."

   But right anon the worthy Knyght bigan,

   Whan that he saugh that al the peple lough,

   "Namoore of this, for it is right ynough!

   Sir Pardoner, be glad and myrie of cheere;

   And ye, sir Hoost, that been to me so deere,

   I prey yow that ye kisse the Pardoner;

   And Pardoner, I prey thee, drawe thee neer,

   And, as we diden, lat us laughe and pley."

   Anon they kiste, and ryden forth hir weye.

Here is ended the Pardoners Tale.

~

482/ everychon = every one. 483/ grote = silver coin. 485/ so theech = I swear. 486/ breech = underpants. 488/ with thy fundement depeint = stained with excrement (skidmarks). 489/ croys = cross; Seint Eleyne = St. Helen. 490/ coillons = testicles. 491/ seintuarie = box for relics. 493/ shryned = enshrined; toord = turd. 495/ wrooth = angry.

THE WIFE OF BATH'S TALE

The Wife of Bath is the most dynamic personality among the pilgrims, and is often considered Chaucer's favourite because of the care he takes in developing her character. The Wife of Bath's autobiographical *Prologue*, which is more than twice as long as her *Tale*, chronicles her past relationships and establishes her credentials as an expert on questions of marriage and the battle of the sexes: "Experience, though noon auctoritee / Were in this world, is right ynogh for me / To speke of wo that is in mariage" (Personal experience, though not any written authority in the world, gives me the right to speak about the pain of marriage). When we meet her in *The Canterbury Tales*, the Wife of Bath has already been married and widowed five times, and is on the lookout for husband number six: "Welcome the sixte, whan that evere he shal." Despite her dismissal of written "auctoritee" in the opening line, the Wife of Bath's amorous autobiography is punctuated with classical and scriptural references justifying her overt sexuality and colourful background, exposing her pride and also her sensitivity to the subject:

> For hadde God commanded maydenhede,
> Thanne hadde he dampned weddyng with the dede.
> And certes, if ther were no seed ysowe,
> Virginitee, thane wherof shoulde it growe?

> (If God had commanded virginity,
> Then he would have condemned marriage.
> And surely, if there were no seed sown,
> Then where would virginity come from?)

The Wife of Bath uses logical and scriptural arguments to flaunt her sexual empowerment while disarming her potential critics with their own weapons: "In wyfhod I wol use myn instrument / As freely as my Makere hath it sent." In this case "instrument" is more than just a quaint euphemism, since the Wife of Bath constantly uses her sexuality as a tool to achieve her goals: social status, wealth, and especially freedom.

The Wife of Bath's first three husbands were "goode men, and riche, and olde," and she married the first of them when she was only twelve. She doesn't differentiate between them or give details about their individual personalities, since they all represented the exact same challenge and opportunity in her eyes. Despite the authority a wealthy old man could potentially wield over a teenaged bride, the Wife of Bath explains how she managed to completely dominate her first three husbands using sex as leverage. Whenever there was a conflict or an argument between them, she would simply deny them sex: "I wolde no lenger in the bed abyde, / If that I felte his arm over my side, / Til he had maad his raunson unto me." The Wife of Bath's ransom could be whatever she chose, but the result was that she "hadde hem hooly in myn hond" (had them completely in her power).

The relationship between wealth and sexuality displayed in the Wife of Bath's *Prologue* also provokes a constant dialogue in rap music: the players vs. the gold-diggers. This dialogue is the inspiration for Jay-Z's song "Can I Get A ... ," in which he asks, "If I was broke, would you want me? ... If we couldn't see the sun risin' on the shore of Thailand, / Would you ride then?" and Amil answers, "Never test my patience / Nigga, I'm high-maintenance, / High class, and if you ain't rollin', bypass!" The Wife of Bath has no problem describing her relationships in similarly stark terms: "What shoulde I taken keep hem for to plese, / But it were for my profit and myn ese?" (Why should I bother to please them if not for my profit or my enjoyment?) There is certainly an element of prostitution in this arrangement, but the Wife of Bath is unrepentant and capable of answering any moral condescension with intelligent argument and a counter-charge of hypocrisy. The same sexually liberated and self-empowered attitude is the basis of Lil' Kim and Foxy Brown's "pussy is power" rap personas, which they present as a form of realism: "No romance without finance." The Wife of Bath states her case in equally pragmatic terms: "With empty hand men may none hawkes lure." These observations partially have their roots in biology, since the division of labour has always required relationships to be accompanied by financial arrangements. Overstatement of this case is where the conflict arises, leading to Kanye West's acute appraisal: "Now I ain't sayin' she a gold-digger, but ... " in which the "but" says as much as all of the other words combined.

The Wife of Bath's initial strategy died with her first three husbands, but as she got older and less able to exploit her allure she also got increasingly wealthy, inheriting a fortune each time she was widowed. As a result she was financially independent at a relatively young age, and had the freedom to travel Europe and go on pilgrimages, run a cloth-making business, and generally enjoy as much autonomy as a woman could possibly have in the

Middle Ages. Her fourth husband was her equal, but was unfaithful, and her relationship with him was a reciprocal game of jealousy and provocation. She repaid him for his adultery by making his life miserable and had the last laugh simply by outliving him: "By God, in erthe I was his purgatorie, / For which I hope his soule be in glorie."

The Wife of Bath's fifth husband was a poor student she flirted with while her fourth was still alive, and he was the only one she married out of pure attraction: "I trowe I loved hym best, for that he / Was of his love daungerous to me" (I think I loved him best because he played hard-to-get). At her fourth husband's funeral the Wife of Bath caught a glimpse of this young student and was smitten: "[M]e thoughte he hadde a paire / Of legges and of feet so clene and faire / That al myn herte I yaf unto his hoold." This physical infatuation with his beautiful legs wasn't instantly reciprocated, since she was forty by this time and he was only twenty, and he was able to exploit this attraction in the same way that she had exploited her first husbands. Once they were married he tried to control her in various ways, criticizing her, limiting her freedom, and reading constantly from his "book of wikked wyves," a collection of stories about women who brought their husbands to ruin. This came to a head when she ripped pages out of the book and he hit her so hard she went deaf in one ear. Husband number five was so sorry for hitting her that he reformed himself and said, "Myn owene trewe wyf, / Do as thee lust the terme of al thy lyf" (My own true wife, do as you wish for the rest of your life). This is the Wife of Bath's happy ending, and she claims that afterwards "He yaf me al the bridel in myn hond" (He let me take the reins in my hand) and there was always peace between them, at least until he died and left her a widow once again.

The Wife of Bath's Tale is foreshadowed by her life story. Her tale is an Arthurian legend, in which one of King Arthur's knights commits a rape and is sentenced to death. Queen Gwenyvere gives the knight one chance to redeem his crime by going on a quest to discover what women desire most of all. The knight faces a series of trials that teach him to respect women and let go of the desire to control them, much like the transformation of the Wife of Bath's fifth husband. The Wife of Bath has established her credentials: "Of five husbondes scoleiyng am I" (I was schooled by five husbands), and the tale is a vehicle for delivering the central message of her life experience: that men will only be happy when they accept the dominance of their women. This proto-feminist propaganda is remarkable for its modern thinking, but the Wife of Bath is not advocating for real social equality. Instead she is proposing a domestic sphere in which women will have total dominance to compensate for their social disadvantage. The idea that relationships can exist in a state of perfect equilibrium is a modern construction, a pipe dream that the Wife of Bath dismisses as logically impossible: "Oon of us two moste bowen, doutelees, / And sith a man is moore reasonable / Than woman is, ye moste been suffrable" (One of us has to submit, of course, and since men are more reasonable than women, you must be tolerant). Recent psychological studies have borne this wisdom out, demonstrating a statistical link between a man's ability to accept his wife's influence (Yes, dear) and their relationship's chance of success. The Wife of Bath has always treated this principle as a matter of course, asserting her dominance over whoever she happens to be married to: "Upon his flesh, whil that I am his wyf, / I have the power durynge al my lyf."

The Wife of Bath's Tale

In th'olde dayes of the Kyng Arthour,
Of which that Britons speken greet honour,
3   All was this land fulfild of fayerye.
The elf-queene, with hir joly compaignye,
5   Daunced ful ofte in many a grene mede.
This was the olde opinion, as I rede;
I speke of manye hundred yeres ago.
But now kan no man se none elves mo,
For now the grete charitee and prayeres
10 Of lymytours and othere hooly freres,
That serchen every lond and every streem,
12 As thikke as motes in the sonne-beem,
13 Blessynge halles, chambres, kichenes, boures,
14 Citees, burghes, castels, hye toures,
15 Thropes, bernes, shipnes, dayeryes –
This maketh that ther been no fayeryes.
17 For ther as wont to walken was an elf,
18 Ther walketh now the lymytour hymself
19 In undermeles and in morwenynges,
20 And seyth his matyns and his hooly thynges
21 As he gooth in his lymytacioun.
Wommen may go saufly up and doun.
In every bussh or under every tree
24 Ther is noon oother incubus but he,
25 And he ne wol doon hem but dishonour.

≈

3/ fulfild of fayerye = filled with fairies. 5/ mede = clearing. 10/ lymytours = friars
who beg in certain areas; freres = friars. 12/ motes = specks of dust. 13/ boures =
bedrooms. 14/ burghes = boroughs. 15/ Thropes = Towns; shipnes = stables; dayeryes =
dairies. 17/ wont = was once the custom. 18/ lymytour = friar. 19/ undermeles = late
mornings; morwenynges = early mornings. 20/ matyns = prayers. 21/ lymytacioun =
prescribed area for begging. 24/ incubus = spirit that seduces women. 25/ ne wol doon
hem but = will do them nothing but.

Back in the days of the dark ages,
When King Arthur made his mark, and courageous
Knights—with tight young pages—embarked
On outrageous quests and fought for ladies' hearts,
The shady parts among the hills and knolls
Were filled with fairies, elves, and trolls,
And dwarves were known to dwell in holes,
And nymphs to succour willing souls.
These thrilling folds, in time, emerged as
Badly out of line with churches,
Which cursed all fairy-kind and purged us,
To cleanse us of our primal urges.
To try and discourage us from growing tense,
The hills were filled with "holy men,"
And now women could lie alone, content
Without the old incubi, only them.

And so bifel that this kyng Arthour
27   Hadde in his hous a lusty bacheler,
28   That on a day cam ridynge fro ryver,
And happed that, allone as she was born,
He saugh a mayde walkynge hym biforn,
31   Of whiche mayde anon, maugree hir heed,
32   By verray force he rafte hir maydenhed;
33   For which oppressioun was swich clamour
34   And swich pursute unto the kyng Arthour,
35   That dampned was this knyght for to be deed,
By cours of lawe, and sholde han lost his heed –
37   Paraventure, swich was the statut tho –
But that the queene and othere ladyes mo
39   So longe preyeden the kyng of grace,
Til he his lyf hym graunted in the place,
And yaf hym to the queene al at hir wille,
42   To chese wheither she wolde hym save or spille.
    The queene thanketh the kyng with al hir myght,
And after this thus spak she to the knyght,
Whan that she saugh hir tyme, upon a day:
46   "Thou standest yet," quod she, "in swich array
47   That of thy lyf yet hastow no suretee.
I grante thee lyf, if thou kanst tellen me
What thyng is it that wommen moost desiren.
Be war, and keep thy nekke-boon from iren!

∾

27/ lusty bacheler = young knight. 28/ ridynge fro ryver = bird hunting. 31/ maugree hir heed = despite her resistance. 32/ rafte hir maydenhed = took her virginity. 33/ swich clamour = such an outcry. 34/ pursute = complaint. 35/ dampned = condemned. 37/ Paraventure = Perhaps; swich = such; statut tho = law then. 39/ preyeden the kyng of grace = begged the king for mercy. 42/ spille = kill. 46/ swich array = such a position. 47/ suretee = assurance.

And so it went that from King Arthur's court,

A strong young warrior marched his horse,

And through the woods he charted his course,

And he met a young girl in the heart of the forest;

And with heartless force, in less than a minute he

Committed an act of criminal obscenity,

And since there was no one else in the vicinity,

No one prevented him from taking her virginity.

    This sinister deed was so repugnant

That the knight was thrown in the castle dungeon

To await judgment, but what should be done with him?

King Arthur favoured capital punishment,

A tactic of governments that live in fear,

But the queen, Gwenevere, whispered in his ear:

"My Lord, his remorse is not insincere;

I suggest we let the poor kid live a year.

In fact, give him here; let *me* deal with him."

And King Arthur granted her appeal, a decision

That revealed he was a man of vision and real wisdom,

That is, a husband able to still listen.

    And from his steel prison the knight was brought

To the queen, who said, "Boy, you're in a tight spot:

Your guilt is certain, but your life is not.

Your head might head right to the chopping block,

Or you might just walk, and get clemency,

But only if you can tell me what women need.

"And if thou kanst nat tellen it anon,

Yet shal I yeve thee leve for to gon

53   A twelf-month and a day, to seche and leere

An answere suffisant in this mateere;

55   And suretee wol I han, er that thou pace,

56   Thy body for to yelden in this place."

57   Wo was this knyght, and sorwefully he siketh;

But what! He may nat do al as hym liketh.

59   And at the laste he chees hym for to wende,

And come agayn right at the yeres ende,

61   With swich answere as God wolde hym purveye;

And taketh his leve, and wendeth forth his weye.

63   He seketh every hous and every place

Where as he hopeth for to fynde grace

To lerne what thyng wommen loven moost,

66   But he ne koude arryven in no coost

Wher as he myghte fynde in this mateere

68   Two creatures accordynge in-feere.

Somme seyde wommen loven best richesse,

70   Somme seyde honour, somme seyde jolynesse,

Somme riche array, somme seyden lust abedde,

And oftetyme to be wydwe and wedde.

Somme seyde that oure hertes been moost esed

Whan that we been yflatered and yplesed.

~

53/ seche and leere = search and learn.   55/ suretee = your promise.   56/ yelden = surrender.   57/ siketh = sighed.   59/ chees hym for to wende = decided to depart. 61/ purveye = provide.   63/ seketh = searched.   66/ coost = coast.   68/ accordynge in-feere = in agreement.   70/ jolynesse = happiness.

"Answer me what it is every woman's tendency
To want, and I'll suspend sentencing.
Now let your penance bring you some cheer;
Come here again after one year,
And then I want to hear from you some clear
Response; now, I suggest you run, dear."
And Gwenevere gave him his walking papers,
And the knight thanked her, and set off on this caper
To save his life, and began to talk to his neighbours'
Wives, and got them to list off their favourites,
Like a census taker; he took to the streets,
And spent the year asking every woman he'd meet:
"If you could have just one thing, what would it be?"

75   He gooth ful ny the sothe, I wol nat lye,

      A man shal wynne us best with flaterye,

      And with attendance and with bisynesse

78   Been we ylymed, bothe moore and lesse.

         And somme seyen, how that we loven best

80   For to be free, and do right as us lest,

81   And that no man repreve us of oure vice,

82   But seye that we be wise, and nothyng nyce.

      For trewely ther is noon of us alle,

84   If any wight wol clawe us on the galle,

85   That we nel kike, for he seith us sooth;

86   Assay, and he shal fynde it that so dooth.

      For, be we never so vicious withinne,

      We wol been holden wise, and clene of synne.

         And somme seyn that greet delit han we

90   For to been holden stable and eek secree,

91   And in o purpos stedefastly to dwelle,

92   And nat biwreye thyng that men us telle.

93   But that tale is nat worth a rake-stele,

94   Pardee, we wommen konne no thyng hele.

95   Witnesse on Myda, – wol ye heere the tale?

96   Ovyde, amonges othere thynges smale,

97   Seyde Myda hadde, under his longe heres,

      Growynge upon his heed two asses eres,

      The whiche vice he hydde as he best myghte,

      Ful subtilly from every mannes sighte,

≈

75/ gooth ful ny the sothe = goes near the truth. 78/ ylymed = caught. 80/ as us lest = as we like. 81/ repreve = reproach. 82/ and nothyng nyce = and not stupid. 84/ clawe us on the galle = touch a sore spot. 85/ nel kike, for he seith us sooth = will not kick, if he tells us the truth. 86/ Assay = Test. 90/ eek secree = also secret. 91/ o = one. 92/ biwreye thyng = betray anything. 93/ rake-stele = rake handle. 94/ hele = hold secret. 95/ Myda = Midas. 96/ Ovyde = Ovid. 97/ heres = hairs.

But you wouldn't believe the diversity;

They just couldn't agree; once asked,

Some said this, and some said that.

They said: confidence, compliments, comfort, class,

Compassion, fashion, or for their passion to come back,

That, save his wyf, ther wiste of it namo.

He loved hire moost and trusted hir also;

He preyede hire that to no creature

104   She sholde tellen of his disfigure.

    She swoor him nay, for al this world to wynne,

She nolde do that vileynye or synne,

To make hir housbonde han so foul a name.

She nolde nat telle it for hir owene shame.

109   But nathelees, hir thoughte that she dyde,

110   That she so longe sholde a conseil hyde;

111   Hir thoughte it swal so soore aboute hir herte

112   That nedely som word hir moste asterte;

113   And sith she dorste telle it to no man,

114   Doun to a mareys faste by she ran;

Til she cam there, hir herte was a fyre,

116   And as a bitore bombleth in the myre,

She leyde hir mouth unto the water doun:

118   "Biwreye me nat, thou water, with thy soun,"

Quod she, "to thee I telle it and namo;

Myn housbonde hath longe asses erys two!

Now is myn herte al hool; now is it oute.

I myghte no lenger kepe it, out of doute."

Heere may ye se, thogh we a tyme abyde,

Yet out it moot; we kan no conseil hyde.

The remenant of the tale, if ye wol heere,

126   Redeth Ovyde, and ther ye may it leere.

104/ disfigure = disfigurement. 109/ dyde = would die. 110/ a conseil hyde = keep a
secret. 111/ swal so soore = swelled so painfully. 112/ nedely ... asterte = some word
had to escape. 113/ dorste = dared. 114/ mareys faste by = marsh near by. 116/ bitore
bombleth in the myre = bird cries in the marsh. 118/ Biwreye = Betray; soun = sound.
126/ leere = learn.

And as the months passed, the knight realized
That he would soon be deceased unless he arrived
At a conclusion, and he badly needed to be advised,
'Cause with all this confusion he could only theorize,
And he wouldn't be alive to end the debate;

This knyght, of which my tale is specially,
Whan that he saugh he myghte nat come therby –
This is to seye, what wommen love moost –
Withinne his brest ful sorweful was the goost.
131   But hoom he gooth; he myghte nat sojourne;
The day was come that homward moste he tourne.
And in his wey it happed hym to ryde,
In al this care, under a forest syde,
Wher as he saugh upon a daunce go
Of ladyes foure and twenty, and yet mo;
137   Toward the whiche daunce he drow ful yerne,
In hope that som wysdom sholde he lerne.
But certeinly, er he came fully there,
140   Vanysshed was this daunce, he nyste where.
No creature saugh he that bar lyf,
142   Save on the grene he saugh sittynge a wyf –
143   A fouler wight ther may no man devyse.
144   Agayn the knyght this olde wyf gan ryse,
145   And seyde, "Sire knyght, heer forth ne lith no wey.
146   Tel me what that ye seken, by your fey!
147   Paraventure it may the bettre be;
148   Thise olde folk kan muchel thyng," quod she.

~

131/ sojourne = delay. 137/ drow ful yerne = approached eagerly. 140/ nyste = didn't know.
142/ wyf = woman. 143/ wight = creature; devyse = imagine. 144/ Agayn = Towards.
145/ heer forth ... wey = there is no path here. 146/ by your fey = by your faith.
147/ Paraventure = Perhaps. 148/ kan muchel thyng = know many things.

And after eleven months and twenty-six days,
He still wasn't sure what he intended to say,
As he headed back to the court to be handed his fate,
And what could stand in his way? On the road home,
The knight ran into an ugly old crone,
Whose face was so wrinkled he thought it had no bones,
And as he passed, she heard a low moan
And asked, "So alone, without any company?
Something's eating you, boy; anyone can see,
But what could upset someone so young and sweet?
It's gonna be okay, son; you can come to me
If you need comforting."

149   "My leeve mooder," quod this knyght, "certeyn

150   I nam but deed but if that I kan seyn

      What thyng it is that wommen moost desire.

152   Koude ye me wisse, I wolde wel quite youre hire."

153   "Plight me thy trouthe heere in myn hand," quod she,

154   "The nexte thyng that I requere thee,

      Thou shalt it do, if it lye in thy myght,

      And I wol telle it yow er it be nyght."

      "Have heer my trouthe," quod the knyght, "I grante."

158   "Thanne," quod she, "I dar me wel avante

159   Thy lyf is sauf, for I wol stonde therby;

      Upon my lyf, the queene wol seye as I.

      Lat se which is the proudeste of hem alle,

162   That wereth on a coverchief or a calle,

      That dar seye nay of that I shal thee teche.

      Lat us go forth withouten lenger speche."

165   Tho rowned she a pistel in his ere,

      And bad hym to be glad and have no fere.

      Whan they be comen to the court, this knyght

168   Seyde he had holde his day, as he hadde hight,

      And redy was his answere, as he sayde.

      Ful many a noble wyf, and many a mayde,

      And many a wydwe, for that they been wise,

172   The queene hirself sittynge as a justise,

      Assembled been, his answere for to heere;

174   And afterward this knyght was bode appeere.

~

149/ leeve = dear; certeyn = certainly. 150/ I nam but deed = I am as good as dead; but = unless. 152/ wisse = inform; quite youre hire = repay you. 153/ Plight me thy trouthe = Swear to me. 154/ requere thee = ask of you. 158/ avante = boast. 159/ sauf = safe. 162/ coverchief or a calle = headscarf or hairnet. 165/ Tho rowned she a pistel = Then she whispered a message. 168/ hight = promised. 172/ justise = judge. 174/ bode appeere = summoned.

And the knight was so distressed,

That he lowered his defences and took a load off his chest,

And wept, and told the oldest woman he'd met

The whole messy story of his hopeless quest

And the approach of his death; and when she got the gist

Of his predicament, she said, "Promise me this:

The next thing I ask for, you'll honestly give,

And I'll tell you what the answer to your quandary is."

"As long as I live," the knight frantically stressed,

"I promise, if I can, I'll grant your request!"

And with that, she laid the man's panic to rest,

And taught him the bottom line, the way to answer best

The standing question that had been on his mind:

"How in God's name do you please womankind?"

The knight had spent a year listening blind

To opinions, and found all women differently inclined.

But when his time was finally expired,

Again the knight stood in the line of fire,

Before the court and queen, in their fine attire,

175   To every wight comanded was silence,
176   And that the knyght sholde telle in audience
       What thyng that worldly wommen loven best.
178   This knyght ne stood nat stille as doth a best,
       But to his questioun anon answerde
       With manly voys, that al the court it herde:
          "My lige lady, generally," quod he,
       "Wommen desiren to have sovereynetee
       As wel over hir housbond as hir love,
184   And for to been in maistrie hym above.
       This is youre mooste desir, thogh ye me kille.
       Dooth as yow list; I am heer at youre wille."
       In al the court ne was ther wyf, ne mayde,
188   Ne wydwe that contraried that he sayde,
       But seyden he was worthy han his lyf.
190   And with that word up stirte the olde wyf,
       Which that the knyght saugh sittynge in the grene.
       "Mercy," quod she, "my sovereyn lady queene,
       Er that youre court departe, do me right.
       I taughte this answere unto the knyght,
195   For which he plighte me his trouthe there,
       The firste thyng I wolde of hym requere,
       He wolde it do, if it lay in his myght.

∾

175/ every wight = everyone. 176/ telle in audience = declare in public. 178/ best = beast.
184/ maistrie = mastery. 188/ contraried = contradicted. 190/ up stirte the olde wyf =
the old woman stood up. 195/ plighte = promised.

And he said, "Strike me dead if you think I'm a liar;
Women desire to have sovereignty
Over their loves, and to have their husbands be
Happy if wives live above them, free.
Now, is there any woman here who doesn't agree?"
And everyone could see that the knight had it right,
And he didn't deserve to be sacrificed,
And the queen was about to give him back his life,
When at that precise moment, that old nasty wife
Who just last night was so happy to save him,
She stood up and smiled with the face of a raisin,
And said, "He just recited the answer I gave him,
Now he owes me a favour, and I'm ready for payment!"

"Bifor the court thanne preye I thee, sir knyght,"
Quod she, "that thou me take unto thy wyf,
200   For wel thou woost that I have kept thy lyf.
201   If I seye fals, sey nay, upon thy fey!"
202   This knyght answerde, "Allas and weylawey!
203   I woot right wel that swich was my biheste!
204   For Goddes love, as chees a newe requeste!
205   Taak al my good, and lat my body go!"
206   "Nay, thanne," quod she, "I shrewe us bothe two!
For thogh that I be foul, and oold, and poore,
208   I nolde for al the metal, ne for oore,
209   That under erthe is grave or lith above,
But if thy wyf I were, and eek thy love."
     "My love?" quod he, "nay, my dampnacioun!
212   Allas, that any of my nacioun
213   Sholde evere so foule disparaged be!"
But al for noght, the ende is this, that he
215   Constreyned was; he nedes moste hir wedde,
And taketh his olde wyf, and gooth to bedde.
217   Now wolden som men seye, paraventure,
218   That for my necligence I do no cure
219   To tellen yow the ioye and al th'array,
That at the feeste was that ilke day;
To whiche thyng shortly answere I shal:
I seye ther nas no ioye ne feeste at al;
223   Ther nas but hevynesse and muche sorwe.

∾

200/ woost = know. 201/ upon thy fey! = (swear) on your faith! 202/ weylawey = woe is me. 203/ biheste = promise. 204/ as chees = choose. 205/ good = possessions. 206/ I shrewe us both two = I would curse us both. 208/ oore = ore. 209/ grave = buried. 212/ nacioun = social status. 213/ disparaged = degraded. 215/ Constreyned was= Was caught. 217/ paraventure = perhaps. 218/ I do no cure = I take no care. 219/ th'array = the splendour. 223/ nas = was nothing.

And instead of evasion, the knight cheerfully
Agreed, "Fair is fair, what kind of care do you need?"
And she turned to the queen and said, "He's very sweet,
And I'll get all the care I need when he marries me!"
The knight stared in disbelief at the smiling face
Of this tiny old granny of at least ninety-eight,
Whose eyes kept climbing his thighs in a slimy way,
And he realized there was no line of escape.
Though he still tried to beg, and barter and plead,
And he offered the deed to his father's property,
And sobbed, "Take whatever you want, please;
Impoverish me, just let my body go free!"

   But it was obvious she needed no persuading;
She said, "Oh baby, you know I'm an old lady,
Decades over eighty; there's no way you can pay me
Enough, now take me before I go crazy!"
And since there was no debating, the knight refused to get
Too upset, for fear he might lose his head,
And that very same night the "I do's" were said,
And with the queen's blessing the two were wed,

For prively he wedded hir on a morwe,

And al day after hidde hym as an owle,

So wo was hym, his wyf looked so foule.

    Greet was the wo the knyght hadde in his thoght,

Whan he was with his wyf abedde ybroght;

229   He walweth and he turneth to and fro.

His olde wyf lay smylynge everemo,

231   And seyde, "O deere housbonde, benedicitee,

Fareth every knyght thus with his wyf as ye?

Is this the lawe of Kyng Arthures hous?

234   Is every knyght of his so dangerous?

I am youre owene love and youre wyf;

I am she which that saved hath youre lyf.

And certes, yet dide I yow nevere unright;

Why fare ye thus with me this firste nyght?

Ye faren lyk a man had lost his wit.

What is my gilt? For Goddes love, tel it,

And it shal been amended, if I may."

    "Amended," quod this knyght, "Allas! nay, nay!

It wol nat been amended nevere mo;

244   Thou art so loothly and so oold also,

245   And therto comen of so lough a kynde,

246   That litel wonder is thogh I walwe and wynde.

247   So wolde God, myn herte wolde breste!"

∽

229/ He walweth and he turneth = He twisted and turned. 231/ benedicitee = bless you. 234/ dangerous = unaffectionate. 244/ loothly = loathsome. 245/ lough a kynde = low class. 246/ walwe and wynde = twist and turn. 247/ breste = burst.

And went straight to their bed and began undressing,

But when his manly flesh felt those wrinkled hands caressing,

The knight decided he just couldn't stand the rest,

And he cried, "I can't handle this; it's scandalous!"

And his wife grinned with lips like an empty cave,

And asked, "Is this how all men behave

On their wedding day, when their lives have been saved

By their wives, and they've escaped knives with thin blades?

Other knights have been brave when their freedom's suspended,

But I can see by your face that you believe I've offended

You, though I never intended to; perhaps it can be mended;

Just tell me what I did, and I'll try to amend it."

   "When this marriage is ended, then I think I'll be happy!"

Said the knight, "'Cause you're low-class, wrinkled, and nasty,

The type that would do anything to entrap me!"

"Is this," quod she, "the cause of youre unreste?"

"Ye certeinly," quod he, "no wonder is!"

"Now, sire," quod she, "I koude amende al this,

251 If that me liste, er it were dayes thre,

252 So wel ye myghte bere yow unto me.

253 But for ye speken of swich gentillesse

As is descended out of old richesse,

That therfore sholden ye be gentil men,

Swich arrogance is nat worth an hen.

Looke who that is moost vertuous alway,

258 Pryvee and apert, and moost entendeth ay

To do the gentil dedes that he kan;

Taak hym for the grettest gentil man.

261 Crist wole we clayme of hym oure gentillesse,

Nat of oure eldres for hire old richesse.

For thogh they yeve us al hir heritage,

264 For which we clayme to been of heigh parage,

265 Yet may they nat biquethe, for no thing,

To noon of us hir vertuous lyvyng,

That made hem gentil men ycalled be,

268 And bad us folwen hem in swich degree.

  Wel kan the wise poete of Florence,

270 That highte Dant, speken in this sentence.

Lo in swich maner rym is Dantes tale:

'Ful selde upriseth by his branches smale

≈

251/ me liste = I want. 252/ So wel ... unto me = Then you might be nicer to me.
253/ gentillesse = nobility. 258/ Pryvee and apert = In private and public; entendeth ay =
always tries. 261/ Crist wole = Christ desires. 264/ heigh parage = high birth. 265/
biquethe = pass down. 268/ swich = such. 270/ Dant = Dante; sentence = subject.

And she asked, "Do you really find these things distracting
When we're interacting?"
                    "Definitely!"
Said the knight, "How else would you expect it to be?"
And she said, "Then all I ask is that you listen to me,
And we'll see if after you think differently.

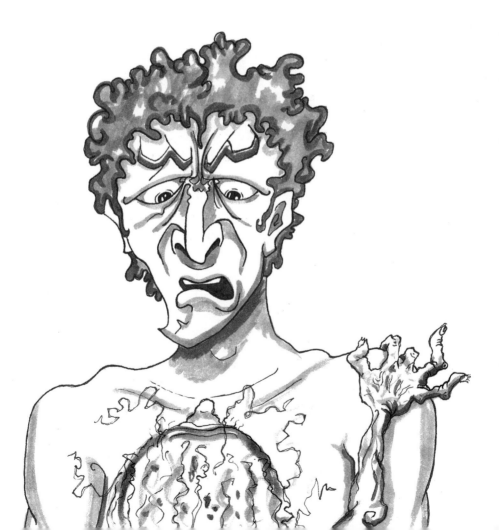

"Prowesse of man, for God, of his goodnesse,
274   Wole that of hym we clayme oure gentillesse.'
      For of oure eldres may we no thyng clayme
276   But temporel thyng, that man may hurte and mayme.
277   "Eek every wight woot this as wel as I,
      If gentillesse were planted natureelly
279   Unto a certeyn lynage doun the lyne,
280   Pryvee nor apert thanne wolde they nevere fyne
281   To doon of gentillesse the faire office;
      They myghte do no vileynye or vice.
           "Taak fyr and ber it in the derkeste hous
284   Bitwix this and the mount of Kaukasous,
285   And lat men shette the dores and go thenne;
      Yet wole the fyr as faire lye and brenne
      As twenty thousand men myghte it biholde;
288   His office natureel ay wol it holde,
289   Up peril of my lyf, til that it dye.
290   Heere may ye se wel how that genterye
291   Is nat annexed to possessioun,
292   Sith folk ne doon hir operacioun
      Alwey, as dooth the fyr, lo, in his kynde.
      For, God it woot, men may wel often fynde
      A lordes sone do shame and vileynye;
296   And he that wole han pris of his gentrye,
297   For he was boren of a gentil hous,
      And hadde hise eldres noble and vertuous,

〜

274/ Wole = Desires. 276/ mayme = maim. 277/ Eek every wight woot = And everybody knows. 279/ lynage = family. 280/ Pryvee nor apert = In private or public; fyne = cease. 281/ faire office = virtuous acts. 284/ Kaukasous = Caucasus. 285/ shette = shut; go thenne = go from there. 288/ office natureel ay = natural qualities always. 289/ Up peril of my lyf = I bet my life. 290/ genterye = gentility. 291/ annexed = connected. 292/ Sith folk … operacioun = Since people don't act right. 296/ pris of his gentrye = praise of his nobility. 297/ boren = born.

"You've given me two reasons why you can't love me;
You find me disgusting because I'm low-class and ugly;
Well, as for low-class, you can't rashly judge me;

299   "And nel hym-selven do no gentil dedis,

300   Ne folwen his gentil auncestre that deed is,

       He nys nat gentil, be he duc or erl;

302   For vileyns synful dedes make a cherl.

303   For gentillesse nys but renomee

304   Of thyne auncestres for hire heigh bountee,

305   Which is a strange thyng to thy persone.

       Thy gentillesse cometh fro God allone.

       Thanne comth oure verray gentillesse of grace;

308   It was no thyng biquethe us with oure place.

309   "Thenketh hou noble, as seith Valerius,

310   Was thilke Tullius Hostillius,

311   That out of poverte roos to heigh noblesse.

312   Reedeth Senek, and redeth eek Boece;

313   Ther shul ye seen expres that it no drede is,

       That he is gentil that dooth gentil dedis.

       And therfore, leeve housbonde, I thus conclude:

316   Al were it that myne auncestres weren rude,

       Yet may the hye God, and so hope I,

       Grante me grace to lyven vertuously.

       Thanne am I gentil, whan that I bigynne

320   To lyven vertuously and weyve synne.

           And ther as ye of poverte me repreeve,

       The hye God, on whom that we bileeve,

323   In wilful poverte chees to lyve his lyf.

~

299/ nel = won't. 300/ deed is = is dead. 302/ cherl = thug. 303/ renomee = renown.
304/ bountee = virtues. 305/ strange = foreign. 308/ place = place in society.
309/ Valerius = Roman author. 310/ Tullius Hostillius = third king of Rome. 311/ roos =
rose. 312/ Senek = Seneca; Boece = Boethius. 313/ no drede is = no doubt. 316/ Al were
= Although. 320/ weyve = renounce. 323/ wilful = deliberate.

"Class is just something that holds us back, and nothing
Goes bad as fast as the souls of nobility,
Whose workloads leave them with gold, but no ability
To show compassion, cash but no humility,

"And certes every man, mayden, or wyf,

May understonde that Jesus, hevene kyng,

Ne wolde nat chesen vicious lyvyng.

Glad poverte is an honeste thyng, certeyn;

This wole Senec and othere clerkes seyn.

329   Who so that halt hym payd of his poverte,

I holde hym riche, al hadde he nat a sherte.

331   He that coveiteth is a povre wight,

332   For he wolde han that is nat in his myght;

But he that noght hath, ne coveiteth have,

334   Is riche, although ye holde hym but a knave.

Verray poverte, it syngeth proprely;

336   Juvenal seith of poverte myrily:

337   'The povre man, whan he goth by the weye,

Bifore the theves he may synge and pleye.'

Poverte is hateful good and, as I gesse,

340   A ful greet bryngere out of bisynesse;

341   A greet amender eek of sapience

To hym that taketh it in pacience.

343   Poverte is this, although it seme alenge:

344   Possessioun that no wight wol chalenge.

Poverte ful ofte, whan a man is lowe,

Maketh his God and eek hymself to knowe.

347   Poverte a spectacle is, as thynketh me,

Thurgh which he may hise verray freendes see.

~

329/ halt hym payd = contents himself. 331/ coveiteth = covets; povre wight = poor creature. 332/ han that is nat = have that which is not. 334/ knave = peasant. 336/ Juvenal = Roman poet. 337/ povre = poor. 340/ bryngere out of bisynesse = stress reliever. 341/ amender eek of sapience = also an aid to wisdom. 343/ alenge = miserable. 344/ chalenge = desire to take. 347/ spectacle = lens.

"Besides, with the middle-class and upward mobility,
The only gentility left with any importance
Proceeds from a person's actions, not their fortunes,
So no more ill-informed class distortions!

"And therfore, sire, syn that I noght yow greve,
Of my poverte namoore ye me repreve.
351   "Now sire, of elde ye repreve me,
And certes, sire, thogh noon auctoritee
Were in no book, ye gentils of honour
Seyn that men sholde an oold wight doon favour,
355   And clepe hym fader for youre gentillesse;
356   And auctours shal I fynden, as I gesse.
          "Now ther ye seye that I am foul and old,
358   Than drede you noght to been a cokewold;
359   For filthe and eelde, al so moot I thee,
360   Been grete wardeyns upon chastitee;
361   But nathelees, syn I knowe youre delit,
I shal fulfille youre worldly appetit."
          "Chese now," quod she, "oon of thise thynges tweye:
To han me foul and old til that I deye,
And be to yow a trewe, humble wyf,
And nevere yow displese in al my lyf;
Or elles ye wol han me yong and fair,
368   And take youre aventure of the repair
That shal be to youre hous by cause of me,
Or in som oother place, may wel be.
371   Now chese yourselven wheither that yow liketh."

~

351/ elde = old age. 355/ clepe hym fader = call him father. 356/ auctours shal I fynden = I can find authors to support this. 358/ Than drede … cokewold = Then have no fear of me being unfaithful. 359/ al so moot I thee = so might I prosper. 360/ wardeyns = guards. 361/ delit = delight. 368/ And take youre … repair = And take your chances with the visitors. 371/ wheither = whichever.

"And as for the fact that I'm not exactly gorgeous,
Perhaps you're just gonna have to be grateful
That you're in a marriage that you're actually able
To trust, 'cause I pretty much *have* to be faithful;
But if you'd rather have me attractive, just say so,
'Cause I can magically change to the shape of a blushing
Young maid with a face that's both graceful and lovely,
But in that case, you'll never be able to trust me.
Would you rather a sexy, disgracefully lusty,
Insatiable slut, finding ways to annoy you,
Who raises up your jealous rage to a boil,
Or would you rather have me this age, and loyal?"

372   This knyght avyseth hym and sore siketh,
      But atte laste he seyde in this manere:
      "My lady and my love, and wyf so deere,
      I put me in youre wise governance.
376   Cheseth yourself which may be moost plesance
      And moost honour to yow and me also.
378   I do no fors the wheither of the two;
379   For as yow liketh, it suffiseth me."
          "Thanne have I gete of yow maistrie," quod she,
      "Syn I may chese and governe as me lest?"
          "Ye, certes, wyf," quod he, "I holde it best."
383   "Kys me," quod she, "we be no lenger wrothe,
      For, by my trouthe, I wol be to yow bothe!
      This is to seyn, ye, bothe fair and good.
386   I prey to God that I moote sterven wood,
      But I to yow be al so good and trewe
      As evere was wyf, syn that the world was newe.
389   And but I be to-morn as fair to seene
      As any lady, emperice, or queene,
      That is bitwixe the est and eke the west,
      Dooth with my lyf and deth right as yow lest.
      Cast up the curtyn; looke how that it is."

~

372/ avyseth hym = checked himself; sore siketh = sighed heavily. 376/ plesance = pleasure. 378/ I do no fors = I won't force. 379/ suffiseth = satisfies. 383/ wrothe = angry. 386/ sterven wood = die insane. 389/ to-morn = tomorrow morning.

But the knight couldn't say which way would make this enjoyable,

And which way would spoil the mood, and he sighed,

"You are truly wise, my toothless bride;

I think *you* should choose between the two sides,

And I'll make do with whatever you decide."

And as soon as the knight let his wife get control

Of his life, and truly decided to let go,

The next moment she changed from a grey, decrepit old

Creature to a young lady with such incredible

Features, the knight was speechless, and stood in a trance,

More deeply enchanted each time he took in a glance,

And his wife saw him standing as stiff as a wooden lance,

And whan the knyght saugh verraily al this,
That she so fair was, and so yong therto,
396   For ioye he hente hire in hise armes two,
His herte bathed in a bath of blisse.
398   A thousand tyme a-rewe he gan hir kisse,
And she obeyed hym in every thyng
That myghte doon hym plesance or likyng.
    And thus they lyve unto hir lyves ende
In parfit ioye; and Iesu Crist us sende
Housbondes meeke, yonge, fressh abedde,
404   And grace t'overbyde hem that we wedde;
And eek I praye Iesu shorte hir lyves
That nat wol be governed by hir wyves;
407   And olde and angry nygardes of dispence,
God sende hem soone verray pestilence!

Heere endeth the Wyves Tale of Bathe.

⁓

396/ hente = took. 398/ a-rewe = in a row. 404/ t'overbyde = outlive. 407/ nygardes of
dispence = penny pinchers.

And said, "Few understand the union of woman and man;
Common sense says we should be treated the same,
But what's really needed to keep people sane
Is for men to treat women like queens with free domain;
And as soon as you agreed to give me the reins,
It allowed me to change, and become graceful and beautiful
And young, and still remain faithful and dutiful,
'Cause you'll never *make* me behave in an unsuitable
Way, now that you understand the undisputable
Root of all happy relationships!"
And with that she leaned forward and gave him a kiss,
And the knight was bathed in a sense of weightlessness,
And they lived out the rest of their days in bliss.

The End.

Acknowledgements

> With soutil pencel was depeynted this storie.

First of all I would like to thank my brother, Erik Brinkman, for contributing his creative vision to these stories, and for supporting me with his time and honest criticism over the years. As my stage manager and technician at the Edinburgh Fringe 2004/2005 he watched me perform "The Rap Canterbury Tales" more than sixty times, and no one could have rendered these characters on paper with more feeling and wit. Erik and I would also both like to thank our esteemed grandmother, Charlotte Murray (a.k.a. "Grandie"), who consulted on every single drawing and added her artistic and architectural expertise.

Second, I would like to thank the many teachers of English literature who fostered my enthusiasm for poetry and language arts. I was lucky enough to find a series of inspiring mentors who encouraged me to both create *and* understand, instead of separating the one process from the other. Dana Morin, Michael Ferguson, and Doreen Zaiss all made a lasting impact in my pre-university days, and Paul Budra, Don Grayston, and Wayde Compton provided valuable guidance during the undergraduate genesis of this project. I would also like to thank Kathryn Kerby-Fulton, John Tucker, and Gordon Fulton for their support and insight during the graduate research phase, and for inviting me to road-test my performance in their classes. It takes a special kind of medievalist to invite a rapper to the lectern.

The instructor and mentor who deserves by far the most gratitude for the realization of this book is Sheila Roberts, who had the open-mindedness to accept a thesis proposal comparing rap music and traditional literature, and who encouraged and supervised the writing of that thesis back in 2000. Sheila set the stage by compelling her students to creatively interpret and perform literature as a living experience rather than just study it as an artifact, and her approach has kept me engaged ever since. I would also like to thank her for proofreading sections of this manuscript and offering her comments (and for resisting the temptation to grade it).

Additional thanks are due to the other proofreaders and copy-editors who took the time to help me with the introduction of this book, especially my team of experts in England. Sarah James at Cambridge University read multiple drafts and provided meticulous comments, and Anna Goodman helped me clarify the scientific analogies. Also in England, Paul Alborough (Elemental) and Daniel Silverstein (Anomaly) deserve gratitude for reading drafts and offering the perspective of underground MCs overseas. I would also like to acknowledge the time spent by Michele D'Acosta, JanaLee Cherneski, Michelle Lynch, Fainne Martin, Shirarose Wilenski, Chelsea Mara, and my father, Dirk Brinkman, who all helped me proofread and copy-edit for errors.

My final acknowledgement goes to the late Geoffrey Chaucer, who has endured six centuries of imitators and translators producing countless adaptations of his work, of which this is only the latest and certainly not the last. No person I haven't met has affected me more, or taught me more about how to exist in the world. I have included his words here so as never to stand between any reader and Chaucer's enduring storytelling genius.

NOTES & BIBLIOGRAPHY

NOTES

Preface

Page 5

"Whoso shal telle … ": I (A) 731–36.
(Whoever tells another person's story / Must repeat as accurately as possible / Every word of it, if that is his task, / Even if he has never spoken so rudely or so freely, / Or else his tale will be untrue, / Or he will mislead, or invent his own words.)

General Prologue

Page 9

"There is no newe gyse, that it nas old": I (A) 2125.
(There is no new style that isn't old.)

"But he that departed … ": *Troilus and Criseyde* (Tr) 1.960–66.
(He that is divided in every place / Is nowhere whole, as wise scholars have written, / Is it any wonder if such a person is unfortunate? / And you know how it goes with some activities, / Like planting a tree or herb, in various ways, / And the next day pulling it up as quickly! / No wonder if it never grows.)

Page 10

"I was not born under a rhyming planet": *Much Ado About Nothing*, 5. 2. 39–40.

"I ain't choose to rhyme; rhymin' chose me": Bubba Sparxxx, "Ugly," *Dark Days, Bright Nights*.

"Diverse scoles … ": III (D) 44c–d.
(Diverse schools make perfect scholars, / And diverse practice in many different endeavours.)

Page 11

"My style's got the rhythm that of an Anglo Saxon": The Roots, "Respond/React," *Illadelph Halflife.*

"It's the Abstract Poet, prominent like Shakespeare": A Tribe Called Quest, "Excursions," *The Low End Theory.*

"I'm breakin' the laws of physics … ": Sway & King Tech f. DJ Revolution, "Canibus Freestyle," *This or That.*

"… one article that stood out for me was about the Latin roots of hip-hop": see Del Barco.

Page 12

"[Black people] are obviously shining our light to the world … ": see Chappelle 131.

John Skelton's "Philip Sparrow" vs. (Skelton 60)	DMX's "Rough Rider's Anthem," *It's Dark and Hell is Hot*
When I remember again How my Philip was slain, Never half the pain Was between you twain,	What was that look for, When I walked in the door? Oh, you thought you was raw? Boom! Not any more!

"Then seek no more … ": Wyatt 97–99.

"The final destination … ": Blackalicious, "4000 Miles," *Blazing Arrow.*

Page 13

"And though I nat the same wordes seye … ": VII 959–62.
(Although I don't say the same words / As you have heard, yet still I ask you / Not to blame me, for, in my substance / You won't find any difference.)

Page 14

"No mistakes allowed … ": Eric B. and Rakim, "Eric B. is President," *Paid in Full: The Platinum Edition.*

Page 15

"And therefore … ": III (D) 413–14.
(And therefore every man this tale I tell, / Get what you can, because everything is for sale.)

"I'm from an environment … " High and Mighty f. Wordsworth and Thirstin' Howl III, "Open Mic Night Remix," *Home Field Advantage.*

"It was also repeated often in books on hip-hop … ": see Cross.

Page 17

"And now they say they wanna get me signed … ": Immortal Technique, "Freedom of Speech," *Revolutionary Vol. 2.*

"Hip-hop fans, … " Wyclef Jean, "Pullin' Me In," *The Ecleftic.*

"For what man … ": IV (E) 10–11.
(Whoever is entered into a game / Must play by the game's rules.)

Page 18

"If you can talk you can sing, … ": Talib Kweli and Hi Tek, "African Dream," *Reflection Eternal.*

"Claimin' that you got a new style, … ": Fugees, "How Many Mics," *The Score.*

Page 19

"I can not se … ": *Parliament of Fowls* (PF) 538–39.
(I can't see these arguments working, / So it seems there must be battle.)

Page 20

"For soothly, he that precheth … ": VII 1044.
(Certainly, whoever preaches to those who don't want to hear, his speech will only annoy them.)

Page 21

"Fuck what you've done; if you've got skills, reveal it": Dilated Peoples, "No Retreat," *The Platform*.

"Too many MCs, not enough mics": Fugees, "How Many Mics," *The Score*.

Page 22

"The Host proposes a game for the 'sport' and 'comfort' of the journey … ": I (A) 775–76.

Page 23

"According to the Host, the stories must be 'aventures that whilom han bifalle,' … 'moost solaas' (most solace)": I (A) 795–99.

"… marchel in an halle": I (A) 752.

"Though I right now sholde … ": III (D) 424–25.
(If I make my confession right now, / I don't owe them a word that wasn't paid back.)

"'quite' the Knight": I (A) 3127.

"[L]eveful is with force force of-showve": I (A) 3912.

Page 24

"One of the only published links I found … was an essay comparing hip-hop freestyle … to Homer's versification techniques in *The Iliad*": see Pihel.

"Whiche layes … ": V (F) 712–13.
(They sang these songs with their instruments / Or else read them for their enjoyment.)

Pages 24–25

"… there is a well-documented change in the social function of minstrels … the 'household poet'": Green 103.

Page 25

"One important outcome of these combined factors was an increase in competition among amateur poets … such as riddles and verse improvisation contests": see Green 116.

Page 26

"Also I prey yow … ": I (A) 743–46.
(Also I ask you to forgive me / If I haven't put the various people / In this story where they deserve to be; / My wit is short, you understand.)

Page 27

"oure Hoost hadde the wordes for us alle": X (I) 67.

"What man artow?": VII 695.

"All of the other pilgrims are named after their profession, so Chaucer would perhaps bear the title of 'the Poet'": Although there is no external evidence of Chaucer being a professional poet, there is some internal evidence (such as "The Complaint of Chaucer to His Purse") that his living allowance was connected to his poetry at the very end of his life, which is when I believe he wrote *Sir Thopas*.

"Thou lookest as thou wouldest find an hare, ... ": VII 696–97.

"He in the waast ... ": VII 700–09.

Page 28

" ... scholars have demonstrated by comparison to be below Chaucer's usual versifying standards": see Benson 917; see also Bradbury 119.

"Sire Thopas wax a doughty swayn ... ": VII 724–29.

Page 29

"'Namoore of this, for Goddes dignitee,' ... ": VII 919–25.

Pages 29–30

"'Why so?' quod I, ... ": VII 926–32.

Page 30

"I don't get on stage and waste your time ... " Reflection Eternal f. Bahamadia, "Chaos," *Soundbombing II.*

"Nowadays everybody wanna talk ... ": Dr. Dre f. Eminem, "Forgot About Dre," *2001.*

"A million MCs and they ain't sayin' nothin'!": Pharoahe Monch, "Rape," *Internal Affairs.*

"And whan this ... ": VII 1045–46.
(And when this wise man saw that he had no audience, all embarrassed he sat down again. For Solomon says: "If you don't have an audience, keep your mouth shut.")

"Lat se wher thou ... ": VII 933–35.

Page 31

"geestours for to tellen tales": VII 846.

"He thurgh the thikkeste of the throng gan thresete ... ": I (A) 2612–13.

Page 32

"mirth or some doctrine": VII 935.

"sentence and solaas": I (A) 798.

"Thou liknest it also to wilde fyr; ... ": III (D) 371–73.
(You can compare it to wild fire; / The more it burns, the more it desires / To consume everything that can be burned.)

Page 33

"Why, she would hang on him ... ": *Hamlet* 1. 2. 143–45.

"Any control system in which feedback is used to compare ... ": Morris 812.

Page 34

"And for ther is ... ": Tr V 1793–99.
(And since there is so much diversity / In English, and in writing the language, / I pray that no one makes mistakes / In copying this book, or reciting it aloud, / And wherever it is read or sung, / Let it be understood, I pray to God, / But now back to what I was saying before.)

Page 36

"[B]eing but an ornament and no case to poetry … ": Sidney 485.

"the Invention of a barbarous Age": Milton 249.

"[T]he language of every good poem can in no respect differ from that of good prose": Wordsworth 147.

Page 37

"I kan nat geeste … ": X (I) 43–44.
(I don't know alliteration, 'rum, ram, rough' by letter / And, God knows, my opinion of rhyme isn't much better.)

Page 38

"the unacknowledged legislators of the World": Shelley 765.

"Literature is but a branch of Religion … ": Carlyle 926.

"I don't think what poetry does is express emotion … ": Margaret Atwood, quoted in Geddes 489.

Page 39

"Just let our spirits live on … ": Eminem, "Sing for the Moment," *The Eminem Show.*

"Ye knowe ek … ": Tr II 22–25.
(You know that speech changes its form / Over a thousand years, and words that / Once had value, now seem silly and strange/ To us, and yet that's how they were spoken.)

"Rhyme in poetry has four recognized functions … ": see Lanz.

"Before the written word was invented … ": see Diamond 218.

Page 40

"However, rhyme was certainly known in England at this time … its absence from virtually all Old English poetry implies that it was deliberately avoided in favour of alliteration": see Macrae-Gibson.

"Philip Sidney pointed this out in 1595 … ": see Sidney 498.

"… modern linguistics has recently expanded the picture": see Harmon.

Page 41

"In surveys of the linguistic roots of words … ": see J. Wimsatt.

"… the word 'experience' appears for the first time in English … ": see Fisher 103–05.

"In wommen vinolent is no defence – … ": III (D) 467–68.
(Drunk women have no defenses; / Lechers know this by experience.)

"I kan right now … ": II (B) 46–49.
(I can't tell you any worthwhile story / That Chaucer, with his crude understanding / Of metre and of skillful rhyming, / Hasn't already told in his best English.)

Page 42

"This may well be rhyme dogerel": VII 925.

"Some verse theorists have proposed that it is a quality of surprise that makes rhyme effective … ": see W. K. Wimsatt.

Page 43

"For instance, a survey comparing Chaucer's rhymes for 'knight' … ": see Burnley.

"'Ye, that is good,' quod he; … ": VII 710–11.

"Comparisons have shown that other medieval poets … ": see Woods.

"I know not whether to marvel more … ": Sidney 495.

Page 44

"Who koude ryme in Englyssh proprely?": I (A) 1459.

"I shouldn't have to pay these shrinks … ": Eminem, "Kill You," *The Marshall Mathers LP*.

"Don't push me 'cause I'm close to the edge … ": Grandmaster Flash and the Furious Five f. Melle Mel, "The Message," *Adventures on the Wheels of Steel: 20th Anniversary Sugar Hill Anthology*.

Pages 44–45

"Write a rhyme in graffiti … ": Eric B. and Rakim, "I Ain't No Joke," *Paid in Full: The Platinum Edition*.

Page 45

"Packin' like a Rasta in the weed spot … ": Nas, "It Ain't Hard to Tell," *Illmatic*.

"When I attack … ": Nas, "Halftime," *Illmatic*.

"I feel like I'm walkin' a tightrope … ": Eminem, "Rock Bottom," *The Slim Shady LP*.

Page 46

"Diverse folk … ": I (A) 3857–58.
(Different people said different things, / But mostly they just laughed and joked.)

"cleped us / precius": III 147–48.

"wyvys / alyve is": III 39–40.

"Swownynge … ": I (A) 2819–20.

"And with my deth … " V (F) 1363–64.

"For curteisie … ": I (A) 3351–52.

"Beside, he was a shrewd philosopher … ": Butler 127–28.

"Profound in all the nominal … ": Butler 153–54.

"What men call gallantry … ": Byron 503–04.

"But – Oh! ye lords … ": Byron 175–76.

"Prose poets like blank-verse … ": Byron 1605–06.

Page 47

"oratorical – less to be read than heard": Gerard Manley Hopkins, quoted in Ellmann and O'Clair 90.

Pages 47–48

"The Song of Eärendil": Tolkein 228.

Page 48

"But nathelees, this meditacioun ... ": X (I) 55–58.
(Nevertheless, this theory / Is always open to correction / By scholars, for I'm not well-read; / I offer only the essence, believe me.)

Page 49

"Showed her my boarding pass ... ": Mos Def f. Q-Tip, "Mr Nigga," *Black on Both Sides.*

"Then in the middle of Little Italy ... ": Big Punisher, "Twinz (Deep Cover 98)," *Capital Punishment.*

Page 50

"For whoso wol ... ": Tr V 757–59.
(Whoever listens to every word they hear, / Or is ruled by everyone else's opinion, / Will never succeed, without a doubt.)

Page 51

"'an enemy of free verse'": McEvoy 10.

"I speak in schools a lot ... ": Talib Kweli, "Beautiful Struggle," *The Beautiful Struggle.*

A Note on the Text

Page 57

"For myne wordes ... ": Tr III 1331–37.
(For my words, here and elsewhere, / I speak them all under the correction / Of you that have feeling in love's art, / And put it under your discretion / To increase, or make reductions / Of my language; that's all I ask of you, / But now back to what I was saying before.)

Prologue to *The Knight's Tale*

Page 63

"Chaucer opens the contest with *The Knight's Tale*, the longest and most detail-rich of all *The Canterbury Tales*": Actually *The Parson's Tale* is longer than *The Knight's Tale*, but it is a moral handbook in prose rather than a rhymed story, which sets it aside from the rest.

"worthy man,/ ... / ... loved chivalrie, / Trouthe and honour, fredom and curteisie": I (A) 43–46.

"He was a verray, parfit gentil knyght": I (A) 72.

"Theseus, the governor of Athens": Theseus's army carries a flag embroidered with the image of the Minotaur, the beast with a man's body and bull's head that the young Theseus killed in the labyrinth beneath the palace of Crete, in another story.

"What with his wisdom ... ": I (A) 864–65.

Page 64

"in this world ... ": I (A) 902–03.

"'What folk been ye ... '": I (A) 905–08.

"rente adoun bothe wall and sparre and rafter": I (A) 990.

"walken in the wodes wilde": I (A) 2309.

"my lady, whom I love and serve": I (A) 1143.

Prologue to *The Miller's Tale*

Page 189

"noble storie … ": I (A) 3111–13.

"I kan a noble tale … ": I (A) 3126–27.

"Tel on, a devel wey! … ": I (A) 3134–35.

"Anyone who has seen the diameter of Busta Rhymes's mouth fully dilated … ": Check out the CD artwork on the album *When Disaster Strikes* for an example of this.

"Woo-hah!!": Busta Rhymes, "Woo Hah!! Got You All In Check," *The Coming*.

"Ther was no dore … ": I (A) 550–51.

Page 190

"janglere and a goliardeys, … ": I (A) 560–61.

"Ooh baby, I like it raw!": Old Dirty Bastard, "Shimmy Shimmy Ya," *Return to the 36 Chambers: The Dirty Version*.

"R. A. the Rugged Man": This underground rap veteran from Long Island is the Miller incarnate. It's uncanny.

"for I moot reherce … ": I (A) 3173–75.

"he caught her by the queynte": I (A) 3276.

Page 191

"C U Next Tuesday vibe": see Sprague.

"And therefore … ": I (A) 3176–77.

"Where the demons live … ": Jay-Z, "Squeeze 1st," *The Dynasty*.

"Avyseth yow …": I (A) 3185–86.

Prologue to *The Pardoner's Tale*

Page 249

"But with thise relikes, … ": I (A) 701–04.

"C.R.E.A.M. = Cash Rules Everything Around Me": Wu Tang Clan, "C.R.E.A.M.," *Enter The Wu Tang: 36 Chambers*.

"The professor says … ": Wyclef Jean, "Street Jeopardy," *The Carnival*.

"heer as yelow as wex": I (A) 675.

Page 250

"voys … as smal as hath a goot": I (A) 688.

"Swiche glarynge eyen hadde he as an hare": I (A) 684.

"No berd hadde he, … ": I (A) 689–90.

"I trowe he were a gelding or a mare": I (A) 691.

"This has provoked endless critical speculation on the Pardoner's sexuality … ": See explanatory notes, *The Riverside Chaucer* 824.

"… the Pardoner later asks the Wife of Bath for advice": see III (D) 185–87.

"I peyne me …": VI (C) 330–34.

"For to make hem free … ": VI (C) 401–02.

Page 251

"Myn entente … ": VI (C) 403–04.

"I wol have moneie … ": VI (C) 448–51.

"pop bottles with models": The Notorious B.I.G., "The World Is Filled," *Life After Death*.

"I wol drynke … ": VI (C) 452–53.

"I got hos in different area codes ": Ludacris, "Area Codes," *Word of Mouf*.

Page 252

"[h]ath trespased to my bretheren or to me": VI (C) 416.

"Thanne wol I … ": VI (C) 413–14.

"Thus spitte I out … ": VI (C) 421–22.

Prologue to *The Wife of Bath's Tale*
Page 295

"Experience, though noon actoritee … ": III (D) 1–3.

"Welcome the sixte, whan that evere he shal": III (D) 45.

"For hadde God commanded maydenhed … ": III (D) 69–72.

"In wyfhod … ": III (D) 149–50.

"goode men, and riche, and olde": III (D) 197.

Page 296

"I wolde no lenger … ": III (D) 409–11.

"hadde hem hooly in myn hond": III (D) 211.

"If I was broke, would you want me? … ": Jay-Z, "Can I Get A … " *Vol. 2 … Hard Knock Life*.

"What shoulde I … ": III (D) 213–14.

"pussy is power": Foxy Brown, "I Can't," *Chyna Doll*.

"No romance without finance": Foxy Brown, "JOB," *Chyna Doll*.

"With empty hand men may none hawkes lure": III (D) 415.

"Now I ain't sayin' she a gold-digger, but … ": Kanye West, "Gold Digger," *Late Registration*.

Page 297

"By God … ": III (D) 489–90.

"I trowe I loved hym best … ": III (D) 513–14.

"[M]e thoughte he hadde a paire … ": III (D) 597–99.

"book of wikked wyves": III (D) 685.

"Myn owene trewe wyf, … ": III (D) 819–20.

"He yaf me al the bridel in myn hond": III (D) 813.

"Of five husbondes scoleiyng am I": III (D) 44.

Page 298

"Oon of us two moste bowen, doutelees, … ": III (D) 440–42.

"Recent psychological studies … ": for instance see Gottman and Silver.

"Upon his flesh … ": III (D) 157–58.

Acknowledgements

Page 337

"With soutil pencel was depeynted this storie": I (A) 2049.
(This story was painted with a subtle pencil.)

BIBLIOGRAPHY

Abrams, M. H., ed. *The Norton Anthology of English Literature.* 6th ed. 2 vols. New York: W. W. Norton, 1993.

Alden, Raymond Macdonald. *English Verse: Specimens Illustrating Its Principles and History.* New York: AMS Press, 1970.

Auslander, Philip. *Liveness: Performance in a Mediatized Culture.* London: Routledge, 1999.

Benson, C. David. *Chaucer's Drama of Style: Poetic Variety and Contrast in the* Canterbury Tales. North Carolina: University of North Carolina Press, 1986.

Boitani, Piero. *Chaucer and the Imaginary World of Fame.* Cambridge: D.S. Brewer, 1984.

Bradbury, Nancy Mason. "Chaucerian Minstrelsy: *Sir Thopas, Troilus and Criseyde* and English Metrical Romance." In *Tradition and Transformation in Medieval Romance,* ed. Rosalind Field. Suffolk: St. Edmundsbury Press Ltd., 1999.

Bradley, Henry, ed. *A Middle English Dictionary.* London: Oxford University Press, 1891.

Bragg, Lois. *The Lyric Speakers of Old English Poetry.* Cranbury, N.J.: Associated University Press, 1991.

Burnley, David. *A Guide to Chaucer's Language.* London: Macmillan Press, 1983.

Burrow, J. A. *Medieval Writers and Their Work.* Oxford: Oxford University Press, 1982.

Butler, Samuel. *Hudibras.* In *The Norton Anthology of English Literature,* 6th ed., vol. 1, ed. M. H. Abrams. New York: W. W. Norton, 1993. 1983–89.

Byron, George Gordon. *Don Juan*. In *The Norton Anthology of English Literature*, 6th ed., vol. 2., ed. M. H. Abrams. New York: W. W. Norton, 1993. 566–620.

Carlyle, Thomas. *Characteristics*. In *The Norton Anthology of English Literature*, 6th ed., vol. 2., ed. M. H. Abrams. New York: W. W. Norton, 1993. 923–32.

Chappelle, Dave. "Amerikaz Nightmare." *XXL* 64, October 2004.

Chang, Jeff. *Can't Stop Won't Stop: A History of the Hip-Hop Generation*. New York: St. Martin's Press, 2005.

Chaucer, Geoffrey. *The Riverside Chaucer*. Ed. Benson, Larry D. Boston: Houghton Mifflin Co., 1987.

———. *The Canterbury Tales: The New Ellesmere Chaucer Monochromatic Facsimile*. Ed. Daniel Woodward and Martin Stevens. Lunenberg: The Stinehour Press, 1997.

Clark, Arthur Melville. *Studies in Literary Modes*. London: Oliver and Boyd, 1946.

Considine, P. E., ed. *Van Nostrand's Scientific Encyclopedia*. 8th ed. New York: Van Nostrand Reinhold, 1995.

Cosman, Madeleine Pelner. *Medieval Wordbook*. New York: Checkmark Books, 1996.

Costello, Mark, and David Foster Wallace. *Signifying Rappers*. Echo, N.J.: The Echo Press, 1990.

Cross, Brian. *It's Not About a Salary!* London, New York: Verso, 1993.

Davis, Norman et al. *A Chaucer Glossary*. Oxford: Oxford University Press, 1979.

Del Barco, Mandalit. "Rap's Latino Sabor." In *Droppin' Science: Critical Essays on Rap Music and Hip Hop Culture*, ed. W. E. Perkins. Philadelphia: Temple University Press, 1996.

Dorsey, Brian. *Spirituality, Sensuality, Literality: Blues, Jazz and Rap as Music and Poetry*. Wien: Braumüller, 2000.

Dupriez, Bernard. *A Dictionary of Literary Devices*. Toronto: University of Toronto Press, 1987.

Ehrlich, Dimitri, and Gregor Ehrlich. *Move the Crowd: Voices and Faces of the Hip-Hop Nation*. New York: MTV Books / Pocket Books / Simon & Schuster, 1999.

Ellmann, Richard, and Robert O'Clair, eds. *The Norton Anthology of Modern Poetry*. 2d ed. New York: W. W. Norton, 1988.

Fisher, John H. "Chaucer's French: A Metalinguistic Inquiry." In *The Emergence of Standard English*. Lexington: University Press of Kentucky, 1996.

Gaylord, Alan T. "Sentence and Solaas in Fragment VII of the *Canterbury Tales*: Harry Bailly as Horseback Editor." *PMLA* 82 (1967): 226–35.

———. "Chaucer's Dainty 'Dogerel': The 'Elvyssh' Prosody of *Sir Thopas*." *Studies in the Age of Chaucer* 1 (1979): 83–104.

———. "The Moment of *Sir Thopas*: Towards a New Look at Chaucer's Language." *The Chaucer Review* 16, no. 1 (Summer 1981): 311–26.

Geddes, Gary. *20th Century Poetry and Poetics*. 4th ed. Oxford: Oxford University Press, 1996.

George, Nelson. *hip hop america*. New York: Penguin, 1998.

Gottman, John M., and Nan Silver, *The Seven Principles for Making Marriage Work*. New York: Three Rivers Press, 1999.

Green, Richard Firth. *Poets and Princepleasers*. Toronto: University of Toronto Press, 1980.

Harmon, William. "English Versification: Fifteen-Hundred Years of Continuity and Change." *Studies in Philology* 94. no. 1 (Winter 1997): 1–37.

Hollander, John. *Vision and Resonance: Two Senses of Poetic Form*. New York: Oxford University Press, 1975.

Johnson, W. R. *The Idea of Lyric*. Los Angeles: University of California Press, 1990.

Kerby-Fulton, Katheryn. "Langland and the Bibliographic Ego." In *Written Work: Langland, Labor, and Authorship*, ed. Steven Justice and Kathryn Kerby-Fulton. Philadelphia: University of Pennsylvania Press, 1997.

Kiser, Lisa J. *Truth and Textuality in Chaucer's Poetry*. Hanover, N.H.: University Press of New England, 1991.

Knapp, Peggy. *Chaucer and the Social Contest*. New York: Routledge, 1990.

Koff, Leonard Michael. *Chaucer and the Art of Storytelling*. Los Angeles: University of California Press, 1988.

Lanz, Henry. *The Physical Basis of Rime*. New York: Greenwood Press, 1968.

Lerer, Seth. *Chaucer and his Readers*. Princeton: Princeton University Press, 1993.

Macrae-Gibson, O. D., ed. *The Old English Riming Poem*. Cambridge: D.S. Brewer, 1983.

Mayes, Frances. *The Discovery of Poetry*. New York: Harcourt, Brace, Jovanovich, 1987.

McEvoy, Beth. "Ripping the Rapper." *The Cambridge Student*, January 27, 2005.

Milton, John. *The Complete Poetry of John Milton*. Ed. John T. Shawcross. New York: Doubleday, 1963.

Morris, Christopher, ed. *The Academic Press Dictionary of Science and Technology*. San Diego: Harcourt, Brace, Jovanovich, 1992.

Neal, Mark Anthony. *What the Music Said: Black Popular Music and Black Public Culture*. New York: Routledge, 1999.

Ong, Walter. *Orality and Technology: The Technologizing of the Word*. London: Methuen, 1982.

Pearsall, Derek. *Old English and Middle English Poetry*. London, Boston: Routledge and Kegan Paul, 1977.

———. "The Origins of the Alliterative Revival." In *The Alliterative Tradition in the Fourteenth Century*, ed. Bernard S. Levy and Paul E. Szarmach. Kent, Ohio: Kent State University Press, 1981.

———. "The Alliterative Revival: Origins and Social Backgrounds." In *Middle English Alliterative Poetry and Its Literary Background*, ed. David Lawton. Suffolk: St. Edmundsbury Press, 1982.

———. *The Life of Geoffrey Chaucer*. Oxford, U.K.; Cambridge, Mass.: Blackwell, 1992.

Perkins, Eric William. *Droppin' Science*. Philadelphia: Temple University Press, 1996.

Pickering, Michael, and Tony Green, eds. *Everyday Culture: Popular Song and the Vernacular Milieu*. Philadelphia: Open University Press, 1987.

Pihel, Erik. "A Furified Freestyle: Homer and Hip Hop." *Oral Tradition* 11 (1996): 249–69.

Powell, Kevin, ed. *Step into a World: A Global Anthology of the New Black Literature*. New York: John Wiley and Sons, 2000.

Ro, Ronin. *Gangsta: Merchandizing the Rhymes of Violence.* New York: St. Martin's Press, 1996.

Rose, Tricia. *Black Noise: Rap Music and Black Culture in Contemporary America.* Hanover, N.H.: University Press of New England, 1994.

Rose, Tricia and Andrew Ross, ed. *Microphone Fiends: Youth Music and Youth Culture.* New York: Routledge, 1994.

Saintsbury, George. *Historical Manual of English Prosody.* London: Macmillan, 1930.

Schipper, Jakob. *A History of English Versification.* New York: AMS Press, 1910.

Shakespeare, William. *Hamlet.* In *The Arden Shakespeare Complete Works,* ed. Richard Proudfoot, Ann Thompson, and Scott Kastan. London: The Arden Shakespeare, 2002. 291–332.

———. *Much Ado About Nothing.* In *The Arden Shakespeare Complete Works,* ed. Richard Proudfoot, Ann Thompson, and Scott Kastan. London: The Arden Shakespeare, 2002. 913–40.

Shelley, Percy Bysshe. *A Defence of Poetry.* In *The Norton Anthology of English Literature,* 6th ed., vol. 2, ed. M. H. Abrams. New York: W. W. Norton, 1993. 752–65.

Shusterman, Richard. *Performing Live: Aesthetic Alternatives for the Ends of Art.* Ithaca: Cornell University Press, 2000.

Sidney, Sir Philip. *The Defence of Poesy.* In *The Norton Anthology of English Literature,* 6th ed., vol. 1, ed. M. H. Abrams. New York: W. W. Norton, 1993. 479–99.

Skelton, John. "Philip Sparrow." In *The Complete Poems of John Skelton,* ed. Philip Henderson. London: J. M. Dent & Sons Ltd, 1959. 60.

Sprague, David. "The Week in Weird." www.rollingstone.com. July 29, 2005.

Stanley, Lawrence A., ed. *Rap: The Lyrics.* New York: Penguin Books, 1992.

Strohm, Paul. *Social Chaucer.* London: Harvard University Press, 1989.

Swanton, Michael. *English Literature Before Chaucer.* London, New York: Longman, 1987.

Tolkein, J. R. R. *The Lord of the Rings.* London: Harper Collins, 1994.

Toop, David. *The Rap Attack.* London: Pluto Press, 1984.

Wesling, Donald. *The Chances of Rhyme: Device and Modernity.* Berkeley: University of California Press, 1980.

Williams, George. *A New View of Chaucer.* Durham: Duke University Press, 1965.

Wimsatt, James I. "Rhyme, The Icons of Sound, and the Middle English Pearl." *Style* 30, no. 2 (Summer 1996): 189.

Wimsatt, W. K. *The Verbal Icon: Studies in the Meaning of Poetry.* Lexington: University of Kentucky Press, 1954.

Woods, Susanne. *Natural Emphasis: English Versification from Chaucer to Dryden.* San Marino: Huntington Library Press, 1984.

Wordsworth, William. *Preface to the Lyrical Ballads.* In *The Norton Anthology of English Literature,* 6th ed., vol. 2, ed. M. H. Abrams. New York: W. W. Norton, 1993. 141–51.

Wyatt, Sir Thomas. "My Mother's Maids." In *Sir Thomas Wyatt: Collected Poems,* ed. Joost Daalder. London: Oxford University Press, 1975. 108.

DISCOGRAPHY

A Tribe Called Quest. *The Low End Theory.* Zomba Recording Corporation, 1991.

Big Punisher. *Capital Punishment.* Loud Records LLC, 1998.

Blackalicious. *Blazing Arrow.* MCA Records, 2002.

Bubba Sparxxx. *Dark Days, Bright Nights.* Beat Club Records/Interscope Records, 2001.

Busta Rhymes. *The Coming.* Elektra, 1996.

Dilated Peoples. *The Platform.* Capitol Records Inc., 2000.

DMX. *It's Dark and Hell Is Hot.* Rush Associated Labels Recordings, 1998.

Dr. Dre. *2001.* Aftermath Entertainment/Interscope Records, 1999.

Eminem. *The Slim Shady LP.* Aftermath Entertainment/Interscope Records, 1999.

———. *The Marshall Mathers LP.* Aftermath Entertainment /Interscope Records, 2000.

———. *The Eminem Show.* Aftermath Records, 2002.

Eric B. and Rakim. *Paid in Full: The Platinum Edition.* Island Records Inc., 1998.

Foxy Brown. *Chyna Doll.* Violator Records, 1999.

Fugees. *The Score.* Sony Music Entertainment, 1996.

Grandmaster Flash and the Furious Five. *Adventures on the Wheels of Steel: 20th Anniversary Sugar Hill Anthology.* Sequel Records, 1999.

The High and Mighty. *Home Field Advantage.* Rawkus, 1999.

Immortal Technique. *Revolutionary Vol. 2.* Viper Records, 2003.

Jay-Z. *The Dynasty: Roc La Familia.* Roc-A-Fella Records, 2000.

———. *Vol. 2 ... Hard Knock Life.* Roc-A-Fella Records, 1998.

Kanye West. *Late Registration.* Roc-A-Fella Records, 2005.

Ludacris. *Word Of Mouf.* The Island Def Jam Music Group, 2001.

Mos Def. *Black on Both Sides.* Rawkus Records, 1999.

Nas. *Illmatic.* Sony Music Entertainment, 1994.

The Notorious B.I.G. *Life after Death.* Bad Boy Records, 1997.

Old Dirty Bastard. *Return to the 36 Chambers: The Dirty Version.* Elektra, 1995.

Pharoahe Monch. *Internal Affairs.* Rawkus Records, 1999.

R. A. the Rugged Man. *Die, Rugged Man, Die.* Nature Sounds, 2004.

The Roots. *Illadelph Halflife.* Geffen Records, 1996.

Sway & King Tech f. DJ Revolution. *This or That.* Interscope Records, 1999.

Talib Kweli. *The Beautiful Struggle.* Rawkus Records, 2004.

———, and Hi Tek. *Reflection Eternal.* Rawkus Records, 2000.

Various Artists. *Soundbombing II.* Rawkus Records, 1999.

Wu Tang Clan. *Enter The Wu Tang: 36 Chambers.* BMG Music, 1993.

Wyclef Jean. *The Carnival.* Sony Music Entertainment, 1997.

———. *The Ecleftic.* Sony Music Entertainment, 2000.